"Saddling La Gringa"

Recent Titles in
Contributions in Women's Studies

"Saddling La Gringa"

Gatekeeping in Literature by Contemporary Latina Writers

Phillipa Kafka

Contributions in Women's Studies, Number 183

GREENWOOD PRESS
Westport, Connecticut • London

Library of Congress Cataloging-in-Publication Data

Kafka, Phillipa, 1933–
    "Saddling la gringa" : gatekeeping in literature by contemporary Latina writers /
Phillipa Kafka.
        p. cm.—(Contributions in women's studies, ISSN 0147–104X ; no. 183)
    Includes bibliographical references and index.
    Contents: Judith Ortiz Cofer—Cristina Garcia—Julia Alvarez—Rosario Ferre—
Magali Garcia Ramis.
    ISBN 0–313–31122–6 (alk. paper)
    1. American fiction—Hispanic American authors—History and criticism. 2. American
fiction—Women authors—History and criticism. 3. Women and literature—United
States—History—20th century. 4. Hispanic American women in literature. 5. Sex role in
literature. 6. Ethnic identity in literature. 7. Women in literature. 8. Patriarchy in
literature. I. Title. II. Series.
PS153.H56 K34 2000
813′.5099287′08968—dc21   00–023957

British Library Cataloguing in Publication Data is available.

Library of Congress Catalog Card Number: 00–023957
ISBN: 0–313–31122–6
ISSN: 0147–104X

First published in 2000

Greenwood Press, 88 Post Road West, Westport, CT 06881
An imprint of Greenwood Publishing Group, Inc.
www.greenwood.com

Printed in the United States of America

The paper used in this book complies with the
Permanent Paper Standard issued by the National
Information Standards Organization (Z39.48–1984).

10 9 8 7 6 5 4 3 2 1

To

Maria Del Carmen Rodriguez
Angela Lopez
Annette Lopez
Maria Obondo
Maria Perez
Myriam Quiñones
Jose Adames

For The Way We Were

Contents

Preface

DEFINITIONS OF THE TERM LATINA

When I refer to Latinas, I apply the term to women whose cultural origins and histories are diverse, whose cultural diversity is obvious across nationalities, and to women who differ in their educational acquirements, their abilities to speak Spanish, and class rankings (Horno-Delgado et al. 1989a, 8). All the same, their discourse is "distinguishable" because it is "culturally unified" (Horno-Delgado et al. 1989a, 6, 11).

Asunción Horno-Delgado et al. expand the term Latinas to include women who served as "storytellers or as participants in oral histories, took part in the Civil Rights movement," the Chicano La Raza movement, the Gay liberation movement, "or the progressive and revolutionary movements of Latin America." Under their definition of Latinas, women whose "views have been informed by the Women's Movements of the U.S. and Latin America" (Horno-Delgado et al. 1989a, 8–9) were also included. Reaching out even further, the term Latina is expanded to include writers from other than Mexican and Puerto Rican cultures who "form alliances with, and draw on, traditions from those groups established with a longer history, that is, Chicanas and Puertorriqueñas. . . . [I]t is within that alliance that we can begin to speak of a Latina literature" (Horno-Delgado et al. 1989a, 10). However, unlike Horno-Delgado and her colleagues, I do not expand the definition of Latina writing to include the work of Chicanas or of women "from other groups who identify with [Latinas] and their struggle" (1989a, 11). Further, Vicki Ruíz would have the term Latina also include "someone of Latin American birth or heritage." Bernardo M. Ferdman and Angelica C. Cortes agree on the basis of commonalities "with the peoples and cultures of Latin America," as well as a blending "of indigenous, African, and European influences" (1995, 273).

In this text I limit my discussion primarily to Latina authors from the Caribbean, with a focus on Puerto Ricans, Cubans, and Dominicans. All the expansive definitions for the term Latina better fit, not that term so much as the blanket term that Ferdman and Cortes use–Hispanic. This term is used to define people from "a multiplicity of backgrounds and ethnic experiences, encompassing Mexican Americans, Puerto Ricans, Cubans, Dominicans, and Central and South Americans" (1995, 247). Nevertheless the term Latinos/as was and is still also generally used to define a separate group in a parallel grouping with Chicanos/as. In such a structure, both groups are considered separate and equal subcategories under the main category of "Hispanics," and I have adhered to that separation in my work.

The reasons for Latinas' departure from their native countries are varied, but they are primarily political and economic. As the Cubana playwright Dolores Prida writes:

Hispanics are here for many different reasons. Many have been born here. Many were here before parts of this land came to be called the United States of America. Some came a lifetime ago. Some came yesterday. Some are arriving this very minute. Some dream of returning to where they came from. Some will. Some have made this place their home for good and are here to stay. (1989, 187)

Cristina Garcia's profile and that of the characters in her novel *Dreaming in Cuban* match U.S. Bureau of the Census statistics for 1991, the year before this publication. Cubans are the richest, most successful, best-educated group of Latinos, with "the largest proportion of foreign-born elderly among the three major Latino groups." The greatest numbers of Puerto Ricans and Cubans live in New York City, New Jersey, and Florida, and the largest Latino populations live in California, Texas, and Florida. "Some [or their parents] came seeking political asylum [as in the case of Cristina Garcia]; others chose self-exile, as in the case of intellectuals linked to academia" (Heyck 1994, 24).

From different classes and origins, Latina writers are "predominantly from middle-and upper-middle-class backgrounds" (Horno-Delgado et al. 1989a, 7), although like the Puertorriqueñas Esmeralda Santiago and Nicholasa Mohr, they can also emerge from the lower classes. But all have this in common, as Mohr testifies about her family: "I, as a Puerto Rican child, never existed in North American letters. Our struggles as displaced migrants, working-class descendants of the tabaqueros (tobacco workers) who began coming here in 1916, were invisible in North American literature"(1989, 113). "Invisibility," or a "dearth of prominent women writers," is by no means due to a lack of talent, but signals a reflection of "the economic condition of women." Also and equally important, it signals their marginalization in social and literary circles" (López Springfield 1994, 702).

MY AIMS IN THIS TEXT

I will explore selected contemporary Latina writers from the Caribbean and Latin America both in terms of "a material analysis of macrostructures of inequality" (Romany 1995, 389) and in terms of the three-fold alienation their texts reveal. This alienation, what I term "enforced psychic tourism" is the traumatic cultural displacement that occurs after enforced immigration into the second culture of the United States. These unwilling "tourists" see themselves as displaced outsiders forced to adapt to the culture of "Gringolandia" (Horno-Delgado, citing Luz Maria Umpierre-Herrera 1989b, 137) when they would rather be back home in their own culture.

Horno-Delgado et al. argue that it is necessary first to comprehend how Latina subjectivity is constructed by their culture before attempting to "decode" their "discourse" (1989a, 14). This is my task in this text, as well as to decode "the process of codification, not merely the code itself" (Kutzinski 1993, 206). This process impacts on these women's gender and race in terms of "the self" as a "diasporic self" (Rhadakrishnan 1993, 765).

Latina writers describe this process of codified subjectivity in women as both created and overseen by the culture's gatekeepers, primarily the characters' mothers and foremothers, as well as other senior relatives, neighbors, teachers, ·counselors, nuns. The writers also describe this constructed self, what I call "the enforced psychic tourist," as characterized by "multiple-rootedness" (Rhadakrishnan 1993, 762). The "enforced psychic tourist" engages in a quest "to re-territorialize" herself and find her "authentic identity" (Rhadakrishnan 1993, 765, 755). She has been acculturated into two discourses: in this case, Spanish, "the mothertongue" (Horno-Delgado 1989a, 14), and English, the language of the colonizing culture. For these reasons, women are situated like outsiders: cultural tourists who feel forever uncomfortable to some extent with both discourses as they exist. This is because both cultures are "defined by male paradigms" (Horno-Delgado et al.1989a, 14) in which inequitable gendered power relations flourish.

Latinas are forced to immigrate spatially and psychically. They are silenced by inequitable gendered power relations in both cultures and the necessity of contending with the alien language of an alien culture either colonizing their birth culture or confronting them daily when they do emigrate to the U.S. mainland. Hélène Cixous offers a solution to the silencing of women, all women, I presume: "[B]y writing, from and toward women, and by taking up the challenge of speech, which has been governed by the phallus . . . women will confirm women in a place other than that which is reserved in and by the symbolic, that is, in a place other than silence. Women should break out of the snare of silence" (1983, 283).

As becomes evident in this text, Latina writers who depict characters who have emigrated to the United States also convey that they have been "denied the promised American dream of upward mobility." They now have to attempt to express themselves in a racist and sexist world that does not want to hear them on three counts–as Latinas, as women, and as women of color. Here I add one further dimension to Horno-Delgado et al.'s conclusions that Latinas are neither Anglo women, nor Latino men. They omit the issue of race. However, the editors of *Cuentos: Stories by Latinas* do include race when they declare that "[c]lass, race, and education . . . as it combines with sex, are much more critical in silencing the would-be Latina writers than discrimination on sex alone" (Gómez, Moraga, and Romo-Carmona 1983, viii). Vera M. Kutzinski, in her work on Cuban nationalism in terms of race and gender, takes a different tack. Although she agrees that class issues are important, nevertheless, she chooses not to focus on them (1993, 206). I, however, do so in my work. Even the more privileged writers such as Rosario Ferré and Julia Alvarez themselves focus on women by class, that is, on higher class women who are light-skinned and educated, although nevertheless silenced and constrained, as well as on women of the lower classes who are women of color and uneducated. Women may be silenced within gilded rather than straw cages, but silenced globally all the same. Emphasizing Judith Ortiz Cofer's *Silent Dancing*, I explore in the succeeding chapters the variety of ways in which gatekeepers are implicated in this "systemic function of silencing" (Kutzinski 1993, 16), despite the external paraphernalia of differing class attributions and rankings used in their characterizations.

I also analyze how contemporary Latina writers critique women's relationship to "the materiality of oppression and its operation in structural and institutional spaces" (Walters 1995, 86). I do this through an examination of their critiques of inequitable gendered power relations that have created and require the "suppression" (Ebert 1991, 889) of women. Latina writers critique "institutional practices"–the so-called privacy of the home and the family, as well, is also considered institutional–that strengthen and perpetuate "structures of inequality inherent in the capitalist system" (de la Torre and Pesquera 1993, 10). Susanna Danuta Walters, like many Latina and mainstream critics agrees with de la Torre and Pesquera that class rankings of women according to gender and race are characteristic of "patriarchal, capitalist, racist regimes" (1996, 865). I disagree whenever I find such frequently expressed charges of inequitable gendered power relations described as due entirely to capitalism. Patriarchy precedes and supercedes and controls all systems globally. Capitalism is only one system within patriarchy.

Latina writers expose three levels of psychic consciousness in their characters. First, they depict their characters as being indoctrinated into Latino cultures' "organization of human life" so that those ways come to seem "normative" (Levinson 1995, 125). In this text I am concerned primarily with Latino cultures' "normative" models for womanhood as reflected in the works of Latina writers. "Normative" or "naturalized" divisions of "social classes" become, then, "realities" or perceived as such by their characters, because they are commonly assumed as such by those individuals and forces that shape and control the environment around their characters, not least of which are their gatekeepers. These gatekeepers are primarily responsible for creating in the younger generations of women who are in their care a conviction of the reality of "a common and sensible world, the world of common sense." This is the "habitus . . . [that] allows the results of past relations of domination and resistance to appear natural rather than social" (Leps 1995, 179–180, citing and translating Bourdieu 546).

These seemingly normal, natural commonsense models are designed to control and constrain women, to perpetuate their subordination as a "category" in status and class to their menfolk. Marjorie Levinson defines this model as "economies of subjectivization and of value, economies entailed by the qualitative and philosophically founding distinction between subjects and objects" (1995, 115). Walters defines this (as I do) as constructing women "in power relations" (1996, 851). Similarly, Judith Butler sees such constructions for women as "identity categories" used as "instruments of regulatory regimes, whether as the normalizing categories of oppressive structures or as the rallying points for a liberatory contestation of that very oppression" (1991, 13–14).

After having performed a study of Hispanics in the U.S. military in Latino cultures, Paul Rosenfeld and Amy Culbertson concluded that "[a] . . . culture-specific value that differentiates between Hispanics and non-Hispanic[s] is power distance. Cultures high on power distance place a great emphasis on power and status differences, show respect and deference for those in power, and tend to be conforming and obedient to authority" (1995, 221). These dominant personality characteristics of Hispanic men and women serving in the U.S. Navy are widely noted, and readers will observe in my analysis of *Silent Dancing* how these characteristics, shared by Judith's father, a career man in the navy, are instrumental in his tragic fate.

In another study that spanned "40 countries," Ferdman and Cortes found "four major dimensions along which national value systems could be arrayed." These four dimensions were "power distance, uncertainty avoidance, individualism/collectivism, and masculinity/femininity." On the basis of this work, Hispanics in the United States, as well as in Latin American societies, have been found to be more collectivist than Anglos such that the group is emphasized over the individual, the need for consensus is greater, and interpersonal behavior is stressed over task achievements. Ferdman and Cortes call attention to the following as examples of collectivist conduct:

[There is a] prevalence among Hispanics to expect dignity and respect in interpersonal relations, and to emphasize positive and de-emphasize negative behaviors. Latin American societies also have been described as having high-context cultures which value communication based on personal trust and interpersonal relationships over formal, impersonal communication . . . Latin American managers [primarily male] relative to those in the United States [were found] to be high on both uncertainty avoidance and power distance, suggesting a preference for clear delineation of formal rules, and relatively autocratic paternalistic leadership styles. (1995, 248)

I also analyze the patriarchal system–what Jutta Brückner calls "the paternal as an abstraction" (in Kosta and McCormick 1996, 359)–that these Latina writers are confronting, primarily in the form of gatekeepers. I analyze how these authors "explain the roles of social power (gender, race, and class) in establishing and contesting state power and what they think of "the division of the world into public and private and the assignment of class to the world of waged work, politics to the sphere of the military or elections, and gender to the home" (Brush 1996, 435, 443). I do this through an extensive exploration of the role of gatekeepers as mediators in the processes that fix these constraints in all these ways. I observe how inequitable gendered power relations in terms of class shapes the politics of Latino culture.

For me to focus only on external differences in interest and priorities and privileged situations between white mainstream feminists and women of color feminists could well be considered as limited in perspective. When Latina writers show or imply such differences between women, as for example, Julia Alvarez does in *How the Garcia Girls Lost Their Accents*, and Rosario Ferré in all her work, I do indeed take their positions into account. Nevertheless, my focus is on the key role that gatekeepers play in perpetuating inequitable gendered power relations, as depicted in the texts of selected contemporary Latina writers. After illustrating this topic in my first chapter as most completely developed by Judith Ortiz Cofer, I go on to illustrate its use in the works of Rosario Ferré and Magali García Ramis from Puerto Rico, Cristina Garcia from Cuba, and Julia Alvarez from the Dominican Republic, as well as other Latina authors.

As in my other works, another aim of mine in this work on contemporary Latina writers is to bring the literature and criticism of contemporary ethnic and women of color writers to the attention of my colleagues in academia. Although since 1976 I have been doing what she describes as only happening "today," still I concur with Prida when she argues that:

The academic community has a large role to play in bringing Hispanic American theatre and literature into the mainstream of this country's cultural life. Fortunately, today there are many college professors who have a deep interest in our work, are studying it, writing papers, and struggling to include it in their curricula. This is a must. Because they are not only trying to enrich the lives of their students by exposing them to the art and culture of the soon-to-be largest ethnic minority in this nation, but also building theatre audiences for the future.

Unfortunately, these few pioneers face many obstacles from within and without the walls of academia. From the outside, there is the problem of not enough published literary and theatrical works by U.S. Hispanics. From inside the walls, opposition, confusion, misunderstanding, why not say it?–plain, ugly racism from faculty and administrators.

Because, they ask, what is "Hispanic literature"? What is "Hispanic drama"? Is there such a thing? And if so, where is it? Where does it belong in the curriculum? They don't know, or don't want to know, what to do with the whole darned big enchilada.

This metaphorical enchilada, like the small real ones, is meant to be eaten and enjoyed! You can't worry about heartburn a priori! I say, what's wrong with bringing U.S. Hispanic literature and drama into the American Drama Department, along with black and Asian-American works? It also belongs in an interdisciplinary subject in Latin American departments. ¿Por qué no? (1989, 186-187)

In addition, I aim to expose mainstream white feminists to the work of ethnic and women of color feminists and feminist theorists. Familiarity with such work reveals "the intimate connections between political and national history and the constitution of the subject" (Romany 1995, 396–397)–both the Latina subject and the white feminist subject. Both are products of those histories–patriarchal systems–that enact gendered and raced power relations globally. This is the case because "[g]ender is a constitutive element of social relationships based on perceived differences between the sexes, and gender is a primary way of signifying relationships of power" (Romany citing Scott, 1995, 396–397). Similarly, I agree with Birgitte Soland when she asserts that it is possible to understand a culture's construction of power relations in all areas of its fabric, even if we only analyze its gender constructions (1996, 506). I do this through questioning Latino culture's discourse on gender, in relation primarily to their gatekeepers' discourse, as to "why women's realities are not represented as language, and why women in search of a language often consume themselves" (Brückner in Kosta and McCormick 1996, 358).

Kutzinski takes a courageous stance on behalf of Cuba's celebrated Mulatto poet of the nineteenth century, Plácido (Gabriel de la Concepción Valdés) and his poem "La flor de la caña" [The sugarcane blossom]. She critiques certain powerful Afrocentric critics who claim his poetry is "depoliticized" and yet at the same time want to make him into "a martyr for national liberation." Instead, she reads his work as an effort to "reconfigure" the various discourses relative to sugar and the "ideological construction of a Cuban national identity from the viewpoint of a nonwhite writer" (1993, 11). In doing so, she consciously confronts a trend in Afrocentric and, more recently, in Afro-Hispanic criticism, to dismiss and devalue texts by white or non-white writers on the grounds that "their politics of representation do not conform to liberal late twentieth-century expectations" (1993, 11–12). She also critiques the anachronistic tendency by such critics to project a black aesthetic "onto Cuban, as well as onto other Hispanic-American literatures. They do this to make the history "of Afro-Hispanic American literature" fit into one narrative: "a journey toward a thematics of blackness that would compensate for prior elisions of racial issues." What really upsets Kutzinski is that once such a revision is made by the centrics, then other "concerns" that these Cuban authors may have are automatically ignored because those other "concerns" are not considered "correct." In fact she contends that Plácido and others like him were conscious of issues of race and gender. Although she is aware that such writing was intricately interwoven into the fabric of "hegemonic discourses, at times even complicitous with them," she still wishes to give them a fair reading based on the historic situations in which they lived and wrote. Responses such as Plácido's are always "complex" and not just "uncritical embraces of white values" (1993, 11-12).

Kutzinski critiques those who uncritically embrace "black" values and dismiss authors who do not do so, or dismiss authors whose embrace is deemed insufficient. She also deplores those who uncritically embrace the notion that once they have made that decision about certain authors (both white and of color), they feel that they need not bother to read those authors at all. It is these centrics' position that after they have judged certain writers as "oreos" they have no other "redeeming" qualities to make them worth the bother. She finds the centric attitude "inappropriate" and "fruitless." Ignoring both "poemas negros/mulatos" and "poesia negrita" (negroid or fake black poetry, poetry in blackface) by whites as inauthentic and racist," they consider only "poesia negra" to be "'real'or authentic black poetry." Instead, she calls on critics to concentrate on "the social constructedness of race" and to historicize "its discursive effects." She reprimands centrics for "bringing indiscriminate charges of racism against all whites who write about African-American cultures" and, by extension, those whites who write about Afro-Hispanic and any other culture that is not white. Centrics should not "censor those writers whose texts, for whatever reason, stray from what are construed as politically correct thematics and acceptable modes of representation at any given time" (1993, 14).

Kutzinski views Cuba, as well as all of Hispanic America, including the Caribbean cultures, as having "particular masculine biases in the literary and critical discourses" of these cultures. She claims that nonfeminist Caribbean literature specialists considered gender issues less legitimate and appropriate a "topic for discussion" than class issues, not that they paid that much attention to class issues. Further, "theoretical approaches to the race/gender/sexuality nexus" were even less favored and less numerous (1993, 15). Readers will note later on how I apply Kutzinski's arguments to traditional, mainstream critics and other ethnic critics who dismiss Latina writers on grounds that their values are political and not aesthetic and that therefore their cultural productions are inferior.

Introduction: Major Elements in the Works of Latina Writers

THE IMMIGRANT EXPERIENCE

Latina writers focus on what Juan Bruce-Novoa calls "profound links between the exile and/or immigrant experience and that of females in a patriarchal society in which they often exist as foreigners or disenfranchised residents" (1989, 81) and what I call "enforced psychic tourism." Yamila Azize Vargas goes even further in her claims for the influence of the immigrant experience in her analysis of the poetry of Carmen Valle, Sandra M. Esteves, and Luz María Umpierre. She believes that their experience of emigration served as "the catalytic agent" for more than their "radicalism and originality," their "feminine and feminist perspective" and "consciousness" (1989, 163). It may also have forced these Latina poets to experience and react to a racist and discriminatory culture with a literature that consciously defended their own culture, its traditions and history, and their "national identity" (1989, 163). For these reasons, how women characters are represented by Latinas in their works is more than the result of any individual Latina author's abiding sense of "enforced psychic tourism": being forced to be other in an alien culture and triply alien and alienated because of gender and race. Latina writers are also aware of being a part of a much larger "discursive setting" (Kutzinski 1993, 213), a system of inequitable power relations of all kinds as a source for multitudes of voluntary and enforced migrations globally.

THE HOME AND FAMILY

Once Latina feminist writers grow conscious of enforced alienation, they seek to upset the perpetuation of a traditional "feminine world," both in their own native culture and in the colonizing culture. They begin to envision a different world "founded on a counterculture of feminist and Latin American affirmation." As becomes evident in the works I analyze in this text, some of the key elements of their writing follow from those visions of how it might be for women. These dream visions lead to their espousal of "nontraditional" forms of "love" for women, of the "necessity of a militant struggle" both against patriarchal Latino and Anglo cultures, of a "sacrilegious" attitude toward the Catholic religion, and of a feminist "reinvention of children's tales" (Vargas 1989, 163). Through revisioning "the plots of patriarchal culture" in a variety of ways, Latina writers are making concerted efforts, not so much to recover their psychic "wholeness" (López Springfield 1994, 701), as in the hope of accelerating movement into new ways, into a new world.

Regardless of their own original class origins, Latina writers tend to depict oppressed working-class female characters, their experiences of daily life, and their realities "from the perspective of the oppressed classes: workers, peasants, women" (Vélez 1988, 4). Horno-Delgado et al. take this argument one step further. They advise readers to view Latina writers' work from a working-class perspective in many ways: "racial, economic, ethnic, political, social, chronological, culinary, ideological, luminous, and stylistic," as "a springboard" in terms of "cultural context" for any "analysis of Latin American literature" (1989a, 12) readers would hope to make.

Within this lower class context, Latina writers tend to focus on women's lives, on how it is like to live "within a woman's space." They generally depict an all-female family, both to reflect reality and to accomplish this goal. Further, many Latinas are themselves from immigrant or exile families. Migration frequently wreaks havoc on the traditional family organization in Hispanic culture. Authors reflecting their own experience, displace the typical "central patriarchal figure" and, instead, depict "a woman-headed and woman-populated household" (Horno-Delgado et al., 1989a, 12), as in Judith Ortiz Cofer's *Silent Dancing* and Magali García Ramis's *Happy Days, Uncle Sergio*. They are not reflecting their visions for a new-world order, only reality as they know it, because they still show traditional patriarchal family models being followed. This is despite the weakness and/or absence of the patriarch, as readers will observe in my analysis of both texts. I analyze this phenomenon from the context of inequitable gendered power relations as perpetuated and mediated by the family's female gatekeepers.

Horno-Delgado et al. also argue that inequitable gendered power relations as a topic for analysis is ignored and subsumed by traditional culture carriers such as gatekeepers whose perception of diversity is only racial or ethnic. Such a limited perspective perpetuates the "division, oppression, inequality, and internalized inferiority of women [of color], especially in contemporary capitalism" (1989a, 13). Again, it is my contention that although I agree that gatekeepers think and act in total obedience to women's relationship to the "power structures" within Latino culture, they do so in all other cultures as well, regardless of whether the culture is capitalist, or fascist, or communist.

The family setup, as buttressed by religious and secular law, as well as social customs that evolve from them, is the single most critiqued institution in the works of Latina writers. But the family is not the cause of women's problems–inequitable gendered power relations are. As Judith Resnik astutely perceives, "power and subordination–not families–are the place from which to begin." Latina writers view "women's oppression" by men in their cultures as emanating not from the family per se, but from how the family is organized so that "men's dominance is constructed and maintained." To reinforce the restrictions on women in the home, all other institutions outside the home practice and maintain male domination, and in all those institutions "women's conceptual location" is situated basically within the structure of "family life" (Resnik 1996, 965).

Is it any wonder then that in describing and analyzing inequitable gendered power relations between men and women, Latina writers, instead of "sanitizing" their feminine psyches often use violent imagery? Their purpose in doing so not only is to forge in a creative way, through writing, a sense of healthy self-identity in the face of a culture that militates against it. As Janice Haaken puts it:

There is a liberatory aspect to the implicit recognition . . . that feminine spaces are often receptacles for male conflict. Men often do act out their own frustrated longings and displaced rage through women. The feminine recovery of a sense of goodness and entitlement inevitably involves reprojecting the "bad" luck onto the oppressor. But if all discordant and powerful feelings must be projected back onto the oppressor, it leaves women with no space for the integration of unsetttling feelings or destructive impulses into a positive sense of self. (1996, 1086)

For Latina writers, as for feminists everywhere, the act of writing to vent their rage against oppression fills the receptive space that is too often lacking outside of the individual woman. However, I would add to Haaken's observations that beyond merely expressing their own subjectivity fully, especially their outrage against inequitable gendered power relations, Latina writers also wish to serve their community, their society, and their world in an ongoing effort to improve it.

INEQUALITIES

All critics of Latina literature are united in emphasizing that it most frequently confronts "sexual inequality in both Anglo and Latino cultures," as well as racism. Interestingly, the writers I have studied emphasize class issues as well, viewing class as one of the key components in their analysis, with gender and race issues within that paradigm. Horno-Delgado et al.'s analysis of Latina writers in this regard serves as a typical example of the failure by critics to recognize the inclusion of class issues in Latina works, let alone an emphasis on them. They perceive Latina writers as engaged in a struggle to effect social and political change with their primary focus on the need for equality for all, especially equality for women. Activism is necessary to achieve this. Simultaneously Latina writers confront racism in the Anglo culture attitude toward Latinos.

Latina writers also rage "against the double standard." Because they live in a situation where they have to deal with "several oppressions simultaneously," they seek to break the barrier of culturally ordained silence. Periodically expressing themselves through angry venting is characteristic of their writing (Horno-Delgado et al. 1989a, 15–17). I contend that Latina writers not only show anger at the oppressions of racism and sexism in their works, they also show anger at the oppression of "differential class rankings" in their culture and between men and women.

Nancy Saporta Sternbach and others have contended rightly that Latina anger about sexism and their priority of interest about all its manifestations, including the suppression of female sexual subjectivity, is not always seen as a priority for women of color as it is for white feminists. Sternbach and others contend that it is only a priority for white femininsts, not Latinas. Sexism is viewed by Latina writers "concurrently with other issues such as class, ethnicity, cultural norms, traditions, and the paramount position of the family." So "simplistic" (that is, selfish) are white feminists that they have not even "begun to perceive the complexities of being a Latina woman in the U.S., let alone a Latina feminist." As a result, "difficult lessons for white women" (1989, 51) have to be learned by them. The argument that issues relating to sexism are not Latina priorities, but that white feminists only concern themselves with sexism and are not concerned with "other issues" such as "class, ethnicity," and so on is specious. The fact is that these issues are now being "viewed concurrently" by most feminists–white, ethnic, and of color. It would appear that Sternbach is essentializing white feminists when she divides feminists along racial lines. She is, in fact, guilty of what she is accusing white feminists, by taking only one aspect of their agenda into account and not any other issues that they focus on "concurrently." In fact, Latina and white feminist writers' perspectives are similar, far more so than she would grant. Rosario Ferré states the prevailing Latina perspective succinctly and allegorically in "The Bitches' Colloquy": "His misogyny takes my bark away" (1994, 895). That is, the patriarchy silences women. I submit that the primary motive for most Latina writing, as of most white feminist writing, is the attempt through writing to overcome the impossibility "of speaking within dominant discourses without being imprisoned by silencing codes and repressive institutions" (Scorczewski 1996, 320). In this text, I explore how Latina writers depict female gatekeepers as mediators, as wardens, who assist in imprisoning their young charges in the patriarchal institutions of Latino and Anglo cultures.

It is a mistake, as I have argued elsewhere, for groups of women in any and all cultures to separate and distance from each other.[1] We should not continue to be divided and conquered everywhere. We should expand our perspectives to become ever more global. We should emphasize commonalities, regardless of divisions along lines of privilege, or apparent privilege, because as Janice Dewey sees it, "Overshadowed by dominant, partial, and repressive cultural values, all women, women of color, lesbians, are displaced and marginalized" (1989, 46).

CREATING NEW GENRES

The Latina writers are also creating new genres "between poetry and fiction, blurring the line between the short story and the novel, between conversation and literary discourse" (Horno-Delgado et al. 1989a, 17). Judith Ortiz Cofer's *Silent Dancing* serves well as the model in this regard, as readers will discover.

Other Latina writers, such as Rosario Ferré also revise legends and myths and traditional children's tales. Kisenija Bilbija, writing about "The Youngest Doll," states that in the way she writes this tale Ferré thereby situates "a feminist translation of the golem fable into a socio-political space resonant with the United States–Puerto Rico relationship" (1994, 887). Readers will also see Cofer taking the same political stance toward the United States in her myth about Maria Sabida, as does Ramis, as well, in *Happy Days, Uncle Sergio*, through her narrator Lidia and in her haunting characterization of Uncle Sergio. However, Ramis is primarily commited to documenting her characters' lives from a feminist perspective and valorizing and preserving Puerto Rican history and culture.

BICULTURALISM

Latina authors depict many of their female characters exposed to a second batch of success models for women in the United States, in addition to Latino models. Through female gatekeepers, Latino cultures train younger females to reproduce the ways in which they are trained to link their sense of "self-worth" and "self-esteem" to the home and domesticity (de la Torre and Pesquera 1993, 10). Anglo culture only reinforces this training, as Alba Rivera-Ramos puts it, through assigning "the WASPM model as a symbol of superiority." By this means, "any person or group that deviates from this standard is not only different but inferior" (1995, 205). In both their cultures of origin and Anglo culture, gatekeepers work ceaselessly to inscribe into their young female charges notions of female "difference and inferiority." Their goal is to reinforce female obedience to their cultures' construction of discriminatory models for them as ideal women.

Readers will also note an ambivalent quality in Latina writers, despite the fact that they resist both their original and second cultural training and in this sense are "enforced psychic tourists" in two alien cultures. Their resistance is linked to their feminist perspective, but it also includes alert, fully conscious choices to reject as well as to accept certain ideologies from the country of origin and the United States. They make their selections and rejections from a distance, as an observing witness from afar and yet newly, just as a tourist observes an alien culture. Stuart Hall and Donald James define "ideologies" as "concepts, ideas, and images which provide frameworks of interpretation and meaning for social and political thought" (1985, 36). These feminist Latina writers, unlike the gatekeepers they depict, refuse to either acculturate or assimilate to both cultures. Instead they carefully pick and choose what "ideologies" they wish to expose as detrimental for women in both cultures.

They make their choices without making the mistakes of some feminist theorists who substitute the Enlightenment/patriarchal perspective for an essentialist feminist perspective and who substitute "the view from nowhere with the view from womanland" (Romany 1995, 391). For Latina writers' texts are never just expressing a simplistic, "essentialist standpoint of the silenced woman" (Romany 1995, 393). They are describing women of color encumbered by many layers of oppression. In addition, their texts are organized /structured for the most part by what they are attempting to expose in terms of inequitable gendered, raced, and class relations of power in both cultures as mediated and enforced through gatekeepers.

All the authors analyzed in this text also frequently depict issues involving "acculturation" and "assimilation" as themes:

Although no definitional agreement exists, assimilation usually refers to the complete loss of the original ethnic identity, as the person is absorbed into the dominant culture. Assimilation can thus be perceived, from a minority perspective, as a pejorative term implying abandonment of traditional Hispanic values. Acculturation, however, is a multifaceted and gradual process. In the past, acculturation and assimilation were often interrelated, but the emphasis today is beginning to shift toward bicultural or multicultural acculturation; that is, an individual being able to participate actively in several cultures without having to negate one's ethnic identity. (Domino 1995, 57)

Thus Latina writers frequently propose "hybridity" and "syncretism" as solutions to the problem of assimilation. In George Domino's opinion, these are the best available models for ridding their characters of "unproductive polarizations" that inhere in essentialist "narratives of difference" (1995, 57). In this text I analyze how Cofer's distinctions between her mother and father as binaries enable readers to comprehend the complexity of her biculturalism, hybridity, and syncresis. Not only Cofer. All the Latina writers explored in this text object to assimilation or acculturation models by depicting their heroines' torturous quests to find personal meaning and fulfillment in their lives through their insistence on retaining their cultural identity. We also see the authors offering a variety of differing solutions to the issues of assimilation and acculturation. Ramis details the successful struggles for a Puerto Rican identity in both the unyielding nationalistic revolutionary Uncle Sergio and the bicultural, hybridized, and syncretized narrator, Lidia. The Dominican Julia Alvarez depicts her character Laura Garcia de la Torre as consciously assimilating and acculturating into American ways minimally–only to the extent she thinks will benefit her personal agenda of self-fulfillment. The Cubana, Cristina Garcia, through her American-born feminist character Pilar, describes her ultimately successful search for psychic integration of her Americanness and Cubanness through "dreaming in Cuban," through psychic communion with her communist Cuban grandmother.

It appears to me that the psychic condition that Anouar Majid defines as "hybridity and syncretism" stems from Latinas' sense of "enforced psychic tourism" in terms of inequitable gendered power relations in our world. The conditions of "hybridity and syncretism" reflect choice, a significant difference from "enforced psychic tourism, although not always admired. To propagate them unthinkingly leaves those who do so with the risk of "becoming complicitous with the systemic violence inflicted on billions of people worldwide" (1996, 17) because hybridity and syncretism reflect the unself-reflexive perspective "of most diasporic Third World intellectuals" (1996, 17). Suffering "stoically" (1996, 17), they ceaselessly attempt to find a psychic home between a birthplace "that is no longer theirs" and a new home in the west.

Majid concludes with a description of such intellectuals that resonates profoundly, unforgettably for me: the first description I ever encountered in all my reading that matches my own past and current condition of "homelessness-as-home, home-as-homelessness" (Majid 1996, 17). Ironically, he meant this description to apply to Middle Eastern, Third World scholars and Americans of color, not to a descendant of the Jewish diaspora from Cossack pogroms in Eastern Europe.

Critical of any members of his group who conform to and internalize western ways, Majid condemns their hybridization and syncretization. He sees such attempts as playing into the ethnocentrism of the "Western academic apparatus" which can then unjustifiably congratulate itself on its dubious "cultural achievement" at the expense of "the unmitigated pain of both Westernized intellectuals and indigenous peoples" (1996, 17). Once members of these groups become academics in the "Western academic apparatus," they are then bound by "the imperatives of a narrow professionalism that insists on productivity" and not on "genuine emancipation" (1996, 18). I feel more sanguine however. Ethnic and women of color feminists such as myself, and even mainstream feminists, have done hard labor for years in this "Western academic apparatus." We feminists never ceased to struggle for change from within. In the recent and ongoing canon warfare, we dodged through the traditional minefields, expanding and transforming the narrow, provincial Eurocentric university curriculum. The mortality rate was enormous, for many of us were crucified and fired before achieving tenure for attempting to integrate our feminist perspectives into the curriculum. In the process we underwent withering fire from some very big guns, and still do. Nevertheless, I personally have experienced some movement toward "genuine emancipation," integrating feminist theory with a more global perspective in the academy. By the end of the twentieth century, Majid, after all, had his essay published in an academic journal emanating from Johns Hopkins University Press, and I had my works published in academic journals and presses, as well.

Aurora Levins Morales, in her poem "Child of the Americas," expresses a far more positive attitude than Majid's, one in the same mood as Emma Lazurus's, but from a hybridized and syncretized child of the late twentieth century. According to Lourdes Rojas, Morales views herself both as multidimensional as a female and multiracial, as "culturally and socially, rooted in an integrated plurality . . . a cohesive and meaningful voice for the powerful heterogeneity of . . . immigrant women" (1989, 175). Morales's perspective represents the model for the most expansive and yet inclusive worldview that could be expressed by Latina writers. She describes them as "not so much people in the process of leaving one world and entering another as they are people living in two worlds at once" (1989, 175). But Morales, "a child of the Americas," lives in many more worlds than two simultaneously. She is truly global in her philosophical reach, perhaps because she herself embodies diverse, yet syncretized elements. She is a Jewish Puerto Rican American, out of the New York ghettos, and the descendant of immigrants. She is simultaneously "Caribeña," but not African or "taína," or European, although she has African, "taína" and European in her blood. All these genetic elements course through her, but she is a hybridized, syncretic combination. She is new. English is her "passion," Spanish is part of her "flesh," and "[S]panglish" is her first language. In her blood runs the "crossroads" of cultures into which she is born. And she is "whole" (1995, 79). Morales also sees multiple identity as a triumphant source of inspiration and pleasure for herself as an individual.

Still, it cannot be denied that multiple identity continues to recur as a problematic in one guise or another in the work of most Latina writers. Can the suffering from being forced to leave one culture, one's originary home in the world, to enter into another, ever be integrated? Both birth culture and Anglo world are equally alien in regard to the oppressive treatment of Latinas by gender, class, and race. Yet Latinas are forced to observe both cultures from outside their class systems by virtue of being women born into those cultures. This excess, beyond and yet contained within "hybridity and syncretism," is precisely where "psychic enforced tourism" lies. Needless to say, this experience is common to the Latina authors analyzed in this text, as well as to most ethnic and women of color writers.

CLASS RANKINGS BY GENDER AND RACE

Always, perhaps more than any other issue in their lives, Anglo culture reinforces in Latinas their original culture's construction of power relations through class rankings by gender and race. What de La Torre and Pesquera claim is characteristic of Chicana writers is also characteristic of Latina writers, as well. "Chicanas are not only questioning and restructuring feminist and national discourses but also infusing largely unexplored class themes with new forms of identity that have until now been absent from Chicano/a cultural productions . . . by incorporating sex/gender domination and resistance within a colonial dialectic" (1993, 3, 6). To expand this paradigm globally, ethnics and people of color are always placed in subordinate positions in terms of class compared with those in power who are always males, "for all categories are, as [Judith] Butler and others have put it, 'regulatory regimes'"(Walters 1996, 851). Simultaneously, women of all races and classes are always "constructed in power relations" (Walters 1996, 851), that is, in subordinate positions to white men in all cultures where white men rule, when a "white, bourgeois, and masculine fetishistic imaginary reigns" (Walters 1996, 854). However, Walters fails to observe that even in cultures where men of color rule, women of color are situated in subordinate positions in real life, as well as depicted as subordinate to male characters in their literature. I do agree with Walters and Romany however, that everywhere on the planet in every culture, "lines of power . . . mark themselves on the lives of gendered, raced, ethnic subjects." This is done, not only conceptually, ideologically, discursively, but "at the very concrete level of power differentials and unequal distributions of privileges" (Walters 1996, 863; Romany 1995, 395).

All the Latina writers analyzed in this text respond to their firsthand experiences of inequitable gendered power relations with attempts to analyze the patriarchy's diverse manifestations and to oppose its domination wherever those manifestations present themselves. That is, everywhere, from the bed to the boardroom, as the saying goes, except that no Latina authors depict their Latina characters in boardrooms. Rather, they depict their Latina characters as bored in rooms that confine them, in factories, fast-food restaurants, or domestic spaces, for the most part. Latina writers depict the enforcement of inequitable gendered power relations in females from the moment when Latina children begin their training under their gatekeepers at home, again in school, and again when they migrate psychically to the workplace and physically to the United States. They are faced with and forced to conform to racist, sexist, and class oppression all their lives, within and beyond their birth cultures.

VIOLENCE

To find a "space" to vent their rage, Latina writers often choose to do it through violent characters, images, and scenes in their writing. This is a characteristic fairly common among writers from oppressed groups, especially feminist writers, and not only unique to Latina writers. Aurora Levins Morales's work fits this model. She became a feminist in the course of consciousness-raising sessions "in those rooms of women leaning intently toward each other" (1995, 807). She began to feel "indignation," an emotion that "became an anchor" for her in that it sourced her writing as an adult. "Not the poems and fables of my childhood, but thick, black journals full of confusion, like a howling wind, where I raged and mourned and thought and planned, reaching for the clear place, the eye at the heart of the storm" (1995, 807).

Ana Lydia Vega also testifies to the same source for her writing. She believes that the experiences she has had since infancy "with repression, this constant negotiation with a male-dominated world leaves an imprint on one's self." Vega claims that it is not necessary to read feminist theories in order to know them, to be a feminist in practice, to arrive at some positions that frame what one chooses to write about. Although she did study feminist theory while attending university, her feminism strikes her as "more a response to decisions I have made in my life [that] grew out of decisions and positions that are lived experiences" ("Interview," Hernández and López Springfield, 1994, 816–817). In this sense, many of the works of Latina authors can be defined as in the genre of "revenge narratives . . . that . . . unmask patriarchy–lays it bare–in a way that avenges at least some of the wrongs done to women in its name" (Vélez 1988, 2). In addition, as Frederick Jameson has noted about "Third World literature," it "tends to be satirical and allegorical" (1986, 69). This is also a characteristic of the Latina authors I analyze in this text. They frequently vent their rage through irony, satire, and allegory.

LATINA AUTHORS' CURRENT FEMINIST PERSPECTIVES

Finally, Latina authors convey a perspective about inequitable gendered power relations different from any of their characters, male and female. Unlike their characters, the authors' perspective toward their culture(s) is current at the historical moment in which they are writing their texts, as opposed to that of their troubled characters. The authors' perspective is feminist, informed by a conscious, feminist critique of inequitable power relations in terms of class as grounded in and emanating from cultural gendered and raced constructions. Unlike their characters, the Latina writers are entirely conscious of and confront the awful reality: "the self-affirmation of one class [men] . . . as a means of social control and political subjugation" (Foucault 1990, 123). This is also the perspective from which I have written this work. defines this perspective as one that "looks at women as a class oppressed by material conditions and social relations . . . [T]herefore, rather than considering gender polarization as the victimization of only women, material feminism considers it a social construct oppressive to both women and men" (Boesing citing Dolan 1996, 1019).

As if they were writing "ethnographies . . . of their own lives" (Gwin 1996, 874), Latina writers critique their past: their original Latino, and then, sooner or later, Anglo cultures, which have constrained women, ethnic women, and women of color from full expression of their humanity. Both cultures practice what even recent American legal reports define as "systemic discrimination, disparities in treatment [that] do appear to correlate with membership in minority groups and 'even' with gender" (Resnik 1996, 959). In their current critiques, Latina authors, unlike their characters, are now aware of the vast networks and systems of belief that inevitably "engender relations of power within the social order" (as cited in Gwin 1996, 875). Even if all that Latina writers are aiming at in their works is to oppose gendered and raced power relations, at the very least, "contesting the concepts is a benefit. It is the first step" (Bunch in Hartmann et al. 1996, 941).

ECONOMIC PROBLEMS

Another recurring theme with Latina authors, especially Ferré in *The Youngest Doll* and Garcia in *Dreaming in Cuban*. involves economics. In fact, this theme is prevalent with most feminist writers because the experience of poverty is prevalent in women's lives in a variety of ways. Rivera-Ramos expresses a position common to Latina writers:

It is necessary to bring forth a deep change in attitudes both in the male and female populations. . . . This necessary change in traditional attitudes and ideological framework that conceptualize the white Anglo-Saxon Protestant male as the best model to copy and impose and that conceptualize women and particularly Hispanic and Puerto Rican women as the inferior part of humankind will have to be brought about in order to pave the way toward the optimization of economic growth and development. (1995, 195)

GATEKEEPERS

Another element so common in the Latina authors that I have made it the major focus of my analysis in this text is the implication of senior women in Puerto Rican and other cultures as cultural collaborationists, as gatekeepers. Latina writers depict these gatekeepers as the group that perpetuates the patriarchal rules and regulations, acting as their custodians, like vigilant watchdogs. I have chosen *Silent Dancing* as my anchor work because it so brilliantly illustrates the major thesis of my book's title, *Saddling La Gringa*, the role of gatekeepers in perpetuating inequitable gendered power relations. The phrase is used by Cofer's mother as a cautionary tale in *Silent Dancing* to sarcastically describe what happened to a young Puertorriqueña relative, influenced by the mainland culture. She tried to overstep the bounds of her culture's limits for young females, to act like a "gringa" or white woman. Gatekeepers do their cultural work primarily by narrating to their young charges "real-life stories . . . always embellishing them with a little or a lot of dramatical detail." These cuentos [stories] are shamelessly used as propaganda, as "morality and cautionary tales" (Cofer 1990, 4–5) in order to inscribe what gatekeepers deem culturally appropriate female gender roles into their young charges. I have also chosen to feature Cofer's *Silent Dancing* because it incorporates within its pages all the other major elements I previously listed.

Understandably, Latina authors are riddled with ambivalence about their foremother gatekeepers because they are simultaneously nurturers to their culture's female children while serving them as cultural censors and guides into the prisonhouse of adult womanhood in a dystopic patriarchy. Older women–mothers and grandmothers, aunts, teachers, nuns, family members, friends, and neighbors–form loyal cadres of volunteers who train children to be obedient to and serve all the interconnected institutions of traditional patriarchy. They conscientiously pour the young into cultural molds, teaching them to be terrified of breaking the rules on pain of religious, legal, political, economic, educational, social, cultural, community, and family ostracism, even unto death.

I also stress *Silent Dancing* because Cofer's "persistent questioning of . . . the concept of bourgeois motherhood" provides the exemplar for illustrating the role of gatekeepers in other Latina writers, the concept "that defines the mother both in and by her domestic role: passive, submissive, servile, and silent in front of men. In such a definition, the mother is seen as an intermediary for men but never as an active agent of her own life or that of her descendants" (Ortega 1989, 127–128). Eliana Ortega makes these comments only about Puerto Rican women's "poetic discourse." Nevertheless, she could well be summarizing the responses of other Latina writers to inequitable gendered power relations in terms of women's roles. They are committed to "demythify the patriarchal discourse of dominant culture" (1989, 129) through demythifying the role of mother/foremother as gatekeeper. That Ortega notes this response as "subversive" adds a feminist dimension and complexity to the too-often essentialized (and misguided) paeans to foremothers and mothers that critics have tended to make. They assume worshipful poses at the very sight of mother/foremother figures in the works of Latina writers, even though to some large extent they are depicted negatively or with great ambivalence as gatekeepers of Latino and Anglo culture's inequitable gendered power relations.

NOTE

1. See my Afterword, "Asian American Women and the Feminist Movement" in my *(Un)Doing the Missionary Position* (Westport, CT: Greenwood), 1997.

Chapter 1

Judith Ortiz Cofer, *Silent Dancing*

Cofer tracks those moments when she and other Puertorriqueñas are first made unwilling psychic tourists in their own birth culture. They are alienated from and yet simultaneously most deeply enculturated into Puerto Rican models for womanhood, models that give a woman class status and rank in Puerto Rican culture. Cofer tracks defining moments when she and other females are forbidden to attempt to try new models, to modify, to discount, to disobey traditional ones, to change the rules and what occurs to those women who dare attempt to do so. In cuento after cuento, Cofer exposes the training, as well as the results, when unruly women disobey the rules by stepping out of line, going past the boundaries set for their kind, and attempt "numerous subversions of power" of "the patriarchal order" (Vélez 1988, 3).

Cofer's major concern is to describe the results of existing power relations in her two cultures, primarily in terms of gender, as well as of race, in such a powerful and chilling way that readers will be as outraged as she is. Readers will observe through her work the imposition of "touristic" models on one gender by another: the enforcement of rules and regulations that keep the female gender from participating within Puerto Rican culture and that keep them observers of the culture from outside its parameters while simultaneously imprisoned within them. The analogy that springs to mind is that of a park within a town and within that park is a zoo and within that zoo are cages with bars that contain captive animals. They are not part of the culture, yet constrained within its rules and parameters.

At the end of her work, Cofer addresses readers in her own voice, rhetorically. Her voice speaks to readers about certain issues, addressing in what ways she is an exception to the cultural training indoctrinated into her by her gatekeepers: why, to what extent, and at what cost. Throughout the text, embedded in her powerful cuentos and end poems, between the lines, and in the final, personal passages, breathes the author's love for both her cultures. This love is equally balanced by her enduring outrage at the oppression of women, situating them, together with people of color and the working classes into what I call "conceptual otherwheres." These are outlying areas in cultures where women are not fully participatory and self-actualized citizens of those cultures.

HOME AND FAMILY, FAMILISM

In the first chapter, "Casa," we meet Mama, the narrator's remarkable grandmother, as well as other women in Judith's family. They are gathered together in Mama's living room to speak of important matters and to tell stories for the hundredth time, as if to each other. "There is an intimacy," Minrose Gwin claims, "within this space between woman and teller and woman as listener–a shared space whose ideology is the production of pleasure in relation, as opposed to the isolated, patriarchally controlled spaces (the field, the store)" (1996, 896). Gwin romanticizes these constrained home spaces, although Cofer does not, even though she concedes that they do give the female children a sense of intimacy and pleasure. For Cofer also indicts what goes on in them.

In addition, Cofer goes beyond Gwin's examples to indict the patriarchy as displacing, dislodging, and banishing women psychically and physically out of all its institutions so that they never become more than enforced tourists in any institution situated within their culture. So it is that the long reach of patriarchy has penetrated into this warm, intimate space of women, as it does everywhere. This space is consciously used by the female authority, Mama, to make use of the pleasure of enjoying one another's company without the constraints of male presence, while indoctrinating and perpetuating male constraints into the females gathered there. She thereby acculturates the next generation of females into "the [v]arious cultural and religious codes in Puerto Rico [that] classify all women as either 'good' women or whores" (Vélez 1988, 3). Mama does this through the use of cautionary tales or cuentos which are intended to be overheard by the young girls in the room in order to inscribe models for womanly conduct into the psyches of succeeding generations of Puertorriqueñas.

Cofer's ambivalent, complicated responses to her gatekeeper foremothers and mother in *Silent Dancing* result in multidimensional representations. These serve as excellent examples of the deconstructing of "deforming myths imposed on them by the dominant culture" (Ortega 1989, 129), myths that many Latina writers attempt to dismantle in their writing. According to Lourdes Rojas, Rosario Morales fervently believes that "the mother-daughter relation" should be considered "crucial to any significant transformation of the role of women in Laina and Latin American cultures" (1989, 167). As Morales, who is the mother of Aurora Levins Morales, puts it: "The relationship between mother and daughter stands at the center of what I fear most in our culture. Heal that wound and we change the world" (1983, 56).

Generation after generation, primarily through the assistance of a group known as the family and controlled and run by men, upon which the young are of necessity dependent, mothers assault their young charges, as they were assaulted, with what the male group culture decrees as constituting appropriate conduct for women. Turned into "monitors of culture" (Vélez 1988, 9), gatekeeper foremothers and mothers act as family wardens in order to keep succeeding generations from breaking the rules of the hegemony. They do this by training female children all that goes into the making of Puerto Rican women.

Heyck describes problems in the Latino family as arising when this grouping is subordinated to Anglo-American culture. She depicts the Latino family as:

a hierarchical institution with the patriarch as the unchallenged head, and women exercising power behind the scenes. Authority is passed down from father to son, with the oldest son playing an important leadership role. In a traditional Latino family, the male expects to be obeyed and does not necessarily feel obliged to consult with family members before making family decisions. A double standard of sexual morality often prevails, with the wife expected to be absolutely faithful and the daughter to be "pure" until her wedding night. The father and sons, on the other hand, are often encouraged to exercise their freedom through sexual affairs, a sign of machismo. This sexual double standard conflicts with the prevailing North American morality and has come under attack in households where children have grown up in this country more influenced by the attitudes of their peers than their elders. (1994, 18–19)

Disputing this allegation, Cofer and other Latina writers depict female children as having problems from the very beginning because they are subordinated within Latino male culture.

CREATING NEW GENRES

Almost immediately in *Silent Dancing*, Cofer begins to undermine the purpose of Mama's cuentos, tailored to perpetuate female constraint in the Latino culture. Cofer does this by providing readers with a subtext in addition to the point of view of the older Puertorriqueña female gatekeeper who is dutifully dispensing the hegemony's prescriptions. By this means, readers receive a different message from the author than that given to the female children who are the objects of the cautionary tales told by Mama. Thus Cofer's description of Mama's cuentos captures how female indoctrination was and is done historically, while at the same time undermining their purpose.

The first cuento is about a poor soul, Maria La Loca, now middle aged and antisocial. As part of the universal effort of all new human beings to figure out what is going on around them, the children would try to figure out what they overheard being said by the adults about Maria La Loca. It all was like a mysterious maze; if they could put it together, life would make sense. Here Cofer reveals that the Puerto Rican female children are situated as enforced psychic tourists, treated by their family as if they were visitors from afar to what should be their own culture. Receiving their cultural cue and acting on it from Mama's distanced and hostile discourse, the children proceed to insult the woman by calling her "La Loca" [crazy woman] as the adults are doing. Whenever Maria La Loca passes men, they whistle at her, but with mockery. The process of demonizing La Loca through repulsive verbal sounds, signifying contempt and disgust, reinforces the children's indoctrination as to how to treat a *desgracia* [outcast]. By implicit extension, the children are acculturated into an unconscious fear of such treatment being accorded to them should they ever be stupid enough to make Maria La Loca's mistake.

Written as from the perspective of Judith who describes herself as Mama's granddaughter and one of the children herself, Cofer, the grown-up writer seems to identify with the children who have internalized their response to crazy Mary as the result of their training. Yet she also adds a distanced, authorial feminist perspective that identifies far more with the object of the ostracism. Here the observation of postcolonial critics such as Homi Bhabha about colonized people's "mimicry" of their masters, is relevant to Cofer's technique in the sense that she too exposes her outrage by "imperfectly" or overly "perfectly" (1984, 128) emulating the requirements. Many Latina authors employ this technique, as we see Cofer's description of Maria La Loca, presumably from Mama's gatekeeping perspective. They do so to expose an oppressive situation for women through the use of conscious irony so as to retell "stories otherwise forgotten . . . a process that discovers or recovers the discredited histories of groups circumscribed by regimes of repressive discursive practices" (Peréz-Torres 1994, 185–186).

INEQUITABLE GENDERED CLASS RANKINGS

According to Mama, Maria La Loca's life was ruined because she let a macho man gull her. There is much controversy about the meaning of the term "machismo" both within and outside the Latina community. In all cases machismo "connote[s] arrogance and male pride and emotionality" (Knouse et al. 1995, 3), despite Knouse et al.'s contention that this "particularly important yet highly misunderstood Hispanic value" has a negative connotation only for "Anglo Americans." This statement contradicts abundant internal textual evidence in Latina works. As readers will observe, Knouse et al. make only a partially valid claim for what they define as "true" machismo when they state that "[i]n reality" machismo "signifies duty and loyalty and strong bonds of honor in Hispanic cultures" (Knouse et al. 1995, 3). This true statement, so far as it goes, nevertheless entirely ignores the sexism enculturated into Latinos which has a devastating impact on Latinas, because it is combined with culturally sanctioned authoritarianism.

At any rate, Cofer here describes the first and primary rule for Puertorriqueñas: Never under any circumstances allow yourself to be made a fool of by a man, or you will suffer the torments of the damned. This message is also common in traditional Anglo-American cultural success mythologies for women. Girls who followed their sexual urges rather than their training were not considered marriageable and thereby lost what would have been their primary claim to respectable class status; to become wives of successful men. They were trained to respond sexually only to the man they married: to identify with and link the expression of their sexual desire only in marriage to one man, their husband. Even then and forever afterward female sexuality was to be suppressed, disguised, muted, and restrained (that is, submerged and sabotaged). They were trained to become witnesses, observers, to judge from afar, to become control mechanisms, enforced psychic tourists, over their own bodies. The goal was to frighten them so badly somehow that they would do anything rather than be identified as "fallen women," ostracized and declassed, like Maria La Loca.

Patriarchal language discourse controls the culture by imbuing it "with symbols that dictate patriarchal power" (Pérez 1993, 59). Until the post World War II period, gatekeepers used coded terms such as "vulgar" and "cheap" or "shameless" to signify outcast females and females who, by class, were considered of the lowest. No Puertorriqueña who aspired to conventional middle-class respectability would even imagine, let alone indulge in, any conduct that would bring such scornful terms down upon her.

In Mama's cautionary myths, the names always changed, as did the predicaments. Whenever a woman demonstrated sexual desire for a man, the discourse of her culture coded her as a female defeated by love. "Defeat" is a term used in relation to battles in wars. The message is clear. Wanting sex, having sex, and enjoying sex with a man is considered a "defeat" in the life-and-death battle of a female struggling to achieve the lofty goal and status of marriage. Indeed, the institution is depicted as some kind of heaven on earth, precisely in order to motivate girls into conformity with the constraints connected with it.

Frustration, even after marriage; the denial of one's sexuality unless one is married to a man; and from then on acting always only within the bounds of propriety are deemed "victories" for women, according to the Latino hierarchy's discourse of constraint for women. The complaint of Lidia, the young narrator in Magali García Ramis's *Happy Days, Uncle Sergio*, bears this out when in conversation with her aunt she inquires why it was unforgivable to be a bad woman? Moreover, if a woman lives with a man to whom she is not married, does she really go to hell? Her aunt responds that it is always the fault of the woman, anyhow.

Further, note that Mama in *Silent Dancing* uses the term "defeat" for women in relation to free sex with men as opposed to that of "victory." Female children are taught that it will be a victory for them in relation to sex only when they marry. Sexuality is thus overdetermined for males as something won on a battlefield/ground, while sexuality for females is underdetermined–some piece of their material essence lost in a war zone—a contested, then conquered territory–unless and except if they succeed in getting the man to marry them. Only then is that essence "owned" legally and always by the man, never by the wife. The woman is the watchful caretaker, the guardian. Her husband is the possessor of her purity conceptualized as an essence, virginity, which must be doled out under certain legal and religious conditions, or it can be lost in an instant of unguardedness. Before and after marriage, therefore, the concept of "purity" elevates "good" women to "a pedestal" of virginity to be "immobilized" forever; thus, women are prevented from "making their own history" (Vélez 1988, 11).

In actuality, sexuality is nothing more than sexuality: an attribute of many life forms on this planet. Only human beings construct and create a story about this basic attribute of life such as Cofer describes as characteristic of Puerto Rican culture and such as most women describe of their cultures. Interestingly, in all known cultures the constructed resolution to this story always ends in defeat for females and victory for males whenever females indulge in the free expression of sexuality without constraint. Ironically, constraints are all culturally created in the first place and inscribed into women to keep them distracted from the realization that they are being *man*ipulated into positions of servility for the purposes, aims, and goals of the hegemony. When they do become conscious of these artificial constraints by gender alone, women become outraged that men should take this right upon themselves, should embed it into institutions of culture. These women then do battle wherever and whenever they can against inequitable gendered power relations, as is the case with the Latina authors analyzed in this text. But it is always as cultural "outlaws," so that the wheel gets reinvented every generation. When women are passive recipients, obedient to the decrees as sacrosanct, they become oppressed victims. When they inscribe these alien and prevailing decrees into succeeding generations, then they become gatekeepers who oppress and victimize their charges who in turn are oppressed and victimized by their culture.

Cofer situates the constraints by Latino cultural authorities over women as religion, the law, parents, and community dictates. The latter "form of knowledge" is "adopted in various discursive practices . . . especially in politics and education since it is particularly appropriate for generating a passive consumption of hegemonic truths rather than an active participation in their determination or contestation" (Leps 1995, 181–182). In Puerto Rican culture, as Cofer describes it, and in most cultures globally, these hegemonic truths provide the myth of male gendered power relations over women, as well as being perpetuated through mediators, the culture's gatekeepers, with their cautionary plot line about female sexuality.

As in Cofer's Puerto Rico, few people, male or female, born into any given culture, question the predictability of this plot. Nor do they question how relations between the sexes came to be connected with gender asymmetry, with war discourse, and with a polarizing binary plot involving victory or defeat for women. The "problem" then of being a woman in Puerto Rico is not literally a problem in terms of biology. Rather, the problem "lies" in the various "subjective positions" open to women, positions that they assume "as social subjects" (Vélez 1988, 8). These positions are few and are situated outside of the culture's systems in terms of class.

Interestingly, Cofer never depicts men as sexually defeated or women as victorious sexually, despite the fact that she battles this paradigm in her writing. Indeed, most cultures do have such a paradigm used only to serve as the reverse of one already previously defined as appropriate for "good" women. For example, there are Circe and Calypso in ancient Greece, Jezebel in the Old Testament, and fox spirits in Japan. It is no more preferable than modeling the culture's currency in reverse by calling for constraining myths for men rather than for women. In other words, it simply replicates the oppressors' discourse, rather than offering an alternative model.

Before the arrival of Christian missionaries in the early nineteenth century, Samoans and Tahitians conceptualized the enjoyment of sexuality as a natural part of life for all. In this regard, Cofer wonders whether it is necessary to create power relations in terms of gender and race through a process of dividing human beings by class where someone must win and someone must lose in any situation. Is reality not far more complex? Yet human beings in most cultures create relationships of power and take binary positions in the matter. Cultures position one side as losing at the expense of another, although lived reality constantly reveals far more complex outcomes. As postmodernists delight in telling us, as if that in any way changes the fact, there is a global hegemony of male rulers in all cultures, but readers should have hope. There are shiftings and slidings and cracks within the foundation: "counterhegemonic forces." Nevertheless, despite all this rhetorical and philosophical distinction making, the hegemony persists.

Mama's story about Maria La Loca plays itself out so as to conform to Puerto Rican inequitable gendered power relations that noticeably use discursive classification codes in the form of public opinion. Cofer and other Latina authors describe as a play on "pain and terror" terminology for the loser the frightening imagery inscribed into female children's consciousness. To illustrate, after being jilted at the altar, Maria descends into a dark night of mental illness for a long time. Reminiscent of Estelle Havisham in Charles Dickens's *Great Expectations*, after recovering from "her honeymoon with death" (1990, 20), Maria was ruined, undone, insane.

What child could fail to fall prey to such fearful indoctrination? After hearing such a tale so strongly reinforced with such powerful imagery and so disgusting a choice of language, expression, and tone, what child would not come to believe without question that the worst fate in life is to be jilted after experiencing sex? Inevitably, unsanctified sex will result in eternal loneliness, if not death, sudden aging (when humans, especially women, are considered repulsive), and insanity to the pathetic point where the only time the jilted female will hear the longed-for wedding march will be in her own insane humming. The wedding march is the quintessential trope for the crowning moment in a female life of waiting.

Is it any wonder then that by the time of their adolescence most females in such a culture have internalized a sense of lower self-worth, of incompleteness and inferiority in relation to men? Is it any wonder then that very few females ever emerge free of these enculturated convictions without enormous self-reflexivity and painful struggles enduring over many years? This is why Cofer includes herself in her own voice at the end of the text: to inform readers with well-deserved pride about her current enviable situation and condition in life. Her own life's trajectory affords a vast contrast to the price other women have paid who did not make it to where she is. Cofer wishes also to convey the pain she feels, as well as understanding and compassion for her foremothers and mother for not being able to understand or even appreciate her accomplishments. She believes that a fulfilling life should be the birthright of every woman–not just herself.

Suddenly Mama playfully lifts thin little Judith up off the floor and begins to waltz with her, the signal for the end of the coffee break, while the other women in the room laugh about their lives. The message Judith decodes from this cautionary tale is cruel and perverse, though. Embedded into female brain cells as the life-and-death battle of love is the necessity of marriage for women. A female must be obdurate as stone in suppressing her strongest biological drives for the sake of ensuring that men do not triumph over her in terms of gendered power relations. Judith claims that in this way her grandmother was showing her how to be strong in relation to the constraints of the culture that would shape her.

It is only later at her Quinceañera, her fifteenth birthday, when a girl's debut into womanhood is celebrated, that she begins to question and debate this kind of negative capability trained into women. It stems from "the terror of the female body" that Eric Naiman observes is "endemic in many patriarchal societies" (1996, 26).[1] Rosario Morales is more direct, more open in communicating the ugliness perpetuated onto little girls. She is outraged that women should brainwash other women into believing that their bodies are "disgusting" and filthy, that to have sexual desire is "obscene," and that all men are "sick" and only want sex from women. The training is to frustrate men by keeping them from getting what they want until the woman first gets what she wants. There is nothing else a woman has going for her. Therefore it is necessary to get as much as she can from the man before giving it up, and when you have to give it up, then you should clamp your teeth together and put up with it, because there is no other way out (1981, 53).

Morales is more honest, as well, in locating the source of her anger–female gatekeepers–women who have made other women miserable under patriarchy. Not only that. They also perpetuate any objection to such indoctrination as a flaw in the individual woman's unruly character. Morales accuses gatekeepers of betraying other women by always turning to men for their approval. She did turn to white women for support, which they give her, but she found that they were racist about Latinos. As a result, Morales betrays herself and other Latinas by not confronting white feminists whom she feels have betrayed her also, so that she now feels she can no longer trust women in general (1981, 54).

Mama's definition of the nature of strength for women is constructed from within a repressive cultural regime of religio-cultural constraint. Here again it is noticeable to readers that Cofer's current authorial feminist perspective is at odds with such a message. For sadly, as Richard McCormick has pointed out, just "the mere existence of . . . subversive or resistant perspectives in a text [such as Cofer exposes at this point] cannot undo the power of what is still socially 'dominant'" (1993, 662). That a man wins if he possesses a woman: that she ·loses something, everything, again overdetermines female corporeality by linking ideological abstracts to it. "[M]isogyny assigns the corporeal to the feminine and simultaneously places negative value on the corporeal . . . in patriarchally constructed femininity" (Frye 1996, 998).

Strength is strength, whether it is male or female. To link both female and male sexuality to concepts about corporeal strength and weakness is to mix apples and oranges. To be strong or weak, whether male or female, is simply a physiological condition. It is specious, Cofer believes, to link such a condition with sexuality, to conflate sexuality prior to or without marriage as characteristic of weakness in females. It also leads to differentiations in class ranking, not only between men and women, but also between women and women. Antonia Casteñeda speaks to this issue when she differs with those feminist scholars who do not wish to make "an analytical distinction between sex (biological) and gender (sociocultural) categories" (1993, 33). She believes that

The distinction is important because of the distinct oppositions within which each category places women. The biological distinction of sex places women in opposition and in a subordinate position relative to men; the sociocultural distinction of gender places women in opposition and in an inferior position to other women. This sociocultural distinction is based on concepts of sexual morality and conduct that are informed by political and economic values. With few exceptions, however, the sociocultural construction of gender has not accounted for the political and economic dimensions that historically related (if not defined) a woman's sexual morality and gender value to her sociopolitical (religion, race, class) status–and vice versa. (1993, 33).

It is also specious to maintain, on the other hand, that strong sexuality (to the point where they "can't help it") is deemed a natural characteristic only of males at all times: prior to marriage, during marriage, and outside of marriage. If the woman's body is violated, or known and used outside of legal marriage, then she has lost the battle, that is, her virtue, or purity, or honor. To men, the currency of respectability for listing a woman as a bona fide member in the class structure of other culturally accepted, decent women is "virtue."

Whether in traditional Puerto Rican or in American models for gender power relations, the linking of the concept of moral weakness in terms of male corporeality with men's sexuality is comparatively rare. Whenever such a linkage is described, men are invariably depicted as victims, hypnotized into sexuality by women.[2] Under the spell of a witch, a vixen, a female goddess, a femme fatale, and the like, men cannot resist having sex. For example, Sara F. in *Happy Days, Uncle Sergio* tells her niece that women who have sex freely are evil and vicious, whereas there is a wolf inside of men that compels them to have sex. They cannot help themselves. This is a common myth globally.

From Cofer's perspective, it never seems to occur to obedient women of Puerto Rican culture that gender discourse for defeat and victory are male definitions which serve to reinforce church and legal decrees and therefore their control over women. This is a Catch-22 situation, because these are all male models for females created by the same males who then created the restrictive discourse for women, along with the accompanying plots. On the other hand, the men allocated certain freedoms for themselves based on the restrictive rules and regulations within which they constrained women. Thus they signified that they were a higher class of beings than women and therefore the gender rightfully in power in that specific culture.

It also never seems to occur to the majority of the women of the culture that these religious and legal models are often tied to economic wellbeing. Unlike men, if women do not marry, they generally will starve, unless they remain in birth families headed by males. Nor does it seem to occur to many women that these models are political, that whoever controls the power controls the culture. In general, it never seems to occur to most people in Puerto Rican culture–or any other culture–that somehow different rules apply according to gender, that is, rules by which men always "win" and women are always defeated. It can be applied to all of us who are not self-reflexive, who do not examine what we are taught. Walters's reminder on this point to younger feminists who second guess the second-wave feminist movement as essentialist and simplistic reinforces Cofer's:

Do we really want to relinquish a critique of male identification? After all, the feminist insight that a central impediment to women's liberation (yes, liberation) is an identification with and dependence on males and male approval, desire, status, and so on is so obvious as to be banal. Charges of male identification may have been spuriously made at times, but the analysis of male identification is central and important. (1996, 848)

THE ROLE OF GATEKEEPERS

Cofer's female relatives are depicted as serving as cultural gatekeepers for the purpose of religio-social-cultural indoctrination and brainwashing. They serve in the cause of perpetuating the culturally constructed models for female and male conduct by specifying the necessary requisites, terms, and conditions for the built-in superiority of men and the inferiority of women as a class.

These older women also tell their stories in such an indirect way as to comment on younger females' conduct without actually stating that they are doing so. This constant critique succeeds in keeping fledgling women well in line, so that they too, in turn, conduct themselves generation after generation in keeping with the prescribed cultural model for decent females. In this manner the precise nature of what is deemed appropriate conduct and how and in what ways women need to go about achieving that goal are perpetuated.

Again, Cofer uses her delineation of gatekeepers as a double-edged sword for feminist purposes: to destabilize Puerto Rican cultural models about women by exposing these models as unfair and cruel through exposure of the discourse and conduct of the gatekeepers. Men are far less circumscribed, except in complementary ways that ensure that succeeding generations will respond to the appropriate cues. For example, boys are taught to conceive of themselves as superior, and girls respond toward them in ways that reinforce those conceptions.

Mama not only has told the story as a cautionary tale for Judith's benefit, but for that of her own daughter Laura, Judith's aunt. Mama has serious doubts about the wedding between Laura and her fiancé who left for New York in an attempt to improve his chances for a better life. Before doing so he gave Laura a very small ring. At the point in Mama's story where Maria La Loca is left at the altar, just as we are about to approach the tragic dénouement, Judith is disturbed by the noise from her Aunt Laura's rocking chair. But she is not disturbed more than her aunt who stifles her tears because she knew the cautionary tale of Maria La Loca was meant for her. Still, Laura is about to have her wedding gown fitted, even though her mother is upset because a date for the wedding has not yet been confirmed.

The second most important point inscribed into the younger generation of female children is linked to the first one. Mama preaches to the younger generations that if women do not get men to marry them, they lose the men because men do not really want to be married. Men want children, and, therefore, the women have to use that incentive to get men to marry them. It was the entry fee men paid in order to attain the honor of fatherhood. Therefore, only stupid or crazy women would give men entry to their bodies without paying the price of marriage. It cannot be emphasized enough how male children are simultaneously being trained from a reverse point of view more favorable to men, of course. For example, boys are taught that macho men never want to marry. Women manipulate them into marriage.

Most human beings, especially when children, seek approval and conduct themselves so as not to be deemed indecent or stupid. In this way, most of us, male and female, of any race and ethnicity, of any class, are amenable to cultural training, no matter how irrational, oppressive, and unfair. Again, in this regard, note how Mama trains the children through such discourse. She employs the terms "smart" and "decent," not only in connection with female self-deprivation, self-denial, and frustration, but also in connection with the most important achievement of all, marriage.

She teaches Judith and the other little girls that marriage in their culture is the price tag set for men who desire sex and children and that each one of the girls has to be a withholding woman. Marriage is the reward the man confers upon such a woman, the glorious spoils of war for a "smart" woman who does not give away her body "for free." The belief here is that if a woman ever succeeds in getting a man to link with her legally, then the woman has succeeded in turning the tables on the man–through withholding herself and frustrating him to the point where he is willing to marry her. Of course, that she has to experience frustration equally, if not more so, than her suitor is of no consequence or considered as a non-existent problem. As Haaken puts it, "Politically and psychologically, it is more difficult to advance grievances around the deprivations, absences, and constraints that characterize women's oppression than around sexual invasions" (1996, 1089).

That the woman has to swallow the man like a bitter pill if she is not attracted to him is rationalized by justifications always calculated to frighten females into doing so, as in this first cuento about Maria La Loca. If the woman does not accept a decent suitor, she will end up ugly, alone, despised, declassed.

But when a woman is chosen for marriage, she is no longer a conquest to be defeated. She is now the woman who has won the man as a prize of war. Nevertheless, and paradoxically, the man is still in a position of power over her. She has been forced to use the subordinate's strategies to "win" him, and once "won," he still retains his class position of power over her. She is still his social and cultural subordinate in terms of class rankings. "In reconstructing the social boundary between the 'good girl' and the 'bad' one . . . class differences among women in negotiating sexual boundaries and on the sustained legacy of sexual policy as a standard for middle-class womanhood [are used]" (Haaken 1996, 1088). Even as a little girl, Lidia, in *Happy Days, Uncle Sergio*, already knows why she is forbidden to have anything to do with her neighbor Margara, not only because the girl likes men. This liking is somehow translated into the way Margara smells as a woman, which the children associated with the smell of "a lower-class woman" (Ramis 1995, 16). Revealing sexuality automatically lowers a woman's class somehow, but not a man's.

Mama has the disadvantage of being positioned by her culture to perpetuate this sort of nonsense, what she has been taught as the truth–mainly through her Church's strictures. Like most gatekeepers, Mama is devoutly religious. Neither she nor the children she socializes have had the benefits of reading the likes of Friedrich Engels on marriage or Thorstein Veblen on conspicuous consumption, or Catholic Church history on the subject of the sacrament of marriage, or any feminist history of that male-created and controlled institution. These documents all reveal that men, not women, conceptualized marriage and institutionalized it. They then hedged it around with all kinds of prescriptive rules, regulations, laws, and religious doctrines to benefit themselves: to keep women secure in their control, so that men would forever afterward be certain of their heirs and would also prevent other men from attracting or taking their women away. Then the men cleverly claimed that the institution of marriage, as they had set it up, benefited women, not themselves– that it was one of the few potentially safe havens for the female gender!

Marriage, they taught, was a protected site where women could find a place–when they were lucky–in which to live out their constrained lives without further harassment if they toed the wife and mother line. Meanwhile, to reinforce this lie, men made sure that most women would starve otherwise, giving women no alternatives, no safe havens in their culture. Nor do women have safe havens in the majority of cultures, worldwide, in which women can live free and independent from the institution of marriage and the family that is interconnected with it. Both interlocking institutions were constructed by the male hegemony.

Nor was the combination of marriage and the family a safe haven for women who attempted more. Cofer is at her most eloquent when she uses the most powerful imagery on this topic. Marriage and subsequent motherhood securely locked women into institutionalized dependency on a man under penalty of ostracism, torture, and death. The church then added religious sanctions to these institutions, together with a plethora of cautionary tales or myths such as Cofer's Mama recounts. By these means, women have been effectively prevented from doing anything else but to become wives and mothers who are basically locked inside their own homes. Thus "female space under patriarchy" is endlessly reproduced in order to perpetuate this universal patriarchal success model for women "within patriarchal configurations of women's lives" (Gwin 1996, 886, 887).

Legal, religious, and all other institutions–economic, political, social–then reinforced the myth that it was women who sought marriage, because it was to their advantage, not to the men's. Thus it comes about, as Cofer and all the authors analyzed in this text bear out, that most people in most cultures believe in this model without question or historical frames of reference. Feminist critiques of traditional concepts of marriage and the family are characteristic of feminists in all cultures globally, not only ethnic and women of color feminists in the United States, or mainstream white Anglo feminists, for that matter.

For example, in Rosario Morales's short story, "I Never Told My Children Stories," her character Zoreida Alvarez comes of age in the fifties. Narrating her story from the vantage point of middle age, Zoreida tells readers of espousing Communism in her youth, then moving in with her Jewish lover Jacob to whom her parents reconcile because of his goodness and gentle ways. Her gatekeeper mother frequently says "Gracia a Dios, mi hijita tiene un hombre bueno que la cuide" [Thank God, my daughter has a good man who takes care of her] (1981, 120). Zoreida' s protests to the reader at this point expose the reality of gendered power relations in terms of class, namely, that the supposed solution to capitalist patriarchy in terms of marriage did not differ from communist patriarchy. She .found herself doing "a shitload of work" that had not been included in their marriage contract that had specified "a free union, an arrangement between equals." Nevertheless, she ended up doing almost all the work in the home, as well as all the "emotional mending and ironing" (1981, 121).

Cofer's endpoem about Maria La Loca gives an added feminist dimension to the cuento about her. Written in the voice and from the perspective of the outcast woman, as well as that of the author herself, Cofer makes a moving statement from within Maria La Loca's jilted psyche. For the first time in this text, readers can observe Cofer using the technique of creating "a story out of a polyphony of voices" which Vélez calls "a defining element of the newest Puerto Rican prose" and what Mikhail Bakhtin calls "polyglossia."[3] This means that "the text is structured out of a multiplicity of voices. Polyphony, though not specifically feminist, has been usefully appropriated by feminist writers, as they write into their texts the voices of those who have been traditionally suppressed, 'raising' these voices, at times, to the level of narrator" (Vélez 1988, 13–14).

Maria La Loca has long ago turned her wedding veil into doilies and bedroom curtains. Now she makes her living selling live chickens. Because she always smells of blood, dogs are attracted to her and follow her around. Maria forever "imagines her betrayer's face in the chickens' eyes," and when she slaughters them, she forever fantasizes that she is castrating her faithless lover in revenge for his public humiliation of her at the altar.[4]

From Mama's colonized perspective, to accept the training of the traditional unquestioned model is to make it always appear as if the man in question has succeeded in undoing Maria La Loca. Her lover has outsmarted her by taking something so precious from her that she loses her health, sanity, and standing in the community. She becomes an ugly, old outcast. In contrast, the man who jilted her is perceived as living out his life in another village in perfect ease and contentment, a respected member of his community who is doubtless blessed with a loving family.[5]

The flat tone and nonjudgmental description Cofer consciously uses to give her readers this information provokes us to greater anger than we would otherwise experience at so inequitable an outcome. Cofer is neither directly presenting any other alternatives for the betrayed woman, nor satirizing her condition. Instead, by having the wronged woman speak in her own voice from her own perspective, Cofer reveals that Maria La Loca is traumatized, obsessed by betrayal, plotting the destruction of her betrayer. She views herself as an avenging angel, whereas her culture views her only as having been driven crazy. But if the false lover ever did return, there can be little doubt what Maria La Loca will do to him, or where Cofer, the supposedly dispassionate delineator of her culture's customs and values, stands on this issue.

Cofer's representation of Maria La Loca calls for readers to meditate on male and female power relations; on the cruel privileging of men's sexuality over women's and the tragic results for women who express their sexuality in a male-dominant society. Public and private "humiliation" and "symbolic self-maiming" [as well as imagining the maiming of the cause of the shame] leads to "lasting debilitating consequences" (Harding 1995, 152).

In the tale of Maria Sabida, also told by Mama (in "Tales Told under the Mango Tree") in *Silent Dancing*, Cofer, through the use of the fairy tale/fable genre, employs magic realism to provide readers with a contrast to the foolish character and tragic fate of Maria La Loca. Or so it would appear at first glance. From a prodigously wise child, Maria Sabida grows even more so as a girl and woman, primarily because she saw into and through problems, especially those made by men. Born a healer, she was able to speak at birth in order to tell the midwife the herbs that would assist her mother in recovering from childbirth as soon as possible.

Maria Sabida grew up during the Spanish occupation of Puerto Rico, while it was neglected, and as a result, crime abounded. It so happened that in Maria Sabida's district when she came of marriageable age, there was one cruel lladron [robber] who had seized control of the area. He would ride his horse into the stalls on Saturday market days to overturn the tables of produce and steal the chickens for sale there. He would rob the townspeople of their cattle and then force them to buy the cattle back from him. In all this, Cofer is also alluding allegorically to the condition of present-day Puerto Rico in relation to the United States.

The young woman decides either to conquer or kill this robber. For she is courageous, as well as beautiful. She follows him to his fortress in the forest, which she describes significantly as not really a home, "but a man-place" in that it was built like a fortress, without windows but with turrets for men to "stand guard with guns" (70). She cooks delicious soup and pours a sleeping potion into it. Then she goes upstairs to rest, to wait for the robber, whom she now calls her betrothed. After eating her drugged soup, the robber and his men discover the identity of the cook and rush to kill her. All the men fall asleep in their tracks, except the robber who is the only one to make it to her. Each time he tries to attack her, however, she beats him off with a paddle. Then when she is satisfied that he is vanquished, Maria leaves.

The next week the robber and his men come to her house with a cuatro, a giuro, maracas, a harmonica, and wedding supplies. After the robber serenades her with "The Ballad of Maria Sabida," she emerges out onto the balcony of her home in her wedding dress, and the couple is married that day. That night Maria Sabida goes down to the kitchen, gets honey, and returns to the bedroom. There she creates a life-sized doll out of her clothes and pours honey into it. When her husband enters, she blows out the candle. He proceeds to stab the doll's body over and over, while honey splashes out all over his face. He then claims that if he had known she was so sweet he would not have murdered her and prays to her soul for forgiveness. At this, Maria Sabida leaves her hiding place to inform him that she has tricked him once more and that she is not dead. Rejoicing, he swears to her that he will never kill or steal again. Later, he becomes an honest farmer, as well as mayor of the town that was the site of his earlier criminal exploits.

Maria Sabida made a true home out of his den of thieves. Then she had brilliant children, like herself, all of them able to speak as they emerged from the womb. By the time she died at 100, she was the wisest woman in all of Puerto Rico, her reputation having spread even to Spain. Mama concludes the tale with her customary cautionary message for women: "But, she always slept with one eye open" (1990, 74). The crucial meaning embedded in Mama's conclusion is that in order to live decently with men, women must never relax their guard around them. They must be preternaturally alert in every way every day. And every night they must act as if they were sentinels on guard duty because men are all robbers at heart. Again, as in the first cuento, Mama is indoctrinating her young audience into the belief system that men will take advantage of women who follow their instincts.

A model for the successful or prevailing woman according to Puerto Rican cultural values, Maria Sabida is an herbalist, an observer of the natural and social environment around her, so alert at all times that her husband could never catch her off guard. By implication, Maria Sabida provides an alternative to Maria La Loca, the stupid fool. It is no wonder then that later on in life as an adult, Cofer realizes that she received her gift for words not from the school curriculum, or from learned professors in college or graduate school, but from Mama as she related her tales to the younger generation. What Cofer does learn from her formal education is that these myths told to her by her grandmother were in reality rooted in the ancient Greek and Roman myths, continually modified to keep up with changing times.

The tale of Maria Sabida sounds like a combination of Goldilocks, Little Red Riding Hood, and a section of *The Odyssey,* where the hero Odysseus has an affair lasting three years with the witch and minor goddess Calypso. She turns all his men to swine with a magic potion and tries to kill him, but on the advice of Athene, goddess of wisdom, Odysseus does not drink the potion. He thereby outsmarts Calypso, not by using his wits, but by virtue of a goddess's favor. Somehow this seems to bewitch Calypso, instead of antagonize her.

In this text, as elsewhere, Athene is asexual. She can only be a male invention because of the gratuitous cruelty of depriving her of sexual feeling, as if a female entity cannot have both sexuality and wisdom. In fact, this is what the ancient Greeks believed to the point where they celebrated the few instances when women disproved it.

Athene is imagined as having sprung fully formed in an immaculate conception from her father Zeus's brow. She also always serves as an instrument of the hegemony to assure masculine supremacy. She never acknowledges or identifies with the sexual frustration Odysseus's wife Penelope must feel after nineteen long years alone. Indeed, Athene never shows compassion for any females in the epic, nor does she ever work on their behalf unless her work ultimately benefits Odysseus. She does dry Penelope's tears, but only to make her more beautiful for the suitors so that she can keep them dangling until Odysseus can return to wreak vengeance on them. He returns for one night of love and then leaves Penelope languishing alone forever. Again, neither Odysseus nor Athene takes notice of his wife's feelings in the matter, or even that she would have any feelings in the matter. Feeling the same outrage as I do, Marjorie Agosín "advises" Penelope to stop being exploited and start rebelling: "oiga doña Penélope,/avívese,/y por lo menos venda/una bufandita' [Listen, Lady Penelope, rise up and at least cover yourself with a little scarf. I. e., At least, wise up] "(cited in Scott 1989, 243).

Again, in *The Aeneid* by Virgil, Dido, the queen of Carthage, is a widow with whom Aeneas, the hero of the epic, takes shelter after escaping Troy. One day, at the behest of the gods, Aeneas sails away, abandoning her. Observing him as he does so and realizing that she has lost her virtue, she becomes distraught, builds a funeral pyre, and stabs herself in the heart before immolating herself.

Although Mama's tale is evidently a variant of these ancient tales, it is narrated from within the female perspective and with a different purpose in mind from that of Homer and Virgil. Mama creates a larger-than-life heroine in Maria Sabida from the moment of her emergence from the womb. She overcomes male treachery and subterfuge, and with greater intelligence and resourcefulness than any of them. Moreover, she succeeds in her efforts without aid from anyone else, god or human, and certainly not from any man.

Maria Sabida, as does Mama, makes sure, even as she does so, to keep well within the confines of the male-run culture, that is, the men's place, the robbers' fortress. She may put windows and curtains in those openings. She may cook. She may start fresh in her husband's casa, but she never thinks to tear it down.[6]

And therein is contained another subliminal myth for Mama's young charges. Maria Sabida, like Maria La Loca, *is a myth for women, not necessarily a woman's myth.* No female child hearing these cuentos would want to live her life out as a chicken killer in lieu of avenging herself against a false suitor. Nor would any female child want to live her life out like Maria Sabida, forever on her guard against her mate's perfidy, forever worrying about his getting the best of her, his potential treachery.

Certainly, Cofer does not paint pretty alternatives for future Puerto Rican women. This is because the foolish woman and the prevailing woman both lose within the rules of a system that ordains precisely how women prevail and precisely how they are foolish. Men will always be robbers of women's honor so long as women's honor resides in flesh because "[t]he quest for 'womanhood' is still socially defined in sexual terms under the popular emblem of the romantic/erotic" (Alarcón 1989, 104).

The only difference between Maria Sabida and Maria La Loca is that in giving it all up for love, the latter gave her body prematurely, prior to the legal contract of marriage. As a result, she suffered the dreadful consequences for the rest of her life, whereas Maria Sabida did not. Nevertheless, she still had to live on guard against her husband's betrayal in different forms for the rest of her life. This is the deep level moral contained in Mama's cautionary tale.

In actuality, all it means is that by these rules the woman's body has no other value than virginity. If a man enters the woman's body before marriage and does not marry her, she has lost all her value to her culture and therefore to herself. Puerto Rican culture, like most cultures, has no use for the woman except in her flesh, much as Penelope and Dido had no use for themselves, despite their lofty position as queens. They were not important in themselves, so much as that their fathers and husbands were kings. The prevailing woman never gives it away under any other circumstances and conditions than those the (male hegemonic) culture has decreed. The prevailing woman therefore lives always within the prescribed parameters of this rule of purity–whether she has broken it or kept it.

Cofer also muses on the possibility of whether a woman could ever prevail were she to go by her own desires and create her own rules and whether she would be permitted to live and thrive by them. She muses about a woman who might not care for men and sex that much, how easy it would then be for such a woman to conform to rules of chastity. She also muses on a woman who could create or live in a separate community of women which makes its own rules, a woman who could create through revolution a different cultural regime which would make one rule standard for men and women.

There are occasions when I discuss other Latina authors who apply patriarchal cultural role models for men to their female characters for the purpose of provoking laughter–at the patriarchy. Occasionally, although Cofer uses a delightful touch of humor about certain situations she considers unjust and outrageous in the form of delicately expressed sarcasm and irony, in her work the results of female disobedience are always tragic. Women are victims of patriarchy, of the cultural decrees and constraints that create unequal power relations between men and women of their society, generally betrayed by other women they love and trust–their gatekeepers. In either case, whether through laughter or through tears, the gaping chasm thus exposed by contemporary Latina writers between one set of infallible prescriptions for one gender and another set for another gender never fails to reveal a crucial indicator for defining unequal power relations between men and women.

Cofer, like other Latina authors discussed in this text, contributes a political subtext to her own variant to Mama's myth, as well as variants on the Spanish, Greek, and Roman myths. In her version of Maria Sabida, Cofer more openly reveals anti-Yankee, anti-colonial sentiment than in her grandmother's version. In allegorical form, Cofer describes the unequal power relations between Puerto Rico, located at the bottom of the hill, and the United States at the summit. Guarded by a dragon, that is, the U.S. military force, that "large force field of imperialism" (Trask 1996, 909), the Yankee owners have usurped the most profitable and fertile properties.

It is rumored that the Yankees who own the ranch are going to make subdivisions out of it or otherwise commercialize the property, which Magali García Ramis and Esmeralda Santiago, as well as Cofer and all Latina authors, deplore. "The reality of Puerto Rico" is among other things "rampant urbanization that has destroyed thousands of acres of farmland; American businesses that set up shop for as long as they can get tax breaks, then move on to another part of the world where there is no minimum wage and the workers don't expect as much" (E. Santiago 1995, 23).

In fact, the brutal exploitation of the island and its people is a major topic of contemporary Puerto Rican writers. In her novella "Miss Florence's Trunk" Ana Lydia Vega uses a framed story in which Vega introduces the voice of the Englishwoman Miss Florence Jane, who describes her life in Puerto Rico with her "dear benefactress, friend, and employer," Mrs. Susan Lind, who went to live there after her marriage. Vega's novella is based on the life of Susan Walker Morse who became a slave owner as a result of her marriage. Mrs. Lind was the daughter of Samuel F. B. Morse (the famous inventor of the Morse Code and an excellent painter) whom Vega castigates in the novella for his proslavery stance.

Before they are eventually ruined, Miss Florence's observations reveal the injustices of the system that the English and American interlopers benefit from in many ways. The indigenous Puerto Ricans are far more ruined in all these many ways immediately and on into perpetuity. As a friend of Miss Florence's advises her (and as Cofer in her cuento about Maria Sabida subtly advises the landlord on the top of the hill):

[F]lee that luxurious and pleasant prison in which you live, a prison built on the bones of so many of God's creatures. For if you do not, the brilliantly glittering lie of that rotten world will undermine your spirit and your will and turn them into the crushed and desiccated fibers of the sugarcane from which all the sweet-life-juice has been squeezed. (Vega 1994, 217)

Through the use of anti–American discourse in allegorical form, Cofer also reveals herself as joining the "serious efforts being mounted by human rights theorists and activists to recast the issue [of women's oppression] within the public domain. Traditionally, this issue is defined as a 'domestic sphere' or 'private matter'" (James 1996, 467).[7] Further, what Vélez says of Puerto Rican women writers in general can here be said of Cofer, that they

have suffered under U.S. colonialism together with men, they have also suffered because of the sexism of their men. Contemporary Puerto Rican women's writing speaks this reality in no uncertain terms. This writing is, then, a privileged object for undertstanding their particular historical circumstances. It is privileged because it is written by a group of women, all of whom are feminist, all of whom have a complex, subtle understanding of both their social context in national terms and the particularities of their situation as women and as writers in modern-day Puerto Rico. From within that colonial setting, they challenge classism, racism, machismo and especially marianismo. (1988, 10–11)

COFER'S CURRENT FEMINIST PERSPECTIVE

In a significant endpoem to this chapter, Cofer takes on the cause of another abused female, another example of unfulfilled aspirations, and in her own voice, not that of Mama's. Fulana attempts to live by her own dreams and desires. Not surprisingly, grown-ups did not allow Judith and the other children to play with the wild girl who only wanted to use her mother's cosmetics when her mother wasn't home, to pretend to be the wife whenever the children "played house," who didn't want to play anything else. All she wanted to hear about on the radio were love affairs and conflicts between men and women to a romantic musical background. She dreams of becoming a strip-teaser.

Cofer's imagery to encapsulate Fulana's essential self, as opposed to that of other tame, obedient women, speaks volumes. The author describes Fulana as like a young bird winged in youth and hope taking flight from her native town. But eventually she fell to where cows stood chewing their cuds of domesticity. Fulana's return to her community was ignominious. Because her back is visibly lacerated with "jagged scars of wings" (1990, 86) she is labeled a fulana [prostitute], considered less than human. Cofer signifies Latino culture by her use of the landscape, and the cows are all captive women, collaborationists, who blindly follow and perpetuate the rules. The gatekeepers do not permit Fulana's name to be so much as whispered to children. She might influence them. They too might want to fly free above them all, above "the houses of their earth-bound mothers . . . and the schools and churches" (1990, 86) as Fulana once had, too briefly.

Here for the first time Cofer openly and directly separates herself and her own compasssionate voice and sympathetic feminist discourse from the antithetical language and the invalidating discourse of her culture's female gatekeepers. By this means, she positions herself as a "speaking subject . . . in a discursive space once reserved for [males] and launches her own 'war of positions' on machismo and male privilege within [an] 'alternative cultural' production" (Dernersesian 1993, 39). Cofer expresses the culture's strong disapproval of independent women who would attempt to enjoy sexual passion and pleasure. They fly free of constraint, and take such freedoms over for themselves as part of their life experiences.

Interestingly, but not coincidentally, Cofer's later description of herself is like her poetic description of Fulana. Cofer describes herself, like Fulana, as sexual and thirsting for travel–language interchangeable with that which she has used to describe Fulana. What Rosario Ferré is reported as remarking of the great Puertorriqueña poet Julia de Burgos (1914–1953) can here be said of Cofer in describing her "revolutionary eroticism." It "goes against the very foundation of bourgeois society and points . . . towards an unmasking of hypocritical morality and a defense of natural values, such as love and equality" (cited in Olmos and Paravisini-Gebert 1993, 24).

Such a character's and such an author's dreams are unacceptable to their gatekeepers. In fact, both of Cofer's descriptions are reversals of those inscribed by the establishment as models for classing women as legitimate and appropriate specimens of their gender. Cofer does not regard Fulana as sunk in mud, nor as fallen. Instead her wings get pulled off brutally. Why else would she be left only with jagged scars of wings on her back? This is because she has attempted free flight, the expression of sexuality and a desire to move around, a thirst for the unknown, for travel, over and above and beyond the leading institutions of her imprisoning culture–marriage, motherhood, education, religion. Fulana is described as a bird, as having once flown (the coop), and therefore having a perspective (still) above land animals, earthbound mothers. In the beginning, her playmates too were more like her than like "prior generations":

For older women it is expected that she [sic] has had more experiences leading her to change attitudes. Younger women tend to have a more idealistic view of marriage, love, and sex, since they have not yet suffered the frustrations inherent in a nonsatisfactory marriage. Both society and prior generations fulfill their role of pasing down these idealistic conceptions. Once they have had disillusions, frustrations, and hardships both in work and in life, however, they necessarily change their attitudes. (Rivera-Ramos 1995, 198)

But not Fulana. These earthbound mothers are tied down to the lower levels of male rule–to the earth and things of the earth–to houses, fields, and rivers, schools and churches. Only Fulana has viewed them from above. The insulting language applied to her by the culture in order to keep females from aspiring above their lot, as well as above and beyond the values that the word expresses to convey her species, are all summed up in the contemputous name Fulana.

The ugly meaning reinforced by the scornful way this word is sneered is enough to keep impressionable girls in line. However, Cofer the author holds a different view from that which she was trained to espouse by her gatekeeper Mama. She now calls the earthbound mothers by her own harsh name, instead. The grown-up Cofer defines as cows obedient women who are tied to their family domestic routines and define themselves without question as their culture defines them—as good and normal. Her sympathies are clearly with the female social deviant and outcast, with the kind of women classed as the lowest possible level of humanity.

Unlike the author who is writing in the present to an audience of feminist readers and is part of such a community, the problem is that Maria la Loca, La Fulana, La Gringa and Prudencia (whom I discuss later) are isolated and ostracized. This reflects the Latina culture's situating of females gone bad. Each woman has to endure a lonely trial, "a singular and lonely search for the recognition and validation of their sexual and emotional needs. Their solitary quest [is] made more difficult by its being undertaken without the support of their society or of the women's consciousness movement that would emerge in later years" (Olmos and Paravisini-Gebert 1993, 24), which Cofer, in contrast, now enjoys as a result of that movement.

There is yet another area in which support is lacking from the culture: "The negative attributions made to Puerto Rican women are the result of the effective internalization of the ideology of inferiority of any group that departs from the WASPM model. This ideology is disseminated extensively and intensively through formal and informal channels of communication, and the process of internalization starts very early in childhood" (Rivera-Ramos 1995, 199). Cofer joins many feminists in the accusation that masculinist discourse is being used to keep women in line because of women's low self-esteem. This discourse is controlled by the patriarchy and labels, situates, and destroys adventurous, spirited women. In other words, it clips their wings. In "Acróbata" Cofer conceives of *herself* as flying free, as daring to express herself, like Fulana, but through writing. By means of "a trapeze of metaphors," she will be like an acrobat performing life-threatening maneuvers in so clever a way that she will make the forbidden acceptable and receive applause from the public.

When only a little girl of five or six, Cofer begins to create her own alternative stories about Maria Sabida. She did not consciously or overtly do this to contradict her culture or her grandmother's version which reinforces myths, but as entertainment for herself. In the story she relates to us (much as in the traditional Caribbean folktale of the girl who marries the devil), Maria Sabida saves her sick brother from death. Significantly, Cofer's Maria Sabida got her idea of how to save her brother while shampooing her hair in accordance with her grandmother's instructions. Her brother is dying from his unrequited desire for guavas that grow at the top of a slippery hill guarded by a dragon. Not coincidentally, the hill is part of a plantation belonging to the powerful American landowner who owns the house at its summit. So there is more politically to this tale than Cofer's feminism, a tale that equates "sexual domination and oppression of women to the political oppression of Latin America" (Olmos and Paravisini-Gebert 1993, 29).

Once again, we see Cofer reversing the classic male epics when, gluing a concoction of coconut oil and starshine to her mule's hoofs so that the animal was able to find footing, Maria Sabida sets off up the hill in an attempt to save her brother's life. The monster seizes her mule. Nevertheless, Maria Sabida is able to snatch away three enchanted guavas with which she returns to her community. After curing her brother with one of the guavas, she eats another. As a result she is given eternal good health all of her long life. She boils the last guava into a jelly that cures all imaginable children's illnesses.

Cofer creates a character with which she and other females can identify: a heroine, not a hero, who returns to her community bearing gifts, not wealth or fame, but health to all, including herself. Even in her use of an empowering talisman, instead of the traditionally masculinist grandiose or deadly one, Cofer employs a domestic item based on what women use to wash their hair. This is much like her grandmother's method in her story of Maria Sabida when Mama describes Maria Sabida as beating off her future husband with a paddle. This is an instrument used to punish children, Maria Sabida's weapon of choice against the brutal robber who would use the man's instrument, a knife, against the heroine. Although he is creative–writing a romantic ballad of courtship specifically tailored to her identity with which to serenade Maria Sabida–the message here in Judith's grandmother's cuento is that the robber is (ab)using the tender sentiments expressed in his song to beguile her and conquer the heroine.

Cofer does not diminish her grandmother's perspective through overt critique or invalidation. Instead, she historicizes it, adding her own later voice. In this manner she provides polyvocality, with the result that readers experience instead of one voice a veritable cacophony of ambivalent, paradoxical, multiple, diverse voices so characteristic of postmodern and feminist writing. Such realities, such truths are never unified, homogenous, or simple binaries of opposition. Cofer thereby allows the reader to see the difference between various voices such as hers and Mama's, as well as her paternal grandmother's and her own mother's, without making differences an overt issue.

Still, the reader is very well aware of Cofer's difference from her gatekeeper foremothers: their embrace and perpetuation of Puerto Rican tradition, in marked contrast to her feminist opposition to that tradition's stultifying construction of gender roles. Cofer's treatment of her culture with tact, consideration, respect, even love, should not be taken by any readers to indicate weakness or the lack of a powerful difference in perspective. Instead, without any diminution of her strong opinion on the issues arising from inequitable gendered power relations in Puerto Rican culture, the author conveys her differences from its model for women and her deviations from it. She perceives her gatekeepers' crucial differences from herself, not as the result of individual emnity, but as due to historical necessity, to changes in the cultural environment between generations that, in turn, cause changes in generational experiences and perspectives. She is very kind to her foremothers, kinder than they are to her.

There are other, ambivalent elements to Mama's role in this text. Cofer depicts her as both a cultural gatekeeper and an astute critic of her culture's models for women. Her considerable intellectual powers are devoted to justifying or rationalizing these models to the extent she can. Through her cautionary tales, Mama conducts herself as a mediator between these models and her charges in order to guide her female progeny through the minefields as she was once guided.

Also through Mama's voice, Cofer muses on whether a woman could prevail were she to manipulate the rules–pretending to conform to them outwardly while covertly following another agenda entirely. The story about Mama's separating herself from her husband within the confines of their own home in order to hoard whatever health she has left after many pregnancies illustrates this strategy of negotiating private cultural subversions according to one's best interests while taking care to appear to conform outwardly. Such a covert strategy is characteristic of those trapped in a repressive system. Sadly, however, Mama's triumph is not due to her clever manipulation of her husband's assumptions based on his previous experiences of her pregnancies, as Cofer would have readers believe. Mama's success in getting her husband to sleep in another bedroom for the rest of his life does not in fact reside in Mama's cunning, but in Papa's amenable response to her move.

In this story, "More Room," Mama has her own room and sleeps alone in her huge four poster bed. "[n]ullify[ing] her past subserviency" (Dernersesian 1993, 47), Mama removed her husband from this bed "in a famous bloodless coup for her personal freedom" (1990, 26) because she preferred to be healthy and active rather than bed-ridden and ill from having been burdened by too many pregancies. Judith's mother remembers sarcastically about the celebratory occasions following her siblings' births that while the women would be relegated to the kitchen where they shared complaints, the men would be feasting outside and drinking rum, singing and praising one another, "compañeros all" (1990, 26–27).

Mama had lost three children and been pregnant eight times. During each pregnancy she would make up the plans for a new room and her husband would build it. But by the eighth pregnancy, Mama decided that she had had enough, more than enough. All her personal dreams and goals would never be fulfilled if she risked more pregnancies. Also, her body could no longer take it, like a neighbor of hers who had had twelve children. As a result, Flora, who had lost all her teeth, was always sick in bed from asthma. Finally, during the last pregnancy Mama told Papa after he had built the beautiful room that she had designed it for him, not for the children. Cofer then comments in her own voice that this was Mama's way of using birth control, the only kind that the Catholic Church permitted, a woman's sacrifice of her sexuality. Mama felt she had to give this up for something more important, to maintain what health and strength and energy she had so that she could enjoy her grandchildren, and live a life where she was more than just "a channel for other lives" (1990, 28).

But what if, after all, Papa had refused? Conjugal obedience to the father's demands is a requirement in the sacrament of marriage for women in most cultures, regardless of the price on a woman's body and soul. So in no way does Mama impact on the cultural regime: its laws, its religion, its tenets of marriage, its inequitable gendered power relations betwen men and women. She requires the collusion of her man in order to practice abstinence.

I am not here arguing that it makes any difference whether her husband colluded with his wife. I am arguing that Mama's rebellion still keeps the inequitable gender power relations intact. Papa, who made a fair income as a designer and builder, was a gentle soul who wrote poetry, was a spiritualist and healer, and spent his time at home far from the noise and crowds around his wife. Fortunately, he did not refuse. As Cofer herself points out, her grandfather could have prevented his wife from making decisions if he had really wanted to. In "Puerto Rican society, the man is considered a small-lettered god in his home" (1990, 18). But Papa was not by natural disposition interested in confrontations. He preferred to avoid angering his wife by giving her space. He kept his reading and his activities as an espiritismo out of her domain.

In the endpoem to this cuento, entitled "Claims," Cofer uses her grandmother's voice, as she did Maria La Loca's, to expose the true perspective of the women whom the hegemony silences. Mama complains that babies may be made in moments of pleasure at night, but "steal your days . . . the rest of your life" (1990, 18). She does not question why this is so. She does not see that it could be different under a different system of rules for gender relations. The rules seem fixed and eternal to her. It never occurs to her that rules were made by mortal men and perpetuated by mortal women like herself, colluding with men: that what can be made can be unmade and changed to suit. More devastatingly, Mama teaches this way of life to each of her daughters in turn. Meanwhile, whenever she can, she frees herself up from the rules, but always covertly, by subterfuge.

Also to be noted at this point is that Cofer imagines her grandmother's thoughts as one-dimensional, as simplistic concerns about nothing but the well-being of her grandchildren and her plans for their futures. Such one-dimensional projections about their forebears are common to children. The title story, "Silent Dancing," refers to home movies that record the appearance and actions of Cofer's relatives at a party. The author's use of home movies to resurrect past experiences is reminiscent of Marcel Proust's beginning of *Remembrance of Things Past*, with the eating of a madeleine. Both authors use an external object to evoke emotions of nostalgia, loss, pain, and love: in Proust's case to protest French anti-Semitism through the Dreyfuss case. A Jew and a homosexual, Proust despaired of the European form of racism, as well as the legal stigmatizing of forms of love in violation of the patriarchy's prescribed model for intermasculine power relations. In Cofer's case, she is attempting to provoke anger in her readers at her culture's inequitable gendered power relations.

In the scene recorded in the home movies the men are playing Dominoes, not the women. There are also children at the party. Cofer boasts that Puerto Rican women did not use baby-sitters, did not even recognize the concept. No mother would consider even leaving her children with someone unrelated to them. Here Cofer reveals no awareness of the possibility that there could be any other responsible adult involved in cultural role modeling than the biological mother and grandmother. She conceptualizes a mother as tied eternally to her children without a break. Like other Latina feminists, most ethnic feminists, and women of color, she strongly disagrees with materialist and radical feminists that having children and having to raise them help to keep men free while constraining women further and unnecessarily. Patriarchy keeps women out of the man's world, keeps them as "enforced tourists" through the use of taboos of female constraint and subordination in relation to children and mothering. Children in Puerto Rican culture are not considered intrusive anywhere, and for that reason there is no need to leave the children at home. Wherever her mother went there her children went, Cofer maintains proudly. I cannot resist adding, *but not where her father went.* She seems to see no inequality in gendered power relations in according that responsibility only to her mother.

Cofer here represents the situation as if from her mother's perspective, not hers. This narrative voice speaking directly to the reader might simply be stating the situation as it existed when she was a child, without judgment. The confusion arises because the reader expects a clear distinction to be made between the views of the older generation and Cofer's feminist views. When she does not make such a distinction, she thereby gives both views equal weight, equal validity.

Cofer does emphasize that her mother was a teenager when she married, only fifteen at the time. Together with her baby, she lived with her mother-in-law and sister-in-law and was treated like royalty by them until her husband returned from his tour of duty. Jealous at one point of the attention given to her father during his welcome home party, Cofer climbed out of her crib and into the spit where the pig was roasting. Cofer here makes a statement that strikes me as cruel. She proudly informs the reader that because of this self-destructive act of hers, her mother had to accept the fact that all her daytime hours belonged to her daughter from that point in time, whereas her husband enjoyed ownership of her at nights because they belonged to him. She exults that this experience was a sign that her mother had to come to terms with her marital and maternal duties. Like her perception of her grandmother's internal thoughts as solely preoccupied with mothering and grandmothering, of Mama's having no personal thoughts or desires for herself, Cofer here complacently views the duties of a married woman with children as fixed, ongoing, endless burdens of caregiving, with no relief.

To Cofer as a child, school represents not a language barrier, but an institution she and other children resist because they instinctively understand that school signifies the end of the precious, carefree days of childhood. She attributes this to separation anxiety before refuting it or subsuming it to fit her argument of fear of loss of freedom. Her argument is based on what is to her a fact–that it is the mother who is "the guardian of 'the playground' of our childhood" (1990, 53). The word "guardian" exposes Cofer here as apparently harboring no resentment against the cultural fixing of the mother alone in that role. Again, she seems wholeheartedly, and without irony or sarcasm, to assign this responsibility only to the mother, and fulltime, at that.

Does Cofer then hold such a stark view of herself in the role of wife and mother? She has become both and not only dedicates this work to her own mother, Fanny Morot Ortiz, but to her own daughter, Tanya Cofer, as well. In fact, at the end of the text we find that Cofer has a point of view toward wifehood and motherhood that reveals her as different from the culturally conventional voices we hear in these passages in the text. In reality, then, Cofer does not seem to subscribe to this belief, yet here she seems to be doing so. She subscribes to both–to the conventional significance given to motherhood–and, as a feminist, the attempt to find a new way of being a woman, wife, and mother.

In "The Black Virgin," readers discover that when Cofer's mother married two weeks before her fifteenth birthday, she went to live with her mother-in-law, Mama Nanda (Fernanda), and her divorced daughter, Felicita. The young bride relished the grown-up atmosphere of this house, compared with hers. She had been fourth in a family of eight, and her Mama had been six months' pregnant with her last child at her wedding, whereas there were no children at Mama Nanda's.

Recently widowed by an abusive and alcoholic husband, Mama Nanda was just beginning at that time to allow herself a few pleasures such as cigarette smoking. They are private pleasures, private solutions, such as Mama's had been in relation to birth control. They expose nothing publicly that the culture can comment about and rule on. For as long as her husband had been alive, Nanda, astute but timid as a wife and overburdened from raising twelve children, would repair to the back of the house frequently on the pretext to her husband that she was going to work in the herb garden. But she went there to smoke, because afterward she would be able to take some mint to disguise the smell before returning to the house.

Cofer's mother took up the habit enthusiastically, and in private the women whiled away the pregnancy, all smoking and philosophizing, Nanda and Felicita about the hardship it had been to live with Fanny's father-in-law who is the embodiment of the patriarchal regime. These women, just as all women, young and old, learned the "cultural values of marriage and familism." These were "large families, women working in the home, and differential statuses between men and women . . . cultural values that result in Hispanic women being pushed toward submissiveness, compliance, self-sacrifice, and deference of decisions to the male head of household" (Rosenfeld and Culbertson 1995, 225).

Felicita had lived with her husband in New York before her return home. He had divorced her for having been unable to bear children, among other reasons, even though she had been pregnant three times. It was therefore natural for Felicita to take a special interest in Fanny during her pregnancy. She would sleep with her whenever she experienced difficulty at night and she took care of Fanny when she had "morning sickness." And it had been Felicita who had called the midwife to assist in Cofer's birth. As a result, she became very close to her young sister-in-law.

The powerful poem "Quinceañera" conveys Cofer's feelings about the culturally celebrated occasion in the young Latina's life that marks her official passage publicly from childhood into womanhood. This is a time-honored occasion for public celebration: to announce the girl's eligibility for marriage, for official entry into adult female life and all its constraints. Again, Cofer speaks in an angry, bitter tone, exactly like the one she uses in her searing comments about the Catholic Church in "The Black Virgin": it is a man's world and a man's heaven.

Here the cause of the Quinceañera's resentment is that prevailing masculinist discourse trivializes and makes menstruation repulsive. Cofer angrily rails against yet another specious excuse (unfortunately common in most cultures) to justify placing women lower than men in the culture. The speaking voice complains that from this day on she has to clean everything her body touches–her clothes and her bedding, for example–on the assumption that her bleeding is somehow poisonous. How can this small amount of blood be considered something to be ashamed about? What can possibly be so repulsive about women's monthly blood, especially in view of the fact that saints' and soldiers' blood is considered so wonderful, and that "Christ's hands . . . bleed" in front of everyone "from His cross" (1990, 50)?

In daring to situate female menstrual blood on the level of men's shed blood in warfare, or Christ's, shed to save humanity, the Quinceañera is here using shocking, sacrilegious discourse. She is also an unusually strong feminist for so young a female. As in "La Fulana," the Quinceañera's voice reflects Cofer's feminist sensibilities. Once again, it is Cofer's own angry voice that we hear. What is said of the poems of the Cuban Daína Chaviano can equally be said of Cofer's remarkable poetry, that they are "a feminist representation of female consciousness. In her poetry, female sexuality is not placed exclusively at the service of a male; no longer is being for another the whole of women's sexual construction." Her writing calls for "a change in the norms of sexuality and for a critical reexamination of female psycho-sexual and sociosexual experience" (Olmos and Paravisini-Gebert 1993, 32).

ON CATHOLICISM

Cofer's paternal grandmother, Mama Nanda, not only was religious, but also superstitious. She observed mass daily at a famous church where the black Virgin had miraculously appeared during the Spanish occupation. Together with other women, all dressed in black, she made a promise to the Virgin in order to assure the return of their sons from the Korean War. This was to climb the one hundred steps of "La Escalinata," roughly hewn by masses of laborers, to pray weekly at the Virgin's shrine. They believed that because she was a black woman, she was the best auditor for them, the chronically ill, the debilitated, all those without power. In a compassionate tone for the women, yet one that is embittered and sarcastic, Cofer tells us that she can understand how women could find comfort in prayer. They can do this despite their having no idea of the whereabouts of a male relative, or for what reason his precious life was being risked in a war that had nothing to do with them. If indeed God was so all-knowing, then it stood to reason that the Virgin who was a woman, a wife, and mother like them would mediate for them with him on their behalf. These women believed that she could do this, even though it was both "a man's world, and a man's heaven" (1990, 44). Interestingly, their concept of the relationship between Mary and her son and God in heaven somehow exactly matches their relationship with their men on this earth. They obviously cannot imagine an egalitarian relationship.

Although it was a man for whom the black Virgin had originally interceded and although she has her adorers of both sexes, the author notes that women worship her. A small room dedicated to her in a corner of the nave is stuffed with proofs of her help in times of war and personal problems, ranging from crutches to baby clothes, for she can also cure infertility in women. Clearly, the black Virgin is special for her women adorers. She is someone they can pray to as mediator for women, a saint with whom they can truly identify, not least because of her proximity to and influence upon the distant male all-powerful deity. This mediatory influence of a black female deity is especially potent for doubly powerless women, both on earth and in heaven.

On occasion, as in this case, Cofer uses a technique common to contemporary Puertorriqueña and Latina writers–humor–that "question[s] the nature of power and expose[s] the hypocrisy of traditional notions of gender roles; the affirmation of female eroticism and sexuality; an experimental language that embodies new and untried human relations" (Olmos and Paravisini-Gebert 1993, 26).[8] However, despite her deceptively light, humorous tone, Cofer can scarcely contain herself at the blatant sexism inherent in these women's religious belief. She exposes a rage common in Latina texts that inequitable gendered power relations are extended and projected into religion, and consciously so by the culture, as an additional form of oppression in heaven to further reinforce the disempowerment of women on earth.

Cofer does, however, concede later in the text, specifically in relation to her beloved father, that seemingly omnipotent Puerto Rican men are themselves, in turn, oppressed and subordinated to their masters–currently the U.S. government–and prior to that, the Spanish colonizers. These women's menfolk, to whom they are subordinated, are themselves subordinated to their colonizing masters. Nevertheless, Cofer's grandmother and all her female relatives worship within the male constructs, within the parameters of "a man's world" and "a man's heaven." These are Cofer's own feminist words. However, one wonders if her female relatives share her distanced perspective in relation to their culture and religion. Certainly it is one shared by the other Latina authors I discuss in this text. Resentment, bitterness, and anger at the injustice of social and religious inequitable gender power relations does lead to women's creative (re)construction of alternate systems within this oppressive complex of systems that are sourced by the culture's patriarchal hierarchical class structure. For Latina authors, including Cofer, "the Virgin Mary does not constitute a real model for the contemporary woman [who defends] the validity of sacrilegious acts to criticize false religious rites in a consumerist society that has commercialized even our sexual behavior" (Vargas 1989, 161).

The black Virgin sits on an altar within the Catholic God's house. Devout Catholic women make sure to keep within the paradigm of the patriarchal culture's religious institutional parameters. They worship the black Virgin only in her role as mediator to her son, and therefore, indirectly, to God. They dress severely in black with a cord around their waist, which represents Christ's suffering, and they even put sackcloth on beneath their garments, to torture themselves in the extremely hot weather. By these means, the women emphasize only their suffering and their pain, their masochism. Cofer again, with sarcasm, comments about the unquestioning attitude of these women worshipers.

It never seems to occur to these gullible women that instead of turning their suffering inward they should look for its causes externally and unite in a struggle to fight them. Instead, it appears to them as if they can bypass human agency and find a solution through prayer and physical punishment, a discourse within the parameters of their culture's male-constructed limits. They are doing so within the setup of masculinist discourse, of inequitable gendered power relations, even in heaven. They believe that God himself would address their problems if only they use the right discourse, the right self-inflicted punishments. The solution, they have concluded, lies in bypassing men and their male governance and governments. They go directly to the top of the hierarchy, to their men's male God himself to get satisfaction. Indeed, there were plenty of proofs that if one only did it right, the male God their men constructed (although they are unfortunately unaware of this) will intercede on women's behalf and make life better for them. Mama Nanda, who lobbied for God's favor and rewards endlessly, without ever giving up, is an example of these devout women.

The women do not look at the big picture. They only make promesas in isolated cases of unusual seriousness. True, many of these women meet together every night to say the rosary in one another's company and in this way they experience a sense of community and a safe space "to share . . . their troubles" (1990, 45). But this is not done in a manner conducive to seeing broader patterns to their sufferings or for having realizations and insights about the larger causes for their troubles; rather, they have individual crosses to bear. Their purpose is only to share in a sense of common suffering and to pray to God jointly for mercy and assistance. If God saw fit, he might occasionally ameliorate their sufferings, have mercy on them. To look for the source(s) of their miseries, to analyze them, or to imagine that there might exist some practical solutions to their problems that they themselves could try, never occurs to them. Instead, they lobby with God's mother to appeal to him, which is defined as nagging in masculinist discourse. That is, when women make requests for outcomes they are impotent to influence because they have no power to do so.

BICULTURALISM

In "Primary Lessons," Cofer informs readers that in Puerto Rico color-coding was used for school children's uniforms until they finished the twelfth grade. Again, showing that this custom is characteristic of Latin cultures, in Julia Alvarez's *How the Garcia Girls Lost Their Accents*, about a family from the Dominican Republic, we find the same custom used by the mother and objected to on Freudian grounds by her Americanized daughters.

Like many other bilingual, bicultural Americans, Cofer has a doubleness of psyche, especially linguistically. For example, she complains on first being sent to school in Puerto Rico that although she could not speak Spanish, only she fully comprehended exactly what she meant by speaking in Spanish while informing her listeners that she could not speak the language. She spoke Spanish with so strong an American accent that she sounded like an American trying to speak Spanish.[9] From her early childhood onward she had lived with her parents "in a bubble" of fused biculturalism and bilingualism. She could listen to TV in English at the same time as she could hear her parents talking Spanish to each other. Once her family moved to Paterson, New Jersey, Cofer innocently imagined herself to be as American as the children on TV and that all parents communicated with each other in a different, private language when at home alone, as hers did.

When it came to speaking with his children, her father primarily spoke in English; he was doggedly vigilant about correcting any errors they made in pronunciation: "not 'jes' but 'y-es.' Y-es, sir" (1990, 53). On the other hand, Cofer's mother insisted upon speaking Spanish to everyone. Again, in *How the Garcia Girls Lost Their Accents*, the situation is similar, only the reverse is true. Dr. Garcia never masters English (he reads only the Dominican papers), whereas his wife Laura, who had received her education at an élite finishing school in New York, speaks English fluently and reads *The New York Times*.

It doesn't matter what culture is hyphenated with Anglo-American culture, or whether one or both parents is an assimilationist, but it matters that the succeeding generation experiences and claims a double consciousness. In the case of Cofer's parents' generation, they are depicted as more commonly like Cofer's father, wanting to conform wholeheartedly to Anglo-American ways. And like Cofer's father, they attempt to obliterate the hyphenated part of themselves because they have internalized the master's script. They believe that they should strive for anonymity and sameness in the effort to be as typically American as possible in order to protect themselves from suffering oppression because of being "Other." In contrast, staunch separatists such as Fanny Morot Ortiz insist upon their own culture, language, and discourse, and all its ways, no matter where they live.[10] This resistant consciousness remains unitary and single, whether the Puerto Rican remains on the island or migrates to the mainland.

Cofer's description of her own parents' sharply differing perspectives and differing fates comprises a definitive response to Alberto Sandoval's penetrating questions:

What happens to the immigrant [such as Fanny Morot Ortiz] who refuses to give up the native culture and mother tongue, who attempts to stay attached to the ethnic umbilical cord, and continues nurturing the cultural heritage (traditions, norms, values, attitudes, sentiments, practices) of the place of origin? What becomes of the person [such as Judith Ortiz Cofer] who wants to reconcile both cultures and their respective social constructions of reality, while at the same time not succumb to Anglo-American acculturation? (1989, 202)

The second part of the family triangle, Fanny Morot Ortiz's husband and the author's father, is the mirror opposite of his wife. He is a Puerto Rican who seeks total assimilation, whom Sandoval does not describe. As to the third part of the triangle, their daughter, she is pulled between both these polar parental vectors. Because of this, the author becomes the one who is actively engaged in the "traversing, intersecting and defining of two cultures" (Sandoval 1989, 203). Also, influenced by feminism, Cofer is much like Ella (the Cubana psyche) and "She" (the Americanized psyche) in Dolores Prida's one-woman play *Coser y cantar*. Two psyches in one body endlessly struggle in the mind of the female character. At the end of *Silent Dancing,* Cofer describes her own complex subjectivity "as a historical process marked by doubleness, oppositions, divisions, contradictions, and differences" (Sandoval 1989, 203).

In the case of Cofer's generation, their psyches are actually three-dimensional–multicultural, not double or bicultural, as they claim. They are intimately familiar with, have internalized, and in all cases, then separated themselves from Anglo-American discourse, culture, and language, as well as that of their ancestry or their own cultures. They themselves in some ways embrace elements of both parents; in other ways they reject both. And in still other ways, they accept and reject and create a new complex, multicultural mix of an American of hyphenated ancestry and of color. Together, both of Cofer's parents are profoundly conservative, whether separatist like her mother, or bent on assimilating as much as possible like her father.

As in many colonized situations, Cofer informs us that school children in Puerto Rico were forced by law into Americanizing. They were also forced by law to take twelve years of English in order to graduate from school. She blames the U.S. Department of Education for enforcing through law their conviction that English should replace Spanish as the language used in every Puerto Rican school. A product of this time period, Cofer's father was taught to salute the American flag and to sing "America" and "The Star-Spangled Banner" "by rote" (1990, 54). He did not understand one word. The policy failed, Cofer informs us, and by the time she went to school in Puerto Rico, she had to take only one English class a day.[11]

This is a policy universally objected to by all the writers discussed in this work, as well as by other non–Latina Caribbean authors who are subject to "the hegemonic Anglo-American system of power" (Sandoval 1989, 206). Here Sandoval's sharp questioning is relevant, for it reflects the perspective of all of these authors. "To what degree does the official U.S. system of education, which favors English as a Second Language abroad, discredit bilingualism at home, conveying it as a basic antinomy? Could such political strategy impose and install an imperialistic enterprise that comprises the elimination of all that is different or in between boundaries (such as Chicanos and Nuyoricans)?" (Sandoval 1989, 206).

RACE AND CLASS DISCRIMINATION

Through Felicita's experience of marriage, Cofer also critiques the culture's race power relations that assign the lowest of classes to people of color. At sixteen Felicita had eloped with a young black man against her father's wishes. Cofer describes her aunt's situation as evoking support, at least in half the neighborhood (probably those neighbors who were not racists and who were black, as well). When Felicita's fiancé had gone to her father to ask his permission to marry her, her father brandished a machete at him. He then swore that if the young man ever showed his face again, he would cut him in half with the machete. He then beat his daughter and his wife, as well, because she had raised a slut, and he forbade both of them to leave the house. In retaliation, many neighbors colluded with "the star-crossed lovers" (1990, 43), donating funds for them to flee to New York. Felicita did not dare to return home until long after her father had died.

This extreme response is common to fathers in the Latina texts I discuss later in this work. In Julia Alvarez's *How the Garcia Girls Lost their Accents*, Dr. Garcia responds in a way characteristic of Catholic Hispanic fathers' "masculine values" (Alarcón 149) in such a situation–and exactly like Felicita's father. In Cristina Garcia's *Dreaming in Cuban*, Jorge brutally beats his future, dark, and lower-class son-in-law, who in turn brutally beats his wife, Felicia, immediately after the wedding ceremony, whereupon she retaliates with even greater violence.

Cofer notices her teachers' racism, as well as her discrimination against those in a lower class than herself. Judith and a little black boy, a servant's son, were favorites of the teachers. She believes this was the case because Lorenzo strained endlessly to win their favor, to earn their smiles. One year Judith is chosen to host the PTA show because of her outstanding grades. But Judith insists that Lorenzo deserves the honor, not herself. She does not say why. We can only conjecture that it is because Lorenzo was in fact as good a student, or even a better one than the author. At any rate, the result of her comment makes readers aware of the racism underlying Lorenzo being ranked below Judith, of his not obtaining what he deserves. This is the case all too frequently because "many teachers have low academic expectations of working-class and minority children. . . . Thus, within schools, both organizational practices (such as curriculum tracking) and social dynamics–in particular, relations between teachers and students–can negatively affect educational achievement" (Segura 1993, 200).

One day Judith overhears her teacher talking to a colleague about Lorenzo. Interpreting his quick, acute intelligence according to racist stereotypes rather than to his individual ability, she calls him "a funny negrito" and likens him to a parrot because "he can repeat anything you teach him" (1990, 58). As for the other teacher, realizing that Lorenzo's Mama is desperately poor, she is going to ·give the boy her own son's first white communion suit with a bow tie. Judith's teacher protests, laughing, because she imagines that in such a suit Lorenzo would look like a mosca en un vas de leche [a fly in a glass of milk], and then both teachers laughed. Later, Cofer's mother also laughed at the image, after her daughter asked her to explain its meaning. It means that Lorenzo is different, Cofer was told, but she shouldn't worry about it because she didn't need to do so. Nevertheless, she *does* worry about it.

She is also self-conscious about her own skin color, as she points out in a paradoxical statement elsewhere, to the effect that in Puerto Rico she was considered white, but after she migrated to the United States she was considered "a brown girl" (1995, 132). This statement is explained fully by Clara E. Rodriguez when she makes the claim in a survey that "[s]ome recently gathered data" reveals a "browning" tendency on the part of . . . "unquestionably white" Puerto Ricans; the so-called U.S. melting pot seems to "brown" Puerto Ricans. None was classified as "unquestionably white" who saw themselves as black:

There was, on the whole, however, a very strong tendency for respondents of both generations to classify themselves as darker than perceived by the interviewer. This was most evident in the "white possibly" category. This (as defined by U.S. standards) was the most fluctuating and largest category of respondents. It was here that a significant number perceived themselves as brown, black, and Indian. However, it was also here that some perceived themselves as "unquestionably white." Thus while this was the only category in which a few respondents saw themselves as lighter than they were seen, many people in this category also saw themselves as darker than they were seen. (1995, 87)

In any event in *Silent Dancing*, Cofer calls to account the racism and class élitism of white and light-skinned professional women teachers in Puerto Rico. Like most other groups, Puerto Ricans have internalized the superiority of white skin. It is to be recalled that Judith's paternal grandfather attempted to prevent his daughter from marrying a black-skinned Puerto Rican, but half the community conspired in their running off together. In Cristina Garcia's *Dreaming in Cuban*, Felicia's father beats his would-be son-in-law Hugo Monteverde mercilessly because of the difference in the latter's class and race. As in Cofer's text and in most other texts, the darker the color the greater the unquestioned assumption of inferiority, followed by the automatic consignment of an individual to a lower class than lighter skinned classmates.

One day, when she was a little girl, Judith was hit with an eraser by a teacher for seeming to disrespect a command the teacher had put on the board. The teacher did not bother to find out whether the child understood English (which she did not). Judith neither outwardly rebelled against the teacher's overhasty decision, nor did she report her for abuse, or even for racism–for the assumption on the teacher's part that Judith as a Puerto Rican was delinquent and disobedient. Still, Judith began to feel hatred toward the teacher instead of the trust and respect that her parents and Latina culture had inculcated into her. By writing about racism in *Silent Dancing*, Cofer is retaliating in a public way by breaking through her silence, the silence her father advocated and lived by.

Martita Morales also protests this racism within racism. Her parents do not permit her to get involved with a man who has an Afro hairdo or who has dark skin because then he would appear to be a black man. To them it is "dirty" somehow to be black, whereas they think to be a blue-eyed blond with "dead and silky" hair is "supposed to be pure" (1995, 9).

In yet another example of racism, this time on the part of Jews, Cofer's father has convinced the Jewish owner of a candy store into allowing him to rent the apartment above the store. After great effort, her father had finally unearthed what he considered a suitable apartment because it was outside Paterson's "vertical barrio" (1990, 62), the tenement Puerto Ricans called El Building. Her father vehemently maintained to the Schultzes and his brother that he and his family were different from other Puerto Ricans.[12]

Because he had light skin, spoke perfect English, and was in his uniform, Cofer believes her father finally got the apartment on Park Avenue that he coveted. Cofer's mother was beautiful in a Latina way, with very long, luxurious dark hair and a voluptuous body. That is why Ortiz did not take his wife with him when he went apartment hunting or attempted to pass as white. This was despite the fact that everyone (including the Jewish landlord) was fully aware that a Puerto Rican man's wife is his "satellite" (1990, 64). If he was accepted, then so was his family. Rosario Morales recounts a similar experience, but in reverse. Her grandmother, with light skin and fine dark hair, was the one who looked for apartments. She would claim that she was Italian, while keeping her "dark-skinned husband . . . the daughters out of sight" (1981, 54).

Cofer's and Morales's observations are also echoed by Clara E. Rodriguez:

Given the racist perceptions in New York (and the U.S.), Puerto Ricans are not accepted by blacks or whites as a culturally distinct, racially integrated group, but are rather perceived and consequently treated as either black or white Puerto Ricans. Racial distinctions are heightened to a degree unnatural to Puerto Ricans (although blacks may be more aware of the cultural distinctness of Puerto Ricans, they still perceive in American racial terms). Given their racial heterogeneity, different racial perceptions, and awareness of the negative effects of racial reclassification in the U.S., Puerto Ricans generally exhibit considerable resistance to these divisive racial perceptions.

Thus there are only two options open in biracial New York–to be white or black. These options negate the cultural existence of Puerto Ricans and ignore their insistence on being treated, irrespective of race, as a culturally intact group. Thus, U.S. racial attitudes necessarily make Puerto Ricans either white or black, attitudes and cultures make them neither white nor black, and our own resistance and struggle for survival places us between whites and blacks. (1995, 86)

Magali García Ramis in *Happy Days, Uncle Sergio* offers another example of discrimination, but this time of reverse racism in the stereotyping of white American men and women of the middle class, as well as of Puerto Ricans who attempt to assimilate. One of her uncle's Americanized friends changed his name from Arnaldo Quiles to Arnold Killey. He married an American, which Lidia's family criticizes on the grounds that their kids were "untidy," that the wife is "so dull" and wears "awful perfume, that "they make an awful couple" which is what happens when Puerto Ricans marry Americans. They attempt to explain their disapproval on the basis that in different cultures different genders perform differently. Puerto Rican men "are lazier" than their women, whereas American men work very hard while their wives indulge themselves in laziness. American women are "very untidy," neglecting themslves and their families, never ironing "their husbands' handkerchiefs," "making their children wear wash and wear clothing so they don't have to iron." "When two lazy ones [a Puerto Rican man and an American woman] get married their children suffer" (1995, 53–54).

Judith's father internalized American culture's racism and class discrimination against himself and his people to such an extent that he lived in exile from other Puerto Ricans. He despised the loudness of Puerto Rican music and Puerto Rican mothers who continually yelled, "Ay Bendito! that catch-all phrase of our people." In extreme reaction to the sound and noise he associated with his people, this tormented man advocated complete silence, teaching his children to cultivate and practice it. After getting the coveted apartment, Cofer's father made his children take off their shoes as soon as they came in the door in order to prove that he and his family were entirely different from other Puerto Ricans. They were quiet and unobtrusive.

Judith's father suffered intense emotional and psychic stress when at work on shipboard while serving in the navy and whenever he was out in public while on shore. His obsession to appear indistinguishable from mainstream Americans ultimately proved so unbearable that he suffered a mental breakdown followed by institutionalization. Many years after the events Cofer describes in *Silent Dancing*, his daughter has openly espoused a perspective different from her father's about the necessity to Americanize. In what would otherwise be laughable contrast if the source for the couple's difference–U.S. colonialism and racism–were not so tragic, Judith's mother also lapsed into silence, but for a reason different from her husband's. Mrs. Ortiz claims that she has "La Tristeza, the sadness that only place induces and only place cures" (1990, 64). She would have loved nothing better than to remain in Puerto Rico, or barring that, to be close to her people, but she deferred to her husband's wishes until his death.

Cofer explores her father and mother's differences in respect to their attitude toward their birth culture and assimilation not only in terms of race, but of class, as well. Internalizing Anglo prejudices toward the Other, Ortiz links that which is Puerto Rican to lower in class. She records her father's obsession to get out of the barrio (in Paterson, New Jersey). He would never permit any bonding with Puerto Ricans there. He would shop at the supermarket instead of the Bodega, and at department stores such as Sears. He would snack with his children only at Woolworth's soda fountain. He would set up a Christmas tree and give and get presents on Christmas Day, as well as on la Dia de Reyes, as other Puerto Ricans did (1990, 91–93). In marked contrast, his wife only shopped at the Bodega. Although they were a financially secure family, they could not get out of the barrio. He looked forward to doing so, whereas his wife feared more than anything that they would do so. Both pulls are deeply internalized forever in their daughter.

Latina writers also use tastes in food–American food, as opposed to indigenous food–to metonymize racism and classism. They measure the extent to which their characters have internalized American culinary tastes–especially in respect to artificial junk food. Cofer's mother, like Esmeralda Santiago's mother in *When I Was Puerto Rican*, always buys food used in the Puerto Rican diet, whereas Cofer's father takes his children to a typical American fast-food counter of the time. In contrast, Lidia, the narrator in *Happy Days, Uncle Sergio*, resists food other than American fast food in her childhood, boasting that she likes to eat steak and french fries, hot dogs, hamburgers, and grilled cheese sandwiches and drink Cokes. She calls food native to Puerto Rico that her aunt attempts to feed her "junk that hicks eat."

Cofer also discusses class asymmetry in power relations in Puerto Rico. Even if the sources, generally land and titles, of class status have evaporated over a long period of time, they are still respected. People who live in ancient houses falling to ruin still outrank workers in factories who live "in modern comfort in cement boxes" (1990, 56).[13] In contrast, in the United States, a Puerto Rican, no matter of what class status back in Puerto Rico, was always ranked as "a second-class citizen" (1990, 56). Even if factory workers and workingclass Puerto Ricans in the United States were making more money than professionals, the latter were treated with great respect. Although educators and government workers were poorly paid in Puerto Rico, if someone achieved professional status by going to school for their degrees, they were given lofty honorary titles, for example, Cofer's teacher was called "La Mrs" (1990, 56).

Cofer first began to learn class hierarchy in power relations because of the exaggerated respect this teacher, as an official gatekeeper, received. "La Mrs" was never wrong, and parents always jumped to fulfill whatever she required. Apparently teachers were all female and communicated directly with the mothers. Cofer claims that such dialogues created "a matriarchy of far-reaching power and influence" (1990, 57), although she nowhere shows this to be the case in any of her work. Quite the opposite. That both men and women respect the educators regardless of their gender may provide one of the few exceptions to inequitable gendered power relations in Latino culture. In the United States, male educators are respected more than female educators, paid better, and rise in rank faster and higher, and in far greater percentages.

Certainly this statistic might be disproved if women worked to modify or manipulate from within those institutions that conform in all respects to the ruling male hierarchy's criteria. But this is not the case with the women traditionalists who worship the black Virgin, as well as those who form study groups in her honor in their homes. Like these religious women, female teachers still work within the parameters of the cultural regime, a system that the male hegemony forwards and perpetuates; they are still teachers in male-run institutions who work within its framework in terms of its content and context. These institutions do not respect and reward female teachers in particular, except by perpetuating the system by extending the private role of nurturing mother within the institutions of marriage and the family out into the public domain of education. The teachers Cofer describes merely happen to be female, and as such fit into the already-constructed cultural model of inequitable gendered power relations within and outside the teaching institution set up to perpetuate the men as the rulers in power.

In "The Looking Glass Shame," Cofer writes at length of her mother, the most collusive of all the female gatekeeper characters in the text. She describes how Fanny Morot Ortiz created a carefully constructed facsimile of a Puerto Rican home in an apartment in Paterson. Her mother's appearance was radically different from the other children's mothers because she insisted upon dressing as if she were still living in Puerto Rico. This difference in appearance was so great that Judith felt embarrassment at being with her in public. The other children's mothers were plump, motherly, gray-haired. Her mother was young, exotic, beautiful, with waist-length black hair; wore bright colored dresses; and spike heels.[14] Judith felt as if she would die from embarrassment if her schoolmates would see the sexy way her mother walked and the way the men eyed her (1990, 126). It is evident here that Cofer is writing about her reactions to her mother. These are not as they are when Cofer is writing, but as they were when she was a child, after Judith has become Americanized, after she has internalized a second set of cultural inscriptions from those of her birth origin.

Meanwhile, her mother still remains defiantly Puertorriqueña. In Latino cultures, it is the norm for young, single and married women to dress to fulfill male fantasies for sexual attractiveness, while acting virtuously and demurely.[15] Cofer's mother adheres to this cultural model rigidly and defiantly. She never moderated her feelings, or way of laughing, or restrained her hand gestures. She rarely left her apartment, except when escorted by her husband, or to bring a child home from school. Her attitude was that of a prisoner "doing time,"and the United States was her jailhouse. The length of her sentence was a mystery to her, as was the punishment of exile from Puerto Rico. She remained in the United States only for her children's sake.

She kept herself prepared for her eventual return to the island by denying herself a social life on the grounds that she would have then made connections within the United States. She also adamantly refused to speak English and insisted upon re-creating a Puerto Rican casa in the family apartment. She began most of her sentences with the phrase, "En casa" [back home] that was inevitably followed with how things were done at her mother's house. As her means of survival, she chose to be eternally nostalgic, endlessly describing how her life would be after she finally returned home.

Of her father, in the U.S. Navy, Cofer poignantly remembers that after each long absence on a tour of duty he came back to the family ever more withdrawn and silent. He lived vicariously through his children, and he was obsessed with their education. He would read Judith's schoolwork with as much interest as if she had written "a fascinating book" (1990, 129). I wonder whether he lived long enough to do this, to read his daughter's books which indeed had turned out "fascinating." When on leave, Ortiz would listen intently to his wife's description of how the family had spent their time during his absence, as if what she told him were like food and drink to a man lost in a desert. He questioned his family endlessly about everything they had done, no matter how minute, as if he were trying to live vicariously through them. He had been a fine student himself, even having become president of his senior class, and he felt embittered that he could never fulfill his talents because of lack of opportunity in Puerto Rico due to poverty and racism. Cofer likens his depression to "drowning in silence" (1990, 128) and grieves that no one could help him.

The most moving thing, the most telling evidence of U.S. discrimination against Puerto Ricans that Cofer records of her father is that he rarely looked into mirrors. He would not even look at himself when he combed his hair. He did not want to face his face, the face of a terminally disappointed man without hope that his future would change and improve. He was trapped on shipboard for months at a time in an endless grind at his menial job, outwardly assimilated, but always Other, always subjected to discrimination as a Puerto Rican. He lived in a state of continual deprivation–of his wife and family, his birth culture that he outwardly rejected, his own home. Although his work kept his family in comfort, compared to most other families in Puerto Rico, he suffered from a sense of endless exile from all that he loved and from his own frustrated hopes and dreams, and ambitions, given his superb intelligence and early promise. His daughter views his depression and disappointment in life as not necessarily restricted to Ortiz as an individual, but common to "many minds" because of the hardships of "immigrant life" in the United States. She wonders what he was afraid of seeing in the mirror and concludes that "[p]erhaps the monster over his shoulder was his lost potential. He was a sensitive, intellectual man whose energies had to be entirely devoted to survival. And that is how many minds are wasted in the travails of immigrant life" (1990, 129).

Unlike his wife, Ortiz saw his and his family's salvation in Americanizing, assimilating, attempting to pass whenever possible. He advocated living only in the present, wished to give up Puerto Rican culture and language, and did not long to return to Puerto Rico because he saw it as a dead end. Only his wife's need to be with her family is what prompted Ortiz to compromise by devising the complex system of back-and-forth travel of Cofer's childhood. Each time his job would take him away to Europe, his family returned to Puerto Rico, but whenever he returned to Brooklyn Yard, his family would return to the mainland, to Paterson, New Jersey.

COFER'S FEMINIST PERSPECTIVE IN RELATION TO GATEKEEPERS

In the title story "Silent Dancers," Cofer asks her mother about the identity of the silent dancers in the home movie. One of the dancers, she is told, is her cousin's girlfriend who has just come up from the island. The sign of this very recent immigration is the fact that she keeps her eyes down, because, as her mother lectures to Judith, decently brought-up girls never raise their eyes.

Always throughout the text, Cofer's mother is presented as lecturing to Judith in this way: as a dedicated gatekeeper, an ardent transmitter of her beloved Puerto Rican culture. A Puerto Rican girl must act with humility in every thing she does, and if this one is properly humble, she is going to become a proper Puerto Rican married woman. That is, providing Judith's cousin marries her quickly, because he met her only weeks after she arrived here. Otherwise, the city will corrupt her, exactly as it did another cousin of Judith's.

In these family films, readers observe the "strong family values prevalent even among Hispanics who have become highly acculturated into the larger American society." On the other hand, throughout the text, as well as in this instance, we see Cofer as ambivalent toward this "culture-specific value called 'familism'" (Knouse et al. 1995, 2). Women such as Mama and her daughter "accept the symbolic law of the father, perpetuate it, and, in essence, are male-identified women denying a bond with women and affirming men's superiority" (Pérez 1993, 60).

One wonders if the girl just up from the island ends up exactly as the young Puerto Rican wife in Ana Castillo's poem "Milagros." The girl talks to Castillo about how important it is for her to pursue her education. She is knowledgeable about conditions in Puerto Rico and expects to return there in the future. The poet smiles at the sight of Milagros's "beautiful face" shining with hope. But Puerto Rico is really only "a childhood memory" like her hope of some day earning a degree. Milagros is pregnant again, and her husband has no use for "this college business" (1995, 136–137) idea of hers, anyhow.

The cousin Mrs. Ortiz scapegoats as ruined was ambitious; she never spoke Spanish in public. She intended to become a secretary to a lawyer after her graduation from high school and pass for Italian, but she became pregnant by her teacher and has to have an abortion.[16] She vowed that her life would end differently. She boasts about her older Anglo lover with a car. Without her parents' knowledge, she sometimes leaves home in the middle of the night to see him, hoping to obtain an American last name by marrying him. She also hates rice and beans because it makes Puerto Rican women fat.

Cofer presents her before and after her fall as a cautionary tale, as one of the tribe of foolish women like Maria La Loca. Her fate, once she gets pregnant, is to be shipped off to a village in Puerto Rico, so remote from civilized living that visitors can not reach it without going at least a mile off the road. In that village the impregnated girl experiences a great change in environment from the one she had previously known in her short, unhappy life. Cofer's mother, trained all too well to identify totally with the masculinist point of view, mocks her ostracized and exiled niece. Distanced from the outcast young girl emotionally and physically, she shows no compassion, no sense of identity with her niece or any woman whom she has been indoctrinated to believe has been ruined, somehow "corrupted" by a man.

By this point in the text, it is abundantly clear that Cofer is going to reveal her feminist perspective through the strategy of exposing her readers to the Puerto Rican culture primarily through the voices of its female gatekeepers. There are differences in their voices, even so. Sometimes they are ambivalent, as in the case of Mama, sometimes wholeheartedly collaborationist, as in the case of Cofer's mother, sometimes solely its victims, as in the case of Maria La Loca and now La Gringa. As with Fulana we never learn Judith's cousin's given name.

Readers are only treated to her derogatory title, issued in contempt of her futile ambitions to "white womanize" herself–as a La Gringa.

In this way, Cofer induces a much greater sense of outrage in her readers than if the author had expressed in her own voice her outrage at a cultural concept of gender power relations so unjust to women. When Judith's mother's ironically distanced voice continues, she uses a most disturbing metaphor for women's condition, inadvertently, a dazzling summing up of my chosen topic in this text. For these reasons I have memorialized it in my title as the best expression of a gatekeeper's role and perspective. Exiled to this small, isolated village the girl has met another man because women like her cannot bear to live without men around. But Puerto Rican men "know how to put a saddle" on women like Judith's cousin. Now everyone calls her La Gringa. "ha, ha. ha. La Gringa is what she always wanted to be" (1990, 97).

Also in this chilling passage, Cofer's irreverent humor (even at her mother's expense) is characteristic of other Latina authors, as I have previously pointed out. As Olmos and Paravisini-Gebert put it so well: "While examining such serious issues as the appropriation of sexual power and the elimination of age-old taboos proscribing female sexual freedom, they are able to sense the humor and the absurdity of much of what passes for 'normal' behavior" (1993, 30). By this means Cofer exposes the sadism of the culture and of the gatekeeper women who collude with it to destroy La Gringa for daring to be different. The concept of free violence against a woman, saddling a woman, La Gringa, is clearly the product of transposing a woman into a tamed or captive animal figure.

The source of this unfortunately too commonplace a perspective is the global conviction that all men's rights are or should be public rights, the rights of citizens. Women have "different (that is, lesser) rights to citizenship" (Stacey 1996, 15). In most cases, the term "citizen" is not even conceptualized to include a female citizen. At the historic Beijing Conference of 1995, a new paradigm was attempted for the first time in relation to this problem of citizenship: to maintain that violence against women of any kind is a violation of basic human rights. Aruna Rao of the Bangladesh Rural Advancement Commission, who participated in the conference calls for recognition that "violence against women is a public issue, not a private one, demanding public policy response and that freedom from all forms of violence is a basic human right" (1996, 219). This move emulates Malcolm X's brilliant shift in discourse before his death, but unfortunately without giving him the credit for it. From struggling for civil rights for African Americans *within* the United States, he proceeded to publicize *to the whole world* that the United States was in violation of African Americans' basic human rights.

Of course, it never occurs to Fanny Morot Ortiz that if all women united with women like La Fulana and La Gringa in announcing both their sexuality and their right to the free expression of that sexuality; if all women united in refusing to permit the grossly unfair oppression of their own kind and protested it as a group, as a class (action); and if all women refused "to be brainwashed or intimidated into believing rhetorical statements that run counter to their own interests and have no concrete expression in their daily lives" (Dernersesian 1993, 52), then men would no longer be free to continue their oppression.

Men could continue to make up the laws, rules, regulations, and customs, the inequitable gendered power relations. When they violate the rights of women, they should be ignored and disobeyed. This was also Thoreau's point in *Civil Disobedience*, that a critical mass could easily change a situation. More than that, as he and his disciple, Mahatma Gandhi proved, the number could be one and still make an impact.

The male hierarchical establishment in power can make up whatever models they fantasy for appropriate female conduct, including defining erotic parameters for kinds and classes of women, but never for themselves. Women do not have to accede to their definitions, as most of them, such as Fanny Morot Ortiz and Lourdes Miranda King, choose to do. King feels that "It has been basic misunderstanding of the [feminist] movement as anti-male, anti-family, and somehow sexually promiscuous which has made it difficult for more Puerto Rican women–as well as Anglo-American women, I might add–to embrace the cause of feminism" (1995, 109). Such women are what I call in this work and elsewhere "gatekeepers" for patriarchy–women who have internalized and perpetuate inequitable gendered power relations. On the other hand, Cofer and the other authors analyzed in this text believe that the truth lies beneath the exaggeration employed by the culture's gatekeepers and designed to frighten off and away all those women who dread disapproval, ostracism, and cultural sanctioning from the home to the public arena.

The works analyzed in this text reveal that masculinist discourse defines as shameful and heretical whatever will keep women down and out in comparison to the masculinist hegemony. The feminist movement is antipatriarchal, whereas most cultures are patriarchal–run by men and assisted by gatekeeper women. The feminist movement is antifamily in the patriarchal sense of the heterosexist and religiously sanctioned family to which King refers as being viewed as natural and normal by Latinas. The feminist movement also advocates sexual freedom for women.

In La Fulana and La Gringa, Cofer is placing "particular emphasis on the affirming qualities of [women's own] eroticism." She flies in the face of most cultures, not only Latino patriarchal culture. She emphasizes a "category" within gender power relations not permitted to be self-defined by women "that is constantly being challenged and appropriated by women who recognize its possibilities as a vital resource for change and empowerment." This would come to pass if women did "express in direct and critical language" such as Cofer does with La Fulana, "a woman's most intimate needs and desires" (Olmos and Paravisini-Gebert 1993, 27, 28). What Cofer exposes, Lillán Leví testifies to, as well, in terms of contemporary Nicaraguan culture:

The motto for the masculine gender–"make a mark on the world"–can hardly be fulfilled by impoverished Third World men. They are, one might say, deprived of their gender prerogative. This fact exacerbates their tendency to violence, a tendency fostered by the war. Even the most deprived male has one or several women at his disposal. One Nicaraguan male imperative is to "put a belly on a woman"; having a child by her is a sine qua non of Nicaraguan masculinity.

The motto of the feminine gender–to belong to others and live for others–begins to be played out as soon as a girl baby is born. By the age of five a girl child from the lowest economic stratum has become a caretaker for her younger siblings. Her body is already bent under loads almost equal to her weight–a pail of water, a baby. She is unlikely to attend school: family income is insufficient and she must help with domestic chores. By ten she will have witnessed many abuses against her mother; she herself will become the object of violent incest at the hands of one or several males in her own family. At eighteen, after an agitated sexual life but no erotic experience, she will become a mother, still without social services, education, job training, or legislation attentive to her urgent problems. (1993, 15)

If women refused to perpetuate male fantasies; if women laughed them out of existence and stopped taking them seriously as sacred decrees from on high cast in stone; and if women stopped viewing themselves as heretics for disobeying what are actually unfair and inequitable fantasies of petty minds, then there would be no terms like "La Loca" "La Fulana," or "La Gringa," no saddles to put on women. Cofer is saying as much in the story of La Fulana when she describes the sensual woman as having wings which not only are clipped, but cut off down to scar tissue, while the gatekeeper women who assist in this symbolic clitoridectomy do so as earthbound animals.

It takes a great deal of delicate subtlety combined with daring for Cofer to expose her culture's unfair gendered power relations. She relies heavily on the reader's sensitivity to tone and innuendo. Still, it is clear where her sympathies lie and what she would prefer when she exposes the social and religious oppression of women, without comment, while maintaining a totally different view toward ostracized women than that which she herself has been so rigidly trained to take. Like Michel Foucault, Cofer makes it clear that she sees La Fulana as contructed as a prostitute by "the modes by which, in our culture, human beings are made subjects" (1982, 777), as Foucault puts it, and that those "modes" are discursive and social.

We have seen this previously in Cofer's sympathetic attitude toward Maria La Loca, even writing a poem from her perspective. In fact, she always takes the perspective of the female victims of injustice to women, as well as of female rebels against their indoctrination. "The quest for power and control over one's sexuality, and the freedom to explore erotic fantasies are themes which gradually progress from veiled allusions [as in *Silent Dancing*] to a more open and frank expression in the candid and direct writing [that Cofer is here using]. . . . [T]his despite the fact that centuries of patriarchal and machista criteria have left deep roots regarding sexual attitudes in most Latin American countries" (Olmos and Paravisini-Gebert 1993, 31).

The author sometimes even includes herself in this process, as well, for example, in the story "Some of the Characters" where Cofer tropes sexism, injustice, and oppression in general. From a Puerto Rican female child's eyes, life seems to be like a play directed by grown-ups who are the directors and the children who are the actors. If they miss a cue, they are ostracized or punished. So it is that little girls are trained in the script of their lives according to the interpretation of their directors, their gatekeepers. They are not permitted to deviate from the script because the culture, the society, their audience, will not permit them to be out of place, nor to be so bright as to be able to make up their own lines, or make surprising changes from the script (1990, 100–101).[17] Cofer classifies Maria La Loca, La Fulana, and La Gringa in the latter category as women who deviated from the script, and she champions them.

Another deviant female character, Prudencia, attracts Cofer's revisionary pen in an interesting and unusual perspective from which to subvert the traditional script. In Prudencia, Cofer reverses her attitude toward the Maria La Loca female perceived by the culture as abandoned and therefore made insane because she has been foolish enough to have given it all up. As a result, Maria La Loca has turned into a powerful, murderous, avenging force, killing chickens as a means of venting her rage against the betraying male. She stalks through the streets of the town ever in readiness to castrate her betrayer if ever he should come near her again.

In Prudencia, Cofer also reverses the concept of Fulana, who is like Hélène Cixous' preoedipal vision of woman: a high-flying, traveling woman of exuberant sensual appetites, including love for men and children and mothering. Sadly, Cofer struck La Fulana down like a female Daedalus, grounded by a murderously constraining society for flying too close to the sun of her emotional and physical warmth. La Fulana's wings are clipped, and only scar tissue remains in memory of her efforts to be at one with her real nature.

In Prudencia, Cofer also reverses the concept of La Gringa, a young woman attempting to work, to have a career, to make it in American society, who foolishly trusts a white man to help her obtain these goals. In her allegorical connection with the Holy Mother, despite being amoral in her culture's eyes, Prudencia paradoxically destroys "the social order of capitalist class distinctions and of the linguistic order of fixed meaning." She does this by subverting "the bourgeois order of oppression (or, in psychosexual terms, the order of repression)" (Piper 1995, 170). She also serves as a threat to the "decentralization of social life" because of her failure to cooperate with her community. She has created an alternative community, with herself as head of her differently fathered brood of children "that can only be defined negatively" (Piper 1995, 171–172).

In contrast, Cofer made La Gringa ambitious and idealistic; La Gringa is also simultaneously a negotiator who compromises her independence to make her dream come true. She gambles on the Cinderella myth. She trusts in it to the extent of relying on her teacher, a ranking member of one of the major institutions of the patriarchal culture, as the Prince Charming who will marry her and enable her to achieve Americanization, only to be struck down again by her culture's constraints. Could La Gringa not have had an abortion and continued on with her schooling? Could she not have carried the child full term and remained in New York, working as a secretary to lawyers? Could she not have married thereafter and married someone respectful and compatible? Why did her life have to turn out thwarted? Why were these alternative possibilities too much to ask for? Why could La Gringa not carry her child full term, or abort it, as she chose, and still have her ambitions come true?

Why does Cofer make her, like Fulana, so thoroughly, so predictably the victim of her culture? Why do La Gringa's parents have the power to ship her back to Puerto Rico? How could they make her go back, unless she was economically powerless to support herself, unless she was too far into her pregnancy to work? Until she got on her feet, wouldn't she have been eligible for some welfare benefits had she remained in New York, even though minimal?

Cofer does not tell readers under what conditions the parents could immure La Gringa forever with a cruel and vicious husband in Puerto Rico. There the local population looks on approvingly like a cultural Greek chorus and mockingly calls her La Gringa for her aspirations, while this hapless young woman is made into a man's household slave. This formula is much the same as the one Cofer uses for La Loca and La Fulana. Is La Gringa then a cautionary tale, or is it a tale to inspire women readers to further efforts to destabilize and transform culturally constructed models for women that are incompatible with reality? Why, ultimately, would La Gringa give up? Why would she allow this to be done to her, unless she believed that she was as worthless as the hostile community maintained she was? Unless she had entirely internalized the feelings of worthlessness that her culture had inscribed in her because of her sexual activities?

In the story of Prudencia, Cofer takes the depressing situations of La Loca, Fulana, and La Gringa to an even greater extreme and reverses it. These three women all gambled with their bodies and lost. But in Prudencia's case, Cofer wonders what would happen if a woman gambled with her body and was imprudent with her sensual desires to such an extent that she went totally beyond the cultural realm of morality. Prudencia, as Cofer satirically names her protagonist, is a living embodied critique, through extremes, of the Christian mythology of the Virgin and Child. As such, other women ostracize Prudencia. Her public appearances with her brood outrage the neighbor women's fixed notions of female morality, that is, to accumulate children without benefit of known fathers, without being legally entitled to do so within the bounds of marriage and family. She also gives the social workers nightmares.

Cofer describes Prudencia's appearance with admiration as a round mother figure based on pre-Christian typologies, on the statues of mother goddesses found, for example, in Malta, which some feminists theorize as antedating patriarchy. At other times, Cofer contents herself with playing off the image of and associations with the Virgin which Prudencia's endlessly maternal state ironically evokes.

Prudencia brings her children to a public park that has been taken over by homeless men who construct their cardboard shelters over the playground equipment at night and sleep on the benches during the day. Smiling like the Virgin, she sits with these men while she watches her children. Perhaps because of her spirituality, she may not be disturbed by all the sleaziness surrounding her, Cofer theorizes, or perhaps she may not be disturbed by it because she is so out of touch with reality, mentally deficient.

Cofer acknowledges and confronts the Puerto Rican community for condemning women such as La Fulana, Maria La Loca, La Gringa, and Prudencia for breaking the religious and legal strictures and regulations of the Latino male hegemony. Still, she is proud that it does not label any of these women as clinically disturbed, as Anglo-American culture does. As a Puertorriqueña, Cofer emphasizes this distinction, although it seems to me scant and strained in Prudencia's case and even moreso in that of Maria La Loca's. In *Dreaming in Cuban*, Cristina Garcia, a Cuban writer who is discussed later in this text, also points out that harmless souls who would be labeled crazy in other cultures could roam around in the streets without being locked up. What it could mean in both Puerto Rico and Cuba is that the government simply does not have or is unwilling to allocate funds for facilities to house these souls.

Prudencia inevitably becomes a great source of resentment and fear to conventional women. In their outrage, they label her a desgraciada [a shameless woman] because she receives support from the state government, not from a father or husband or brother:

The woman who is defined out of social legitimacy because of the abrogation of her primary value to patriarchal society, that of producing heirs, is therefore without value, without honor. She becomes the other, the bad woman, the embodiment of a corrupted, inferior, unusable sex: immoral, without virtue, loose. She is common property, sexually available to any man that comes along. . . . A woman (women) thus devalued may not lay claim to the rights and protections the society affords to the woman who does have ·sociopolitical and sexual value. (Castañeda, 1993, 38)

Such a definition for Prudencia strikes Cofer as unthinking acceptance: perpetuation through community reinforcement of a kind of institutionalized ostracism based solely on the culture's masculinist models for gendered power relations. Thus other women in her community declass or outclass Prudencia, even though she is in the same class as those who cast her out. They consider that their relationship to their men gives them a class status that she does not have, out of an abiding apprehension that their own status is always precarious. Bruckner defines the workings of this delusion as "social exclusion." I define it as gatekeeping. Further, Bruckner views the ostracism to which Prudencia is subjected entirely in terms of class: "[S]ocial classes are separated by something that is determined not only by money but, above all, by social exclusion. And by a feeling that is connected to exclusion, namely, shame, as a disciplinary measure of capitalist society" (in Kosta and McCormick 1996, 350). Even though Bruckner makes a refreshing class analysis for a change, she unfortunately does not include gender. Either she is unaware of this factor, or gender issues are either invisible or irrelevant in her focus on class issues. She also blames capitalism for these problems, whereas male hegemony pervades societies that are not capitalist. Capitalism is limited, whereas patriarchy with its seemingly inevitable accompanying inequitable gendered power relations is global and imbued in all societies, not only capitalist societies.

As for Cofer, she exposes the gatekeepers as working within a system in which they observe the rule that "a woman's body with its capabilities to produce new lives, is a trump card in the balance of human relationships" (1990, 113). Prudencia's innocent mindlessness disrupts that belief system with which the active concurrence of men seems vitally necessary to this type of woman. She upsets them by not playing by their rules. Instead, she conducts herself as if she were a winner whereas the other women only see all women as losers. Prudencia had babies without benefit of the sacrament of marriage and took money from the state instead of from a husband to support herself and her household.

Cofer sets Prudencia up as her candidate for the reversal of the cultural constraints on women, writing with admiration of the tricks that Prudencia has learned to survive successfully. In her poetic epigraph, "Why Prudencia Has Babies," Cofer calls Prudencia "the welfare madonna"–a joke that she didn't understand for a long time. Prudencia's mother, a prostitute, would leave the child alone when she went out. Prudencia's present lifestyle probably began after she was raped and bore her first child. She believed that her pregnancy meant that she was not alone any longer. By having children around her, she would never again be left alone. Prudencia then imagined that she was the Virgin Mary. Cofer does not describe Prudencia as planning for the future, as most young mothers do. In a few short years, her children will either be taken away from her by the state, or they will voluntarily leave her side. When Cofer wrote *Silent Dancing*, the author herself was the mother of a young daughter. No doubt it was difficult for the author at that stage in her child's life ever to imagine a future when her offspring would not be a large part of her daily life.

In any event, once again as in the case of Maria La Loca, La Fulana, and La Gringa, Cofer's attitude toward Prudencia is different from her mother's or Mama's. In Fulana's case, especially, Cofer makes it clear that she is not on the side of the earth mothers, the traditional and tradition-bound women. In Prudencia's case, on the other hand, Cofer seems to distance herself, even as she gives motivation to her frequent pregnancies. The author conveys an understanding of Prudencia's motives, a distanced compassion for her, but does not identify with her. She does not see the solution to the problem of an imposed, externally contructed notion of unequal gendered power relations as residing for women in exaggeration, in "metaperformnce" in Judith Butler's terms. Nor does she see the solution in essentialism, in making woman the opposite of man, a purely natural force of nature, a giant womb.

Obviously Prudencia endangers conventional women, the gatekeepers, who confine themselves to the rules and regulations laid out for them. They get food and shelter, legal recognition, and their husband's class status if they construct and constrain and distort and imprison their sexuality in the Procrustean Bed of male dictates. By these standards, Prudencia is an outlaw because she refuses to control her sexuality according to their time-honored dictates of religion and law and custom, thus endangering their hard-won and tenuous security.

As long as women accept the conventions of the constructed female conduct necessary for their acceptance into the culture, as long as they do not rebel against those conventions that decree women deviant by male standards, as long as women refuse to accept women like Maria La Loca, or La Fulana, or La Gringa or Prudencia within their ranks, even within themselves–then no change can take place, no destabilization, no transformation of the culture's prevailing conceptions of gendered power relations. As Foucault stated so brilliantly about "sex," it is not a fixed entity, but cuturally deployed and manipulated by "cultural regimes" of power. In most cases, as in Latino culture, this is done by the patriarchy in terms of inequitable gendered power relations reinforced and perpetuated by gatekeepers:

The central issue, then . . . is not to determine whether one says yes or no to sex, whether one formulates prohibitions or permissions, whether one asserts its importance or denies its effects, or whether one refines the words one uses to designate it; but to account for the fact that it is spoken about, to discover who does the speaking, the positions and viewpoints from which they speak, the institutions which prompt people to speak about it and which store and distribute the things that are said . . . What is at issue, briefly, is the over-all "discursive fact," the way in which sex is "put into discourse." (Butler 1990, 140)

As she gets further into her text, Cofer begins to write increasingly in her own voice as it is at the time of writing: direct, strong, angry. In the story "Quinceañera," Cofer describes what she learned at fifteen, about what being a woman means in Puerto Rico. If a girl desires to be left alone, she is considered rude. If she begins to leave a room, she is questioned as to her destination. Women always guard girls, watching them intently as though their bodies were "time bombs" about to go off. They eternally warn young girls to be careful about how they behave with men. Girls must always cross their legs in the presence of a man; they must never be seen in underclothes or nightclothes, and they must "never interrupt" men when they talk (1990, 140).

Cofer also learns that a woman who is pregnant for the first time had the right to receive special attention because everyone knew that she was going to have it much harder afterward. Again, in this story, Cofer tells us of a girl whose life ended at sixteen after she was used and impregnated by an older man. Instead of being sympathetic, Cofer was inexplicably disgusted and furious whenever she came into contact with the girl because of her beaten and apathetic expression. Could this seduced schoolgirl be Judith's cousin La Gringa? The evidence points to such an assumption. In any event, Cofer succeeds at this point in arousing her readers to anger at this girl's lethargy, her reactive sense of victimization. Cofer succeeds in provoking these emotions in her readers by the use of direct means, by openly using her own voice. She does not filter her message through the use of a double-edged irony, as when she had used her mother's voice to mock La Gringa's predicament in Puerto Rico. Up to this point in the text, Cofer has indirectly conveyed her strong emotional responses to the

Puerto Rican culture's indoctrination of women. She has done this by using the strategy of situating the gatekeepers' voices on the surface of her text, while deeply layering, embedding her differing opinions within the text.

When she acts like an automaton programmed for life, Judith's "ruined" young cousin acts much like Mama. She dutifully followed a routine of labor and self-sacrifice into her old age. Cofer claims that even up to the time she wrote this text, her grandmother's programming has remained intact in her psyche. She retains her undying belief in redemption for women through work, not in the pursuit of a career, but always being occupied in "doing for others" (1990, 141). Mama's system of ethics for women, what Carol Gilligan defines as the "ethics of caring," is like that of other women in every culture globally. Here Cofer uses the repetition of the word "doing" to convey her anger and frustration when "doing" for others is carried to the extent of obliteration of one's own sense of self, one's own needs and wants.

Ultimately, Cofer asks, what were the very best possibilities in life for women, according to Latino culture? What acts were defined by this culture as success or failure as models for other women which the women who perpetuated them could hold up as guides for succeeding generations? Mama believed that if a woman were so unfortunate as not to marry, she could spend her time as a nun, nursing, or teaching, but only until she married. The most awful fate for a woman was to die by herself and without children. Within the parameters of the role of mother, Prudencia, however, has attempted to devise a way to avoid this fate, to have as many children as her body could bear.

As I have previously pointed out, the character of Mama is not so simple, however. By the age of fifteen, although Cofer was still enjoying listening to her grandmother's cuentos, the young girl had finally begun to read messages other than those on the surface. She hears their sarcasm, their hints at other attitudes toward female sexuality than those prescribed by the culture, and she hears Mama's "true feelings" about frustrating marriages and "narrowly circumscribed lives" (1990, 142).

Long before this point in the work, however, readers have been made aware that Cofer feels this way in the present moment. But not once before has Cofer shown that her relatives also felt this way years ago, certainly not from any of her mother's statements and actions. However, Mama's cuentos do go both ways, at times, as does her conduct. It may be recalled that she does tell the children about Maria Sabida as well as about Maria La Loca and that she also tells them about her enforced physical separation from her husband. In the course of doing so, she sarcastically reveals the different reactions and different spaces in which the men and women celebrate after a childbirth: the men feasting, drinking, singing, boasting, and male bonding outdoors, the women, laboring in the kitchen, upset and depressed.

After her husband's death, Cofer's mother joyfully returned to Puerto Rico for good. Once there she regressed into the traditional life that she preferred and ceaselessly questioned her daughter's judgment. Lourdes Miranda King informs us that Fanny Morot Ortiz's decision to return to Puerto Rico is more common among women than men, but she fails to include widowhood as a reason for return to one's family: "Studies have shown that women predominate among the return migrants to Puerto Rico. Some are single young women who have lost their jobs; others are older women whose children have left home. A still larger group is composed of women who have returned after a marital breakup" (1995, 104–105). King's purpose in making these remarks is primarily to contrast these returnees with the situation in the United States which has created "different patterns" than are evident in *Silent Dancing*. These occur, however, in other texts, such as Esmeralda Santiago's *When I Was Puerto Rican*, where "[t]he woman is thrust into the role of sole supporter, creating the new immigrant woman and incidentally destroying the myth of the passive female" (1995, 105).

Cofer's ambivalence toward her mother ultimately takes the form of forgiving her for living two lives, for the rewards Cofer reaped for that, especially bilingualism. She proclaims her gratitude for learning to speak in Spanish and continuing to be able to do so with great ease. After all, her mother's obstinate insistence upon clinging to her traditions, her values, and language have provided Cofer with an incomparably intimate knowledge of them all. Only an author such as Cofer, simultaneously both within and outside the system, could understand and actively choose whether to follow it, or to destabilize, subvert, and attempt to destroy it.

Because of her mother's loyalty and abiding adherence to Puerto Rican beliefs and customs, Cofer records that she has trouble whenever her mother attempts to define her daughter by the concepts she believes in. Her mother's definitions are those of the Puerto Rican culture, whereas Cofer's are feminist. Cofer is simultaneously a mother, a teacher, and writer. Her mother "married as a teenager and led a life of isolation and total devotion to her duties as a mother" (1990, 152). Cofer thinks of her as like Penelope waiting endlessly for Odysseus to return to her so that she herself could "return" to Puerto Rico. In marked contrast to her mother, Cofer married a man who was supportive of her needs–writing, traveling–experiencing life for herself. These are needs that her readers remember La Fulana and La Gringa had also, but which were brutally suppressed. Cofer's mother rejoices at her daughter's success, especially as a writer. Still, she expresses anxiety at Cofer's spending time away from her family and home, although Cofer keeps pointing out to her that her husband can do the parenting and cleaning just as well, if not better–that he equals her in parenting and surpasses her in cooking.

Cofer might as well have saved her breath, because her mother has swallowed her training that the woman is everything in domestic matters. Such qualities as Cofer vaunts in her husband are deemed irrelevant to men, are never taken into account, except as expressions of their wives' selfishness and deviance from the expected norm. Cofer's mother would have to see a different reality than that which she has been trained to see by her culture, before she could even begin to hear her daughter. As Cofer points out, "the source of friction in our relationship . . . is my mother's concern about my familial duties" (1990, 153). In her eyes, women can have no other role than that of mother.

Women are burdened forever with the complete responsibility for their family. This is entirely a role indoctrinated into women for many centuries in most cultures globally, not only in Latino culture.

Elsa Barkley Brown, the African American historian, attests to this same belief on her mother's part, even though, unlike Cofer, who differs from it, Barkley Brown has chosen to embrace it and make it a theory of two disparate beliefs acted upon simultaneously. This is the espousal of "no single identity, but rather a multiciplity of sometimes contradictory subject spaces," or, more succinctly, "a de-centered malleability" (Wegner 1993–1994, 149). In my opinion, Barkley Brown's is a clever rationale for the hypocrisy of the gatekeepers who fulminate against their daughters while covertly supporting them against the hegemony.[18]

Cofer titles her mother "my loving adversary," a sad commentary on the latter's insistence on her role as gatekeeper. The author visits her mother every June. The difference in their values, and in their attitudes is not explained as generational, or even temperamental, but as political. Cofer, because of her experience, like that of the other authors in this text, could well be defined as a "postcolonial hybrid." Her work is an effort "to compile a laborious 'inventory of one's self' and on the basis of that complex genealogical process, produce her own version of hybridity and "find political legitimacy for that version" (Rhadakrishnan 1993, 753). Cofer's mother is a conservative who loves the past, is male-oriented, and whose perspective is masculine. She is never once named throughout the whole text, except as the mother. Only in the dedication is she named: Fanny Morot Ortiz. As for Cofer's grandmothers, we discover Mama's name—Pola—only with great difficulty. To differentiate them, Cofer calls her paternal grandmother Mama Nanda. Again, readers find the latter's given name with difficulty because the role of mother has filled, defined, and become their lives. Cofer does not make her mother the heroine of the work, nor does she make her mother's commitment to her values heroic, nor is Mama the heroine, although both women are major characters in this text. Their daughter's and grand daughter's abiding feminist sensibility–pervading every cuento and poem–could be said to be the heroine of this work.

What interests Cofer are Puerto Rican customs and values, especially the Puerto Rican culture, primarily in relation to its inequitable gendered role relations of power, all the training by gatekeepers that goes into making a Puerto Rican woman successful and prevailing or always tragically (and predictably) ostracized as a failure. She describes her mother and grandmothers lovingly, but she is critical of them, as she reveals throughout *Silent Dancing*–in her version of Maria Sabida and in her cuentos about Maria La Loca, La Fulana, La Gringa, and Prudencia. Cofer perceives and reveals the frustration and the narrowly circumscribed lives of Puerto Rican women through her creation of a succession of tragically failed female characters by Puerto Rican standards, all of them declassed victims of their culture.

Cofer's mother, grandmothers, and her Aunt Felicita serve as Maria Sabida, as the enforcers of the culture through cautionary tales. In actuality, however, the author, no matter how modestly, is the only female character who is truly "a prevailing woman," one who does not lead a frustrated and narrowly circumscribed life. To put it more positively, Cofer presents herself as having it all and not having given it all up. Furthermore, such an issue is not even a problem for her or her Anglo husband. But instead of approval, Cofer is given a guilt trip by her mother, the gatekeeper-representative of her culture for her daughter and her daughter's readers. Such conduct on the part of Cofer's mother diminishes her daughter's enjoyment of the life she has carved out for herself in the United States.

How can it not bother Cofer that her mother is so self-righteously complacent in her conviction that her daughter is inferior and deficient as a wife and mother–as a woman–because she does not fit male-defined and male-benefiting notions? Cofer cannot come to terms with her mother's trivializing her and continuing to attempt to confine her in domesticity. Cofer's mother calls upon male demands to cut her daughter down in her flight: to "sacrifice" Cofer's full actualization of her fine writing talents on the altar of appropriate gender roles for women and mothers.

Cofer's mother, much like the other gatekeepers analyzed in this text, has entirely internalized her culture's constricting model for women which her daughter has successfuly bypassed with her own solutions. What is remarkable about Cofer is her genuine ability to be patient, understanding, tolerant, and compassionate toward her mother's perspective. She provides a great contrast to her mother who disapproves of Cofer's Americanized values for women. Cofer confines herself, however, to critiquing the belief system. She accepts her mother and the other gatekeepers where they are situated historically and in terms of their training.

Cofer's relationship to her mother is similar to that exposed in Dolores Prida's wonderful play *Coser y cantar* where two characters, "Ella" and "She," represent two oppositional sides of one person, the Cuban and the American side simultaneously, the dialectics between ethnic identity and assimilation, according to Alberto Sandoval. Whereas Prida describes this as an ongoing process within one character, Cofer's relationship to her mother can be seen as an ongoing process in Mama, her mother, and herself:

[W]hat Ella is really experiencing is a recovery of her historical past, her memories, and her cultural models. She does so by examining and deconstructing cultural codes in order to reintegrate them anew in her present bi-cultural horizon of experience. This cultural examination will be judgmental and critical of both the Anglo-American culture and her own. Each side of Ella's personality criticizes, undermines, and puts down its cultural adversary, in its quest to survive, by the elimination of either Ella or "she." . . . What appears to be an irreconcilable opposition in her is actually a dialectic dependency, molded and vectored toward an ideal cultural synthesis. In this synthesis, Ella will always rescue, re-shape, re-define, and even re-familiarize herself with her native cultural models of/for social action. Ella's struggle to affirm and incorporate her Latina identity in the United States establishes the co-existence of both the Latino and the Anglo cultures. . . . This duality, multiplied to the second power, is not a search for total separation . . . but rather a search to bridge, overlap, and merge cultural borders in order to reinstall subjectivity in at least a partial resolution of reconciliation. (1989, 208–209, 214)

Ella, like Mrs. Ortiz, will always remain "an outsider to U.S. society." As such, Cofer, her daughter, delineates her strong mother's obstinately separatist character, utilizing "irony, sarcasm, laughter, and cynicism to cope with estrangement, alienation, loneliness, abandonment, and disengagement" (Sandoval 1989, 210).

Although Cofer herself did not say the following, it reflects her basic respectful agreement to disagree with her foremothers:

[H]ow important it is that we begin with people where they are. Often, where people are, most immediately, is in the space of their own lives, their own bodies, their own longings and dreams. So much intellectual thought in our culture does not try to engage people where they are; instead, it tries to aggressively push people to move from where they are to some other place. This is not an effective means of educating for critical consciousness. (hooks with McKinnon 1996, 825)

Publicly as a writer, Cofer attempts this as well by focusing on the cultural constraints that keep Puerto Rican women as an underclass to men and that are heavily inscribed into succeeding generations of Puertorriqueñas in order to continue to do so. If Cofer's life as depicted in *Silent Dancing* is seen as her oppositional responses to both her own and other women's experiences within her birth culture, then it would seem that Cofer is presenting alternatives to that culture. She does this by ascribing to women what have always been seen as male prerogatives: success in one's chosen career, sexual fulfillment, the right to roam about this world freely instead of being housebound, companionship, equality, and motherhood, if one so wishes.

Cofer seems truly to have it all, except for the loss of her brilliant father whose insanity and death seems to have been caused entirely by an inimical, racist colonial environment both in Puerto Rico and the United States. Her father's solution was to attempt to blend in to American ways, to assimilate; her mother's solution was to retain her Puerto Rican culture, no matter what, no matter where. This essential difference divides them irrevocably. Always on guard, always self-conscious, tense, and stressed, he aspires to a higher class than that which Americans would place him in by race and ethnicity. His wife attempts to live a separate existence entirely free of American ways and Americans, no matter where she is.

On the other hand, Cofer seems to have achieved all the things that her birth culture prevents women from achieving. And we would like her to tell us how she has succeeded where so many have failed, especially given that her cousin, La Gringa, and all the other girls in the family do not seem to have done so. What did Cofer do differently? How did she become so different? What does she advocate doing to get from frustration and constraint to freedom, fulfillment, and success? *Silent Dancing* does not answer this question. It depicts the constraints and the suffering women endure under the culture's regime, its system of inequitable gendered power relations imposed on the young by its gatekeepers. Then suddenly at the end, Cofer reveals herself as comparatively free from those constraints and the resultant suffering. She shows us what is non-sense for women, but does not show us or suggest to us how to prevent that non-sense from restricting and constricting our lives–as she herself has obviously succeeded in doing. Except for herself, the examples she gives readers are all examples of failure, of women who have tried to fly free and failed, even her own creation Maria Sabida.

Cofer is content to represent to her readers the ways, many of them terrible, in which Puerto Rican culture constrains women. To do this takes enormous courage. As Vélez puts it, "Naming the problem is the first step to its solution" (1988, 16). Further, Cofer does not directly critique the system of power relations in relation to gender and race as a feminist, but as a Puertorriqueña writer. She writes as though specifically concerned with the oppression of Puerto Rican men and women of color because of the Puerto Rican system of power relations in which class rankings are distributed according to criteria of gender and race. In this way Cofer, as an American insider-outsider has used certain strategies, which Charlotte Bunch credits women in other cultures as utilizing to their benefit and from which we can learn. For example, they have made more use of the concept of human rights as an ethical basis for feminism than women in the United States. For many women it has proven to be the primary moral backing they use to counter the cultural religious right language:

When the religious right says family values, we say human rights. What opposing concept has the same legitimacy as the religious family values concept? If they say family values and you say feminism, you are dead in the water. But when they say family values and you say, "We are defending women's human rights," you are on a different level of discourse. (In Hartmann et al. 1996, 944).

Perhaps in the future Cofer will fill in the gap of her silence about the process between her angry responses to injustice against her gender and their transformation through her artistry into powerful cuentos in order to attempt solutions to that injustice.

NOTES

1. Although Irene Blea is writing only of Chicanas, the custom is identical to Latinas. "For the Chicana, her culture is also extraordinarily important because it includes rites of passage, those times in a person's life that symbolize movement from one status to another. For Chicanas these include birth, baptism, beginning school, first holy communion, confirmation, quinceañera, and marriage and death rituals. In a discussion about women the quinceañera is most important. The 'coming-out' ritual marks the end of girlhood and grants womanhood status at the age of fifteen" (1991, 123).

However, within these identical concepts, individual perspectives vary. Cofer's is one of the most depressing and powerful, filled with disillusionment about the patriarchal culture. The Chicana Carmen Celia Beltrán's "Quiceañera/Sweet Fifteen," written in both Spanish and English, is almost cloyingly sentimental. It ends with the author's wish for the girl that "que Aladino te guie con su lámpara de oro/ y te dé Cenicient su chapin de cristal!" ["May Aladin guide you with his golden lamp/and may Cinderella give you her crystal slipper"] (1993, 65–66).

2. The righteous perspective in some quarters taken toward President Clinton's "moral weakness" represented a historical shift in American patriarchal discourse in that it made a move toward sexual repression of men by prescribing a single standard for men and women, a requirement imposed only briefly by the Puritans in the seventeenth century. This move is at odds with the demand by contemporary feminists for a single standard of sexual freedom, based on the assumption of a double standard prevailing in the United States for three centuries. This demand is common to the authors analyzed in this text and feminists, in general.

3. See Mikhail Bakhtin 1988, xxviii.

4. Cofer thus anticipates a similar revenge to Lorena Bobbitt's knife wielding by several years. Lorena Bobbitt, in fact, is a Latina woman.

5. In Amy Tan's *The Kitchen God's Wife*, the heroine Winnie is married for many years to an abusive husband who tortures and torments her endlessly until she finally flees to the United States. He dies peacefully of a heart attack many years later surrounded by a devoted and loving family.

6. See my discussion of Lourdes's attempt to do so in my Chapter Four on Cristina Garcia's *Dreaming in Cuban*.

7. This is a commonly held view among Latinas. See for example, Judit Moschkovich's contention that because "Latin America is a land economically colonized by the U.S.," it therefore can't be compared in terms of oppression against women "with a colonizing culture (the U.S.)" (1981, 82). Why not? Is poverty or wealth a criterion for more or less inequality? Are countries that are not economically oppressed by the U.S. therefore devoid of sexism? Economics is a factor in sexism in that women are underclassed by gender in most cultures of the world and thus far more women live in poverty than men, even in the wealthiest or poorest countries of the world, regardless of the economic status of the countries. Thus inequitable power relations prevails globally, is a global issue, not an issue only of colonialism, and as Moschkovich herself points out, "Oppression is oppression in whatever form or intensity" (1981, 82).

8. The Cubana playwright Delores Prida goes further, when she desribes her musical play *Beautiful Señoritas* as poking "fun at long-standing Latin women stereotypes–from Carmen Miranda to Cuchi Cuchi Charo to suffering black-shrouded women crying and praying over the tortillas to modern-day young Latinas trying to re-define their images" (1991, 182).

9. I have met Cofer personally, as well as Esmeralda Santiago. Both authors describe the self-consciousness and embarrassment that their accents cause them whenever they speak Spanish in Puerto Rico. Santiago emphasizes that the source of her resentment does not lie in her own self-critical attitude toward her American accent, but in the Puerto Ricans' response to the sounds she makes. They insult her when they claim that she therefore cannot be Puerto Rican because she does not sound like one. Cofer seems to have internalized the Puerto Rican perspective and to concur with it, at least as a child, although she has repeated this statement recently, just as it appears in *Silent Dancing*: that because she spoke Spanish with an American accent, she was therefore not speaking Spanish.

10. Lourdes Miranda King makes the interesting point in this connection. A Puerto Rican woman like Fanny Morot Ortiz is "unlike any other woman who has preceded her" .because "she is a member of a group in continuous flux, moving between the United States and Puerto Rico for varying lengths of time throughout her life" (1995, 104).

11. For similar examples, see Merle Hodge, *Crick Crack Monkey*, and Michelle Cliff, *Abeng*, for equally outraged responses to the same problem caused by English imposition of its curriculum and values on indigenous Trinidadians and Jamaicans. Esmeralda Santiago's *When I Was Puerto Rican* reinforces Cofer's point, as well.

12. Apparently Cofer, in attempting to change the landlord's name to protect his identity, unwittingly used a German name, not a Jewish one. Later she points out that "[t]he other Puerto Ricans shopped locally at stores owned by other Puerto Ricans, or by Jewish merchants who had philosophically accepted our presence in the city and decided to make us their good customers, if not neighbors and friends" (93). This somewhat negative perception of Jewish landlords and merchants, holdovers in neighborhoods which had since become Latina, is fairly recent in Latina writing and is also shared by some African Americans (who also critique Korean and other Asian groups exploiting them in their neighborhoods), as well as other racial and ethnic minorities. It perhaps reflects the recent influence of Afrocentricity. Nicholasa Mohr's story "Mr. Mendelsohn," in *El Bronx Remembered*, about an elderly Jew in a once Jewish, but now Puerto Rican, neighborhood, reveals this man to have a different attitude. He and a Puerto Rican family become as close as relatives, thanks to the Puerto Rican mother's inclusiveness and generosity. However, his family's racist attitude toward the Puerto Ricans does bear out Cofer's point.

13. See Nicholasa Mohr's short story about two brothers that stay in New York, while a third brother returns to Puerto Rico because the latter cannot stand to live as a declassé any longer. It is more important for him to live in abject poverty and have this kind of holdover respect in Puerto Rico because of the past grandeur of his family than to remain in the United States where a former employee can be his equal, if not his superior. Rosario Ferré in *The Youngest Doll* and *Sweet Diamond Dust* deals with the same issues.

14. Interestingly, Cofer, a beautiful woman, like her mother, while she does not garb herself in bright colors and high heels, does wears her glorious hair down to her waist.

15. Rosario Morales agrees with Cofer as to the origins of the necessity of a Latina woman having a sexy look, "all decked out in sex." It is due to the enculturation that "you've got to learn how to hold out on 'em just enough to get what you want. It's the only item you can put on the market, so better make it go far, and when you have to deliver, lie down and grit your teeth and bear it because there's no escape." She is much more outwardly bitter about this tradition, however, describing "the tight dress . . . the coquettish, well made-up smile" as "[t]he point of terror, the point of denial, the point of hatred" (1981, 53). On this issue, in keeping with Roland Barthes's gender neutral observation that clothing is used on the body as "a sign or a carrier of signs," Helena Michie extends the point to bear specifically on women. The "dressing of women's bodies" is "representational" (Kutzinski citing Michie, Barthes, and Kristeva, 1993, 221). Kutzinski extends Barthes's and Michie's observations even further through her citation from Kristeva's *The Power and the Horror*, where Julia Kristeva contends that women's bodies themselves are representational, because culture places "significance" as "inherent in the human body" (10).

16. As with Chicana women of the period 1920–1950, who aspired to white color jobs, "[s]kin color also played a role in obtaining office work." That is, very few ethnic women of color were hired, although schools did train them for "clerical positions largely closed to them." When queried as to the motives for falsely enouraging a fruitless endeavor, one educator replied that it was to " teach them respect for the white collar job. "It is noteworthy that La Gringa, like most young Chicana and Latina females, did "respect" office work as a fantasy of female success. Tragically, in many cases such as La

Gringa's, "the media" also influenced such young women's "acculturation . . . Movie and romance magazines enabled adolescents (and older women as well) to experience vicariously the middle-class and affluent life-styles heralded in these publications and thus could nurture a desire for consumer goods." In this regard, Vicki Ruíz cites anthropologist Margarita Melville who concludes that in relation to young Chicana women their "aspirations for upward mobility" emerged as the most distinguishing factor in the process of acculturation" (Ruiz 1993, 111, 112, 114). Her conclusion cannot only be applied to La Gringa and other Latina young women, but to Asian American and other immigrant women, in general. See my *(Un)Doing the Missionary Position: Gender Asymmetry in Contemporary Asian American Women's Writings*, Chapters Two and Three.

17. Here Cofer's attitude is much like that of the Chicana poet Evangelina Vigil who "likens herself to an actress who is exhausted from fulfilling alien roles for a public that doesn't care" without props or supporting actors, and with no friends in the audience (cited in Treacy 1989, 82)

18. We see this covert behavior on the part of female gatekeepers in Asian American literature, as well. And I personally experienced it: the giving of gifts to the daughters, of assistance, while outwardly condemning them for deviant behavior. My mother pawned her rings to enable me to fulfill the demands of a graduate scholarship, while continually invalidating my careerist ambitions and deploring the fact that I wasn't yet married. Nevertheless, I do not feel that these gatekeepers, including my mother, assist their daughters out of covert disagreement with their traditions and religion, but out of their own desire to conform to the definition of a good mother. That is, as Cofer puts it about her grandmother, "giving, giving, giving." To conform to this definition of a good mother, most mothers put the necessity of giving of themselves above their personal convictions and needs. This is why they give support to their unruly daughters: not to make a statement on their behalf, covert as that might be, that although themselves imprisoned, they would assist their daughters' escape when they could. Such mothers give support to avoid guilt, to avoid considering themselves in any way as having fallen below the standard of appropriate behavior for motherhood. It is a blind giving. They would give to any child without conditions, even though they express those conditions, because to be a good mother, the ethic of giving outranks every other consideration. This is cultural training: the erasure of self and not biological instinct.

Chapter 2

Cristina Garcia, *Dreaming in Cuban*

Rather than deploring, defending, or agreeing with her culture's negative conceptualizations in relation to the romantic dreaming of females, Cristina Garcia valorizes the dreaming. In the title of *Dreaming in Cuban*, "Dreaming" includes all the diverse dreams of Garcia's female protagonists about the nature of being Cuban, what it is to be Cuban, to dream, not in American, but in Cuban. This necessitates Garcia's taking into account all the conflicting elements of contemporary Cuban-ness for Cuban and Cuban American women. Amazingly, she never invalidates or disputes the diverse and conflicting perspectives of these different dreamers. She succeeds by giving readers a complexity of experience beyond binaries, where many diverse and conflicting perspectives circle around one another endlessly. These differences are constructed by differences in the various ideologies that the characters embrace—communism, capitalism, traditional gender relations, voodoo, and feminism—and also by differences in their experiences due to varying historical locations in time and place.

The "feisty protagonist" of this novel is "based on [the author's] own grandmother who stayed behind on the island." (Behar 1995, 6). We first meet Celia del Pino, the grandmother, in 1972 at the age of sixty-three; she is an ardent follower of "El Lider" and a devout communist. Replete with binoculars, her job is to guard the area in front of her beach house. Because of the Bay of Pigs invasion by the United States, the location of her house is considered strategically important.

Celia is incongruously clad in a housedress and her best drop pearl earrings. These two disparate elements trope her ambivalent nature. After she enters the water, Celia removes her fancy patent leather pumps, then swims back to her house. The grotesque combination of her magnificent drop pearl earrings; her plain, old, faded housedress; and her fancy shoes reflects the linkage of three discordant elements in Celia's character (in the Cuban character) and tropes the primary qualities of each of the dreamers that we meet in the text. In many ways she is a dreamer, a romantic, an idealist, as represented by the drop pearl earrings. The pearls were a gift from a lover who probably perished in the Spanish Civil War fighting on the Republican side against Generalissimo Franco. Fidel Castro is the beneficiary of Celia's passionate love, the by-product of the communist perspective of her lover Gustavo, a lawyer, like Castro. In her nostalgia, Celia conflates all her romantic feelings for her lost love with his politics and then projects them onto El Lider, Castro, due to the similarities in the two men's ideologies. Behar aptly comments that "[w]omen's resistance to dictators, Alvarez shows us, is fraught with problems, not the least being their susceptibility to the erotic power of charismatic male leaders" (1995, 6) The influence of Gustavo on Celia's outlook is powerful and enduring because she was predisposed to communism from early on in her life. Her concern was never limited only to her own family, but to dreams of justice and equity for all, especially for the struggling masses.

Celia's political dream is for the success of the Cuban Revolution combined with the return or reunion of communism with a disparate concept, a noble, romantic vision of life, as again just as paradoxically embodied in the person of her romantic Spanish lover who is also married. She writes letters to Gustavo for the rest of her life, but does not send them to him because she cannot do so. There is no recipient, no outlet in reality for her hopes and dreams because he does not exist any longer in reality, just as such a linkage in reality between communism and romanticism does not exist for her any longer.

An ardent opponent of fascism, Gustavo leaves her and Cuba in order to fight on the Republican side in the Spanish Civil War. He is never seen or heard from again. To Celia, Gustavo embodies for Cuba the best of the past Spanish heritage. His fate also tropes the death, or nonexistence, the impossibility, of mainland Spain's relevant association with contemporary Cuba, no matter how Cubans might long for it nostalgically.

The pearls her lover gave her long ago never leave Celia's ears, except for cleaning (re-creating and renewing her dream). When she removes them, this extreme act reveals that Celia is renouncing the very essence of herself: her political and personal dreams. Before walking into the sea, she also covers over two photographs in her home, an act that is common before death. One photograph is of her husband: a prosaic, materialistic man, paradoxically again, romantic about her, whom she settles for after the departure of her lover. The second photograph is that of El Lider in uniform. As she covers over his photograph, she fantasies a romantic and sexual rendezvous with him.

To Celia, her Spanish lover and El Lider do not represent opposite poles of the political spectrum, but are woven of the same cloth, because she identifies El Lider with her lover. In her eyes, both men were lawyers whose idealism and visions led them: one to glorious death, the other, to revolutionary victory and leadership of Cuba. Both attempt to reform the political system of their respective countries: her lover, the Spanish fascist, imperial system, El Lider, the corrupt capitalist colonial system.

In one of Celia's letters to Gustavo, she writes of what she remembers seeing during their spring walks through Havana. Surprisingly, this letter does not expatiate on the emotions of being in love, but on the contrasts between their privileged state and the awful condition of those around them. By this means, Garcia reveals Celia's basic qualities of character. In Celia, the idea of romance is interwoven inextricably with her dearest illusions in terms of her political sympathies for the masses, the downtrodden, the homeless. She remembers that "the destitute were everywhere, spread out on the benches in the Parque Central, asleep on yesterday's newspapers." Then she wonders whether Gustavo remembers "the young woman with the dangling wooden leg and the single oxford? The beggar families from the countryside looking for work in the iron-fenced mansions of Vedado? The smart couples in their convertible roadsters driving by without a second glance?" (1992, 98).

If Celia were going to her death still dreaming and still hoping that the communist initiatives would succeed, she would never have let her pearls float away into the ocean, for the pearls represent her illusions. She would have bequeathed the precious jewelry to her beloved granddaughter Pilar who is her psychic successor in the United States. Thus what Garcia is telling readers is that Celia's ardent, lifelong dreams have died in Celia before Celia herself dies. She has no more to live for and that is why she takes her life.

To return again to the beginning. We first come upon Celia dreaming on the beach. Her home there serves for years as the primary lookout for the town of Santa Teresa del Mar. She dreams that if she were able to spot another Bay of Pigs invasion, she would be given a celebration at the palace, an orchestra would serenade her, and El Lider would seduce her in bordellolike surroundings. With his omnipresent cigar, beard, khaki camouflage uniform, and black boots, El Lider provides a crude contrast to the elegant furnishings. Such a contrast reflects Celia's creative linking of her most lush romantic bourgeois dreams with the antiromantic, martial, sweaty, macho grit of Cuban socialism, as troped by El Lider.

Later in the work, in one of Garcia's many flashbacks, Celia, inspired by the same dream, the same linkage of sweat and idealism, is described by the author as willingly performing backbreaking labor in the cane fields as a volunteer in a work brigade.[1] Before the Revolution and after marriage, Celia had been restricted to the life of a housewife. Now she performs public service according to need. Celia's life trajectory here is very common, according to Yolanda Prieto:

The dramatic changes in the role of women as a result of the Revolution has been one of the numerous reasons that many families left Cuba after 1959. According to Cuban men interviewed in a study conducted in Chicago in 1969, the "destruction of the family" was an outcome of the revolutionary government's policies concerning women. These men pointed out that women not only worked outside the home, but also performed rough work in paid and unpaid agricultural labor and participated in the armed forces and revolutionary committees, confirming their fears that socialism had a deleterious effect on women and the family (1995, 164).

At this moment, at the beginning of the text, before Celia leaves her home to walk into the sea, Celia's deceased husband suddenly disrupts her dreaming (as he always had in life). Here Garcia is exposing Celia's occasional disloyalty to her romantic socialism. She has a weakness for aesthetic beauty that can take the form of elitist elegance based on the fruits of materialistic values, as embodied in the person of her bourgeois salesman husband and in the quality of her life with him. Until Jorge's death, Celia never could join El Lider and the Revolution, because her husband prevented her from doing so.

In the 1975 section, Celia is seen in her capacity of civilian judge presiding over a domestic dispute. She has already judged 193 cases. She does so from a feminist perspective and with uncommon wisdom, justice, and prudence. She no longer writes to Gustavo, because since her husband's death, Celia has finally been able to devote herself fully to the Revolution. She is pleased that her decisions are of significance in other peoples' lives and sees herself as contributing to a magnificent future for Cuba. She dreads the thought of how it was twenty years ago, when what she would have been doing, instead, was taking care of her grandchildren and looking forward to nothing but death. That is why after El Lider called for nurseries to be built in the provinces by volunteers. Celia volunteered to work in a microbrigade where she set tiles and operated a construction lift, as well. She also inoculates schoolchildren against malaria and cuts sugarcane every harvest.

In a case involving two women fighting over whether one seduced the other's husband, she sends for the husband. She then sentences him to work as a volunteer for a year at a state nursery to help his compañeras to change diapers, heat milk, wash linen, and organize playtimes for the children. He is going to be the first man there, and Celia will make regular inquiries as to whether he is conducting himself like a model socialist. Still, she is depressed and disheartened about the "unrest." She believes that so much of Cuba's success will depend on what doesn't exist, or exists only rarely: idealism, communitarianism, unselfishness, committing oneself to joint efforts in a great cause without concern for personal reward. Her children are also a source of grief to her because they are each isolated in their separate shells, apolitical, unaware of anything going on outside themselves, about each other and her. She finds no comfort in them.

She responds with animosity to her eldest daughter Lourdes's success with a bakery in New York, as though it were aimed against her heartfelt socialism– eternally reminding her of the food shortage in Cuba. Her other daughter Felicia who has remained in Cuba, has no interest whatsoever in the revolution. She complains wittily that "We're dying of security" (1992, 117). When her mother tries to point out socialism's merits, Felicia responds that indeed people are not starving or living out on the streets. Everyone receives medical treatment and everyone can get a job if they wish to work. But Felicia still does not care for this system.

Celia's son Javier, her only pro-Castro child, left for Czechoslovakia secretly in 1966 without saying good-bye to anyone. He married a woman there whom he now never writes about. Evidently he has made a terrible mistake in his private life, although he is a professor of biochemistry at the University of Prague where he lectures in Russian, German, and Czech. He does write about his little girl, that he speaks Spanish to her so that she can talk with her grandmother some day. Evidently he has hopes of a reunion with his family.

Celia patrols the shore three nights a week. She dresses up for these vigils, fantasying that perhaps El Lider might come along. In the first scene, the final one in Celia's life, written in the form of magic realism as are many others, while Celia paces the shoreline, she suddenly has a vision of her husband who is dying in New York. Dressed nattily in his white summer suit and Panama hat, he then walks toward her on the water. He has blue eyes, which like lasers in the night turn everything blue.

He speaks to her, but Celia cannot hear him because she is unreceptive to his love for her, to uniting with him psychically. He then disappears, and Celia returns to the beach, to pace the shore. There she crosses her arms and hugs them to herself, thus signifying her rejection of him, that her heart is closed to him. She then reads his last letter from New York. As she does so, she remembers his last words to her before he entered the plane in his wheelchair. He is dramatically opposed to her socialism and to her adoration of Cuba's new rulers whom he calls "[b]utchers and veterinarians" (1992, 6).

Before he left for the United States in a fruitless effort to regain his health, Garcia depicts Jorge del Pino's occupation during his lifetime in Cuba as reflecting his political position in a symbolically significant way. That he sells "electric brooms and portable fans for an American firm" tropes the capitalistic materialistic values of Cuba's American colonizers' capitalist ideologies. Jorge tried always to prove to his gringo boss that he was his Cuban counterpart. Jorge's occupation and his colonized mentality clearly reflect a great chasm in class ideology between Celia and her husband. Jorge adores technology. He sells it and identifies entirely with the consumerist, materialistic aspects of the American way of life, but for Celia, this way is soulless.

Again, by way of the technique of magic realism and not the phone, Celia frequently communes through and in Cuban dreams with her thirteen-year-old granddaughter, Pilar, who lives in New York.

We next find Celia in a flashback standing in the summer rain; she is clad in her leather pumps and jade housedress while she waits for her granddaughters to return from their camping trip to the Isle of Pines. Celia feels as if her life has been spent that way–always waiting for others, for something or other to happen. First she waited for Gustavo to return to her from the Spanish Civil War. Or she would wait for the rain in summer to end. Or she would wait for her husband to go off on his business trips so she could be free to sit herself down at the piano and play Debussy. This last forbidden activity gave her some measure of consolation. Ever since her married lover left for Spain never to return she has been inconsolable. She began to lose hair, as well as weight. She tried various remedies, until finally she consulted a santera who saw a body of water in her palms and predicted that she would "survive the hard flames" (1992, 37) of the Revolution.

Garcia is harsh in her antagonism to the Cuban acculturation of gatekeeper women as mothers to their sons, depicting them as degenerating to the point where because they are permitted no outlet for their female sexuality, they become more their sons' lovers than their sons' mothers. Jorge del Pino, fourteen years older than she, who knew Celia since she was a child, insisted that she write her lover. If she were to receive no answer, she would marry him. After the honeymoon, Jorge's mother, Berta Arango del Pino, had pulled the orchid out of Celia's hair and snapped at her that she would have no whorish conduct in her house. She had then called her son "mi corazon," and promised that she would cook a fish for him exactly the way he liked it, cancelling out in two strokes Celia's existence.

In contrast to Fanny Morot Ortiz's supportive mother-in-law and sister-in-law in *Silent Dancing*, Celia's mother-in-law and sister-in-law treat her like a Cinderella. They feed her on scraps, even worse than those thrown to stray dogs without a home. Once in their absence Celia had decided to cook a casserole for them. When Berta Arango del Pino returned, she wrapped the pot in dishrags, carried it through the living room, out of the house, down the stairs, across the yard, and then poured the contents of the pot into the street.

Again, in *Silent Dancing*, Judith's aunt Felicita, her mother's sister-in-law, becomes so close to the young bride that when she becomes pregnant, she acts as her closest attendant. But when Celia becomes pregnant, her sister-in-law Ofelia appropriates her clothes and shoes. Her gorgon of a mother-in-law is perhaps the epitome of all the collaborators and gatekeepers represented in all the texts analyzed herein. She is worse, in fact, because her oppressiveness is matched by her repulsive appearance. Yet her devotion to and preoccupation with her son does not seem exaggerated to anyone familiar with the phenomemon of women globally who take their cultural training as mothers so seriously, especially their roles of mothers to sons, that their whole life becomes about their sons. Berta Arango del Pino takes it to the point of insanity, according to Garcia. Or, rather, one could say that Garcia is exposing a danger when women are so strongly brainwashed by their culture into their roles as mothers that they begin to confuse their sons with their lovers.

In *Dreaming in Cuban*, Berta and her son Jorge and Felicia and her son Ivanito are incestuous, and Celia and her son Javier verge on the edge of incest, as well. Clearly, Garcia disapproves of the hegemony which would so strongly emphasize the relationship of mother to son that women who take it too seriously lose their own individuality, interests, and rights to a fully expressed adult sexuality. They seem, in fact, frozen in time, forever fixed at that point in adolescence when they married their husbands; they are filled with romantic dreams that can go nowhere. Finding no outlet for their romantic desires with their husbands, they project them onto their sons.

In his mother we may observe the source for her son Jorge's admiration for things American, his class and race bias. Berta is a racist, a believer in the class structure of white over black. She is mulatto and uses "bleach paste" (1992, 41) at night to lighten her skin. It is no wonder then that Celia decided that if she had a boy she would flee to Spain, leaving Jorge. She would become a flamenco dancer and her lover Gustavo Sierra de Armas would walk into the nightclub, climb onto the stage where she was dancing, and kiss her passionately to the music of "violent guitars" (1992, 42). This dream endures all her life, even in the form of a similar dream about El Lider and herself.

Before her marriage, Celia had sold cameras at the finest department store in Havana. Even before she met Gustavo, when Celia was still a saleswoman, her identification with the masses was evident, as I have pointed out previously. In one of Celia's letters to Gustavo, she tells her lover how she had been a model in El Encanto, walking about to show off gowns and hats. The store's salesmen had courted her and asked her to go to lunch with them. One of them had in all probability been her future husband, Jorge del Pino. But, Celia complains, they neither noticed the guajiros [hillbillies] sleeping in the parks while Coca-Cola signs flashed on and off over them–signifiers of capitalist materialism–nor did they ever question how these people came to be homeless, sleeping in the parks in the first place.

When her in-laws torment Celia, it does not appear that her husband ever intervened with them on her behalf. In fact, we find out later that Jorge purposely left her with these dragons for a long period of time as a form of retaliation for her affair with Gustavo. It would not appear that Jorge's female relatives were motivated in their cruelty by any sense of class or race superiority to Celia, but they do feel superior to her in terms of hierarchical status in the family. They have no feeling of sisterhood whatsoever with Celia or any other women. Indeed, such intellectual and emotional distance from their own kind is a common characteristic in gatekeepers.

When Berta Arango del Pino discovers from her daughter that Celia is pregnant with her future grandchild, she goes into a fury about how indecent the pregnancy is and wonders rhetorically how her son can possibly feed more dependents. This rhetorical question exposes her transparent desire for her son not to be burdened either with a wife or children. It also foreshadows her later insanity.

In many cultures such a notion of motherhood concerning the "joys of motherhood" has a carrot on the end of the stick for women who obey its demands. The collaborators are all older women who have waited for years to get their rewards–rewards that consist primarily of enslaving the younger generation of women through an unpaid apprenticeship system, while they expect their sons to continue to worship and obey them. Thus Berta Arango del Pino has every reason to prevent her daughter-in-law Celia from threatening her position, but she carries it to the extreme of attempting to foreclose on her own posterity rather than giving up her precedence in the female line.

Both his mother and his sister resent any other calls on Jorge's affection and duties. They expect him to continue supporting them, and he does. In the United States, such demands by the women of a man's birth family would be considered odd and neurotic. They would be ignored or mocked and sent to psychiatric counseling. Nevertheless, this system, alien as it is to the American cultural training of boys in relation to their mothers, where no loop-back is ever taught, expected, or desired, is common in many other cultures,

In Celia's letters to Querida Gustavo of 1950–1955, readers find without comment that her mother-in-law has died, in her madness cursing Celia for stealing her husband (actually Jorge) whom she calls her lover, continually imploring him to come to her bed. As I have stated earlier, such relationships are common in this text. In this way, Garcia exposes what she believes are the extremes of sexual and romantic frustration, when obedience to the cultural decrees about marriage and motherhood are carried out by gatekeeper women who vent onto their own sons, as well as on El Lider.

When she was pregnant, Celia, because of her experience with sexism from her in-laws, determined that if she would bear a girl child she would remain in Cuba. Her reasons for doing so are interesting and germane. She vows that she would not leave a daughter to such a life. She would "train her to read the columns of blood and numbers in men's eyes, to understand the morphology of survival" (1992, 42), so that her daughter would also outlast the hard flames of revolution, as she eventually would. Celia's in-laws are helpless, uneducated, dependent on men, victims of the system, like herself. They consequently see all other women as enemies in conflict with them for the man's scraps. She is not referring here literally to the war that took Gustavo away, or that Gustavo preferred to her. Rather she is referring to the bloody war between the sexes–the cruelty in relationships in the way the hegemonic system is set up in inequitable gendered power relations.

Her determination for Lourdes is fulfilled, but not as Celia could ever imagine. Ironically what happens when the baby does turn out to be a girl creates an enduring ambivalence in their relationship. True, Celia will always assist her daughter and guide her to the best of her abilities, but she begins motherhood by a rejection of Lourdes, which, in turn, prevents Lourdes from ever fully accepting her mother.

After bearing Lourdes, Celia loses her sanity. Clearly she is projecting onto her own female child her deep-level feelings of rejection and abandonment, invalidation, worthlessness, and self-hatred. As a woman she has been rejected by her lover, then tortured by her husband's family with his permission. As for Lourdes, Celia's eldest daughter, she never forgets this story about how her mother had treated her after her birth. It effectively works to keep Lourdes cool and distant from her mother, estranging her forever. Ironically, she comes to place all her trust and devotion in her father whom she adores, instead. Father and daughter are simpatico in every way. It is the youngest daughter, Felicia, who inherits what the world would call the mother's streak of insanity, the painful exposure of vulnerable sensibilities in relation to her sexuality and feelings of love to the point where the woman escapes from reality to some other level of consciousness.

Although not a believer either in Catholicism or Santería, in moments of stress Celia repairs to any spiritual belief system for help. One of them is goddess worship of an old Ceiba tree. Celia was brought up by her Great-aunt, Alicia, whom she had loved. Her cosmopolitanism, atheism, and belief in Santería had been transmitted to her from this elegant and genteel relative. Alicia had worshiped the tree as a woman, a mother, a saint.

When Celia goes there to pray for Felicia's recovery, she discovers that other women agree with Tía Alicia. They have left offerings of all kinds on the ground near the trunk and that the tree itself is bulging with offerings buried underground, some for good purposes, others for evil. This is not so much directly created female goddess worship as the application of Santería which integrates this possibility by worship of the lwa in the tree.

Far more than her mother, however, Felicia will eventually subscribe to a female-oriented and identified aspect within Santería because it gives consolation to those in spiritual trouble. As a child, however, Felicia was a devout Catholic, even suspecting Celia of atheism. She feared that if her mother were an atheist, she would burn forever in hell, as her older sister and her teachers, the nuns, told her.

Generally, Celia assumes a detached stance from both Catholicism and voodoo, except when she needs some spiritual formula that she feels might help her. As a rule, the worst thing Celia, the socialist feminist, can conceive of is for women to be contained within the narrow confines to which "priests and politicians" (1992, 99) consigned them. Before Castro comes to power, she wonders in a letter to her lost lover whether Gustavo can see how between them these two groups are taking control of the entire world, not only Spain and Cuba, and dividing it up among themselves. Survival for Celia then became "an act of hope" (1992, 99). As such an act, Celia joined demonstrations in Havana, demanding that the rebels who survived the attack on Moncada be released. Among those rebels was a young lawyer, much like Gustavo, who was soon to become El Lider. She ends her letters to Gustavo with the Revolution imminent. Interestingly, many years later, her granddaughter Pilar, although living in the United States, feels the same way politically and makes the same arguments as a feminist.

Although not a believer, Celia still feels cautious about spiritual matters and "superstitions" which she does not comprehend on a rational level. And with good reason, as we see in terms of the suffering she experiences when she loses Felicia to them. Paradoxically, although Celia sometimes dabbles in Santería herself, she distrusts the secret ceremonies of African voodoo. She fears Chango, god of fire and lightning. Later on, Felicia becomes his devotée. Celia displays racism in her antagonism to Chango whom she contemptuously refers to as the black people's god. She teaches her children that they will be snatched away from her and become sacrifices to Chango, god of fire and lightning, if they wandered around on the streets by themselves, a prophecy that comes true for Felicia. She forbids Felicia to go to her black friend Herminia's house because her father is a Santería priest. Yet before the Revolution, Celia had respected

Herminia's father, expressing to him the strong political antipathy she had felt for Fulgencio Batista. He had, however, disappointed her by responding that Batista was under Chango's protection and was going to escape Cuba with his life and his fortune, and die a natural death. It should be added at this point that Garcia never represents any Santería priest or priestess as ever making incorrect predictions.

As we already know, Celia prays intensely for her daughter Felicia at the Ceiba tree when Felicia's health fails. There she meets Herminia Delgado carrying healing baskets for Felicia. The contents of the baskets reveal that her friend wants to cure Felicia of hysteria, a nervous condition, and syphilis, as well as to prevent further harm from coming to her. Celia also sees leaves from the Ceiba tree in the collection. After her parents divorced, Celia was raised from the age of four by her Great-aunt Alicia who was an elitist and from the upper classes. Tía Alicia was the profoundest early influence on her life. Instead of resisting, Celia had learned to love her new environment: the museums, the concerts, and the ancient Ceiba tree. And because Tía Alicia had no use for the Catholic Church and its believers, she took the child, instead, to American movies.

At the end of the text, however, in her extreme grief over the loss of her daughter, Celia does fulminate against Santería, Felicia's chosen form of spiritual expression, and commits sacrileges in the temple where Felicia becomes a priestess. Her response is extreme, even considering the circumstances. She comes to feel ever more impotent to change the downward trajectory of Felicia's life, her increasing emotional and spiritual suffering over a period of years. At the end, Celia becomes convinced that she must act: that to have to live on and witness her daughter's disfigurement and death is too much for her. True, Santería finally gives Felicia peace and transcendence at the end of her life when she becomes a priestess, but to balance out Felicia's destruction of men, the gods also take away both her beauty and her life. In a literal sense, so does the apparently untreated syphilis she contracts from her first husband. Felicia's death, coming immediately after her son Javier's disappearance, possibly his death, as well, drives Celia to suicide.

At this point in the text, however, Celia identifies with Dona Inés de Bobadillo, Cuba's first woman governor, who assumed the position after her husband Hernando de Soto left to conquer Florida. Celia likens her lover Gustavo to de Soto. As de Soto had left his Inés to conquer Florida, Gustavo had left Celia to return to the Spanish Civil War to conquer the fascists with his Kodak by indicting them for the murders of countless innocent people. Now that her husband is dead, Celia dreams that Jorge is using one of the brooms that he used to sell as a spear, throwing it at the window of the room at the hotel where she had slept with Gustavo and shattering it, together with her past. In her mind, Jorge has successfully come between her and her dreams by her marriage to him and through the reality of all their years together.

In a sense, she has thereby betrayed all that Gustavo meant to her, all that she had created him as meaning–romance, passion, idealism–living for something greater than herself. Because of this dream, she now resolves to devote whatever time she has left on earth to El Lider, to give herself to his Revolution. Now that Jorge has died and left her free to do as she pleases, she will spend her time volunteering wherever she is needed—vaccinating children, teaching, laboring in the microbrigades. Now she can at last fully live out her idealistic vision of life. Accordingly, for two weeks, at the age of sixty-three, she becomes a sugarcane worker, loving every minute of it: the feel of her muscles hardening as she moves forward swinging the machete, even tearing her skin on the stalks of the sugarcane, her skin browned by the sun. If we did not realize it before, we do now. Celia, as created by Garcia, is a remarkable woman of epic stature.

An example of class antagonism and conflict, not between upper and lower, but between the machetero and even lower class, and between country and city, is depicted here. Such conflict is rarely presented in literature, as occurs when a machetero slashes a volunteer like Celia with a machete because he is furious about lack of recognition for his expertise, for what he has spent a lifetime doing. From his perspective the volunteers imposed on him by the regime are all amateur "Sunday peasants" (1992, 44) whom he consigns to hell.

Celia, however, remains adamant in her romantic dreams about the sugarcane, how after being refined it is exported to Mexico, Russia, and Poland. The people of these countries will be able to use *her* sugar in their drinks or when they are baking. Just as exciting to Celia is her dream of a Cuba grown prosperous, not falsely so, as before the Revolution, but a prosperity in which everyone will share. She is referring here to the former influence and power of the United States over Cuba when Cuba was one of its corrupt dependencies.

She takes pride in her increasingly rough hands. But a recurring dream keeps coming to Celia, a dream that clearly foreshadows her own suicide. In this dream a young girl, dressed as she dresses, is out on the beach to pick shells and gets drowned in an oncoming ocean wave. It is also a dream foreshadowing her loss of innocence, of illusion, of idealism. It is a dream of death in the face of antipathetic, warring forces within her psyche.

Although her husband is newly deceased, Celia wonders why she does not grieve for him, why her vision of him walking on the water in the moment of his death seems a long while ago and even longer since he had flown to New York for his health. She concludes that perhaps this is the case, not because she does not love him, but because all during their married life she had been accustomed to his long absences when he was a traveling salesman.

Celia's epistles to Gustavo begin in 1935, after he left her. She always writes them on the eleventh day of the month, for on that day she lost him. In the first one, where she informs Gustavo that she will marry Jorge, we again see the foreshadowing of her suicide. She fantasies that she is living under the water, the area given over to the worship of Yemaya. She is so distraught by Gustavo's having left her that she hopes that the silence beneath the sea will bring her consolation. She feels as if she is imprisoned in place in Cuba and can no longer sleep. During her honeymoon, she writes about how Jorge attempts to kiss away

Gustavo from her ears and eyes and by making a poultice on her forehead of "moist petals" (1992, 50) to make her forget Gustavo. But all these efforts only make her cry, for she still belongs to Gustavo. She insists on continuing her devotion to this immaterial presence in her past. She uses this devotion as her reason for continuing to live on in the present and into the future, rather than live reality with her life with Jorge in the present. In subsequent letters, she informs Gustavo that she has become pregnant and hopes to die of pneumonia. She then loses her mind and writes him incoherent letters.

She next writes him from the asylum that she has made a friend, Felicia Gutierrez, whose feelings of entrapment in marriage match hers. Only Felicia acts out her feelings in violence, rather than finding solace in letters to a phantom lover as Celia does. Felicia murdered her husband by dousing him with gasoline, then setting him afire. She refuses to repent, and both women are planning an escape together from the asylum. Years later, Celia's daughter, named Felicia after her mother's friend, repeats the original Felicia's act. Only Felicia is never be incarcerated, nor are her children removed from her, because her husband, although horribly mutilated, lives on. He outlives her, in fact, as readers discover during Felicia's funeral.

Celia next informs Gustavo that her friend Felicia was killed by "they," apparently the gods, by burning alive in her bed. Again, this will be her daughter Felicia's fate, to be killed by the gods. Despite Jorge's prediction that she is dooming her daughter, she names her new baby after her deceased friend. Celia then writes in detail about her beloved deceased Tía Alicia, the greatest romantic of all (except for Celia, it might be added). Celia loves Gustavo in much the way she has loved Tía Alicia—for his romantic qualities and for his giving her life a glamorous dimension. She loves the smell of violet water because Alicia had always combed it into her hair. She recollects all the times they walked in parks and boulevards around Havana, while her Great-aunt regaled her with fascinating tales about them.

Celia next writes that Jorge has had a severe car accident. Lodged in his spine were glass splinters that the doctors could not remove. Both of his arms, his right leg, and four ribs were broken. All these assorted "pains in the ass" comprise the trope for Jorge's despair at ever successfully winning Celia over from Gustavo and all the idealism and romanticism that Gustavo represents. Paradoxically, as soon as she set eyes on Jorge swathed in bandages Celia realizes that she does love him, although not with the passion that she has felt and still feels for Gustavo.

When Jorge returns home, Celia has to set up a child's cot right next to Jorge's bed because Lourdes will not allow herself to be separated from her father. This is a foreshadowing of a situation to be repeated much later in New York when Lourdes sets up a cot in her daughter Pilar's room for Jorge. Lourdes, even at two and a half, was extremely devoted to her father to the point where even if he were not due to return until very late at night, she would wait at the door for him in her party dress. This also foreshadows Lourdes's close relationship with her father. They are more like twin souls than father and daughter.

Celia rediscovers the poverty of the countryside as she travels to and from Holguín, the town where Jorge's accident has occurred. At one train station, she describes a horrifyingly unforgettable scene involving a little girl of about six, so poor that she only wore a dirty rag that did not cover her private parts. The child is begging for food at the station. In the bustle of the crowd a man thrusts a finger into the child's genitals. When Celia cries out in horror, the man runs away. She calls the girl over to her and lowers her basket of food through the window for her. The little girl's response is to grab it and run away, "like a limping mongrel" (1992, 55). If Celia's nobility of character comes through nowhere else, it comes through here. In fact, she is beginning to take over the book, to assume such large and diverse dimensions of personality, character, and experience as to interest readers more in her than in anyone else in her family. Perhaps sensing this, perhaps in keeping with the book's structure, polyglossia, Garcia begins to rotate voices.

It is at this point that we also finally meet Javier, Celia's third child. One day after Felicia deliberately burns a customer's scalp with lye, he returns from Czechoslovakia. Garcia tells us that Celia greets him as though he were more a lover than a son, repeating once again the motif she has established for mothers' primary relations with their sons. Javier's wife has left him for a professor of mathematics from Minsk and taken their daughter with her. Celia wonders if he had inherited her passionate nature, or whether passion itself is undiscriminating, haphazard like a cancerous growth. However, this may be, both Celia and her son have this disease. Of her children, Celia sympathizes with her son Javier the most, because his affliction at least, has a name.

After two months of taking over Celia's bed, Javier begins to drink heavily. As a result, Celia cuts back on all her revolutionary activities, even resigning her fulfilling post as a judge for the People's Court. After much difficulty, she finds the santera who had treated her when she was suffering so intensely that she was on the verge of death from the loss of Gustavo. She feels that she must save her son from his depression. If she is unable to save him, then she will not be able to save anyone, not even herself, and her fear turns out to be wellfounded. The santera returns with Celia to her home, and while in her trance, she evaporates. All that is left of the santera is her shawl. In all probability the lwa are punishing the santera for daring the impossible, for interference with those with whom they are dealing. Worse, after Javier disappears, Celia begins to disintegrate too. She finds that she has breast cancer, and after the operation, she is left with a scar exactly like one that Javier has on his back.

Felicia, as I have pointed out, shares her mother's intensity, but in a spiritual way, in terms of her devotion to things spiritual, to indigenous spirituality, rather than Catholicism. Felicia is the embodiment, as well, of the lwa Erzulie, who is irresistible to men. In Erzulie's manifestation of destroyer, she kills those men who, once having become her devotés, betray her. Felicia and her mother are also devotées of Yemaya, goddess of the sea, to whom we see Celia returning in the beginning which is her end.

We first meet Felicia as a flashback from several years ago in Celia's mind after she has returned to her house, while she is making her preparations for her final engagement with the sea. In Celia's memory she sees her daughter rushing onto the scene, upset to find out that her father, when he left Cuba, did not come to say goodbye to her. The last time she had ever seen Jorge was when he had broken a chair over her first husband's back and screamed at her that if she intended to go off "with that sonofabitch" (1992, 12), she should never dare to show her face again in his house. For this reason, she wishes to come to terms with him before he dies in the United States. To achieve that end, she goes to a voodoo ceremony

Manifesting himself as a devoté of the orisha Chango, both in his thunderous temper and his connection with iron in his vocation, Jorge also reveals qualities commonly assigned by law and custom only to Hispanic males, regardless of class. This is the freedom granted to fathers and husbands of all classes to express violence in response to a daughter's (or wife's) disobedience to their will, especially in matters of courtship and marriage. And we have seen Cofer's paternal grandfather's response to his daughter's marriage to a man of color, exactly as Jorge reacts to Felicia's marriage to Hugo Monteverde, also a man of color. Julia Alvarez depicts a similar frightening scene between a representative of the privileged class, Dr. Garcia, and one of his daughters in *How the Garcia Girls Lost Their Accents*, although he does not physically beat her for losing her virginity without the sacrament of marriage. Her lover is a white German, so it is not racism, but sexism that causes this beating.

At the voodoo ceremony Garcia describes an ebony statue of Santa Barbara against the back wall. She is the Black Queen who presides over the participants. Garcia syncretizes this deity and others with voodoo, with African-sourced religion, and with Catholicism. Cofer in *Silent Dancing* describes the black Virgin and her miracles at great length, only in terms of Catholicism, whereas Garcia describes the Catholic deities as the peoples' syncretizations of voodoo and Catholicism. In Cuba, Puerto Rico, the United States and elsewhere, this form of syncretization is primarily due to necessity—harsh and repressive colonial Spanish enforcement of Catholicism on their subjects. How much is Catholic, how much Santería when we see a statue of a Catholic saint?

With Felicia it is not Catholicism. It is the reverse of Catholicism, even with the name she was given in honor of her mother's friend in the insane asylum who had torched her husband and then was put to a fiery death herself in her bed by the avenging gods. Felicia's name is an appropriate foreshadowing for her later manifestation as Erzulie in the association of her husbands with fire, with their death by fire, as well as her burning women unfaithful to or disrespectful of her. Garcia, in choosing such an association for Felicia is appropriating Erzulie's vengeful spirit rather than the Catholic martyrdom of sainted souls, as well as reversing the meaning of the word "Felicia" (happy one). Felicia's life will, in fact, serve as a contrast to all those elements ordinarily associated with mortal "happiness." She will be the vengeful goddess incarnate, as opposed to the god of mercy, and she will never know happiness, except in very brief intervals with her lovers and husbands, and, later, her son-lover, Ivanito, her most loyal and lifelong devoté.

Felicia at one point becomes possessed, refusing to change or clean her filthy nightgown. She restricts her children's diet to coconut icecream, dances constantly with Ivanito, who adores her, and lectures them about how dangerous the sun (reality) is (1992, 46). It may be recalled that Celia too had suffered a mental breakdown. When this happens to her daughter, Celia succeeds in spiriting Felicia's twin daughters away to her home in order to provide them with some semblance of normal maternal care and daily routine. Ivanito, however, refuses to leave his mother. The thought terrifies him.

Hugo, Felicia's first husband and their father, has been with his family a total of three times. The first time he brought presents from China and apologized to his children for staying away so long. The second time he struck Felicia in the eye, blinding her temporarily. The third time he impregnated her with Ivanito and left her with syphilis. Then he had left for good. He is depicted as apelike, as is the third of Felicia's husbands. Hugo's face is destroyed by fire, because Felicia had doused his head with gasoline and set it afire after he had brutally rejected her.

We have seen Garcia depicting Lourdes as preferring Jorge, her father, to Celia, her mother. In addition, Lourdes's daughter Pilar in her turn prefers Rufino, her father, to her mother. Likewise, Felicia's twin daughters also side with their father Hugo against their mother. Ivanito, on the other hand, clings to his mother. The children thus clearly form liaisons strictly along predictable gender lines in this text. Daughters never adhere to mothers, and sons never adhere to fathers. The exception is Berta Arango del Pino, Jorge's mother, and her single daughter Ofelia who lives with her. When Ofelia dies, still single, Berta never recovers and soon dies herself.

Allegorically, Felicia experiences the flames of gender warfare, as her mother experiences the flames of revolution, which the santera had prophesied that her mother would survive and which Lourdes, in turn, had prophesied that Felicia would survive. In her childhood, Felicia had been terrorized with lurid tales by her mother, the nuns in her school, and even by her sister Lourdes. She also seems to have been neglected by her parents who preferred her other siblings. Now Felicia hears voices, sees things, and colors floating before her eyes. Her father had predicted doom for the infant at birth due to the infelicity of the name Felicia given to her by her mother. Later, Felicia identified with the martyred St. Sebastian and wanted his name for her confirmation name. After being balked in this by the nuns, she refused confirmation altogether. Years later, her father blamed all her troubles on this refusal.

Felicia's only sources of happiness are recordings by Beny More, which she never stops playing, and teaching Ivanito all the dances. When she dances with her five year old, everything makes sense, her doubts evaporate. She feels as she did when she was in love with Hugo, centered, in tune with the universe, knowing all its secrets and inmost mechanisms. But as soon as the music stops, she dreams about her husband Hugo. She had met him when she was a waitress at the El Ternero Dorado restaurant. Falling madly in love with him at first sight, she threw off her apron and went with him at once to the Hotel Inglatarra. Even that first time he was abusive. The next time they met, seven months later, Felicia was pregnant and so they married, but without Jorge's presence, for he adamantly refused to recognize the marriage.

The couple moved into her paternal grandmother Berta Arango del Pino's house. Hugo, furious at being beaten by his prospective father-in-law because of his lower class and darker skin and feeling trapped into marriage, threw himself on the couch, staring angrily in silence into space. When Felicia approached him, asking if he would like to make love as he liked best, to be tied down, he pushed his fist into her neck until she could not breathe and warned her that he would kill her if she came near him. The cruel irony that he is now literally tied up and down by marriage, as opposed to how he had achieved his pleasure before marriage, is too much for him. He slept on the sofa and went back to sea the next day, leaving Felicia forever, except for the briefest of flying visits.

At the end of the summer of her father's death, Felicia's psychic malady grows worse. She can now remember when she first decided to murder Hugo in revenge. After he had infected her with syphilis from women he had slept with in Morocco, she has become pregnant with Ivanito. This is actually why she is now seeing visions, is irrational, and is dying. One day she burns Hugo. The flesh on his face and hands were permanently scarred, and for a long time the smell of burned flesh stayed in the air outside.

Much like her niece Pilar, Felicia dreams, grieving about suffering women and children: missing children, prostitutes in India, Cuban women raped in Havana. Thus part of the title of *Dreaming in Cuban* reflects tragic situations such as Felicia experiences and creates. Not only is she suffering over her own husband's betrayal of her romantic dreams, but for all other women's as well. Indeed, the lwa Erzulie, with whom Felicia is identified, will destroy any other woman with whom her male devotés attempt to establish relations, which explains Felicia's attempt to murder Hugo. Once these men dedicate themselves to Erzulie, they can no longer marry or be involved with women in any way.

Finally, Felicia goes to a santero because she wants another husband. No matter how many times he throws the shells, they come up with bad luck for Felicia. He tells her that the gods have willed that she cannot attain what she wishes. Whatever good she gets in life will be transient, like a basket filled with water. Again, as ever in this work, the santero prophesies correctly.

After only four days of marriage to her beloved second husband Ernesto (aptly named, because he is a crusading restaurant inspector), he is burned in a suspicious hotel restaurant fire. Throughout her life, Felicia is closely linked with fire. Here Garcia treats us to a sample of her perverse humor. Ernesto could not be bribed and was committed to the leadership of a detailed campaign to wipe out mice feces. Hysterical at his funeral, Felicia cries out that Ernesto was murdered because of his honesty and thoroughness in not accepting one single mouse dropping. Felicia then writes a letter of protest to El Lider, demanding a full investigation into her husband's death. When she gets no response, she becomes convinced that it is El Lider's fault, that he was somehow responsible for Ernesto's death.

She is clearly paranoid by this point, believing that bright light is being refracted off the glasses of El Lider and his cronies. The light is so intense and bright that it prevents her from seeing them, from identifying the guilty. She becomes convinced that a customer in the beauty shop where she works is one of their spies. Felicia then coats Graciela's head with her menstrual blood and with lye, and places it under a plastic bag. From that moment on, she cannot remember what happens next for a long time. Once again, fire is the cause, this time disfiguring a woman whom Felicia in the guise of Erzulie, believes to be disloyal to her.

In a marvelously written surrealistic passage, Felicia awakens years later, married again, this time to a hulking carnival worker, Otto Cruz. His dearest wish is to escape Cuba for Minnesota. At the point where he announces to her that he had arranged to do so by boat, she becomes conscious that it is over her objections. She murders him, again through burning. The couple goes for a ride on an empty roller coaster. Offering to perform fellatio on him, Felicia gets her husband to rise to a standing position in the falling car. She closes, then open her eyes, and in that instant her husband has disappeared. From Felicia's point of view, Otto's insistence upon going where she does not wish to go is disloyal to her. Therefore she pushes him off the roller coaster and watches him die on "a bed of high-voltage wires." He turns to "gray ash" which is blown north by the wind just as he had desired. Later, the santera's death while in a trance duplicates Otto's, so it is clear that the lwa are taking retribution for this murder.

After the murder, Felicia returns to working in beauty shops by day and attending voodoo ceremonies by night. She believes that the rituals are healing, that she was once again in tune with "the forces in the universe" (1992, 186).

As an ironic contrast to her mother's dreams and hopes for the glorious future of Cuba through active work in the Revolution, we next find Felicia in a prisoner brigade in the Sierra Madre Maestra. A camouflage helmet covers her head, and she wears a rifle on her shoulder. As contrasted to her mother's brigade, Felicia's is comprised of outcasts and social and political dissidents. Unlike Celia, Felicia is critical about Cuba's leadership, with its seemingly endless threats of war and political use of outdoor signs containing clumsy epithets, for example, "Fighters for Learning" (1992, 108) as in communist China, to define teachers.

Ironically, Felicia is not punished by the state for her acts of vengeance against two husbands and one hapless woman, but because she has tried to commit suicide and murder Ivanito. As a result, she is recorded as unfit as a mother and pressured to send her son away to a boarding school where she is permitted to visit him only one Sunday a month. Once she arrives, they never speak to one another, except with eyes and hands, always touching one another.

Garcia presents a variety of reasons for prisoners being assigned to this battalion in order to provide readers with unspoken testimony against El Lider. One member was turned in by her daughter because she demanded that her family say grace before meals. Another young man was carted off to the Isle of Pines to work in the marble quarries there because he liked jazz and his hair was long. The only youth in the troop makes the interesting point that El Lider and his comrades no longer remember what they looked like when they were young rebels. Nowadays they would be "in a Social Disgrace Unit with drug addicts and maricones [gay men]" (1992, 108–109). Although Celia keeps a framed photograph of El Lider by her bed, Felicia believes that he is a common tyrant, much like any other tyrant. Then she, too, like her mother, imagines having sex with him.

Coconuts, which are identified in voodoo with power, purification, and prophecy become Felicia's major diet. The only food she feeds her children is coconut ice cream, which she serves day after day for breakfast, lunch, and dinner. She rips the telephone from the wall and locks the children in the house. When her twin daughters dump their ice cream into the sink, she gives them more. Through it all, Ivanito contentedly eats the ice cream his mother serves him. His sisters, in an attempt to avert the direction he is taking, tell him what happened before he was born. Nevertheless, he remains adamant in his loyalty to her. He insists that he is happy with his mama and that his sisters have joined together against him. Felicia's dreams/obsessions grow worse. She permits no lights in the house, convinced that the sun is evil. Celia visits as much as she can and tries to feed Ivanito normal food, but out of loyalty to Felicia, he will not touch any food that Celia brings him.

One night after falling asleep, Celia dreams she hears someone calling to her and awakens. She does not like the pattern of the moonlight on her sheets. She rushes from her beach home to Havana repeating the words "M'hija" over and over again as if they had the power to cure her daughter, but Felicia is now dying, and Celia, tragically, is unable to save her.

Garcia also takes readers into the consciousness of one of Felicia's twin daughters, Luz Villaverde, when she is fourteen. She resents her mother for having destroyed her father, again providing us with another example of Garcia's division of families along gender lines: boys with their mothers, daughters with their fathers. Nevertheless, however the pairings go, they always reinforce the patriarchal script of the Cuban culture. The mothers live for their sons, serving them better and more devotedly than the best servants, while the daughters live for and serve their fathers, adoring them in their machismo. Thus both girl children and grown women form a subordinate class to their menfolk. For example, instead of resenting her father for never being home, Luz admires Hugo for being adventurous. This pride is revolting, because the adventures she valorizes are adulterous ones with women ill from sexually transmitted diseases which Hugo has, in turn, passed on to Felicia and Ivanito.

Although Luz and her twin sister are not concerned with or angry about their father's having sex with other women than their mother, Pilar, their cousin, an American girl, reacts differently. Brought up during the second-wave feminist movement and herself a feminist, Pilar runs away when she sees her father having sex with a strange woman. By contrast, Hugo's daughters adore him, care for him, and feed him after they are briefly reunited.

Hugo has written them before, but Felicia had always intercepted the cards and burned them. Then, by some accident, they receive one of his communications. They immediately take advantage of their mother's absence at an overnight voodoo ceremony and pay their father a visit. One day he even asks to see Ivanito, but when they do bring him along, they find Hugo having sex with a masked naked woman. Although his daughters still remain loyal to Hugo. Garcia does present the responses of the children to this sight as traumatized.

Again, in her balanced way, Garcia depicts the twin girls as possessed of career ambitions that would have been ridiculed out of existence before the Revolution. Luz's ambition is to become a veterinarian and Milagro wants to be a mycologist. Naturally both girls are glad that they can go to college to fulfill these dreams, that they are living in postrevolutionary times. Their Abuela Celia takes this opportunity to give them a necessary historical and political lesson in this all-important matter for women when she informs them that before the revolution as a rule females did not go to college. They married very young and had children. Here Celia as seen in her role of cultural gatekeeper, trains future generations of women in a positive manner and herself serves as a positive role model for young women, especially in her outstanding decision-making ability as a judge in Castro's Cuba. This ability directly stems from Celia's noble and visionary character, her socialist feminist vision.

Herminia Delgado, Felicia's devoted friend, tells us more about Felicia's character. Like her mother, she collected shells and identified with Yemaya, goddess of the seas. She tells us even more about her own father, who has become a "babaloo, a high priest of Santería" (1992, 184). Sadly, as a result, lies were spread about him to the effect that he tore off goats' head with his teeth and sliced up babies with blue eyes before the sun rose. Herminia herself was called a bruja [evil witch], as was Lourdes, by her nannies.

Unlike Celia, however, Felicia aways defended Herminia from the double discrimination she faced on account of her father's vocation and her blackness. As for Felicia's fascination with the coconut, Herminia explains that it was not just an ordinary coconut, but the "obi," the coconut used for "divining" purposes (1992, 184). Herminia lauds her friend Felicia's loyalty. Although she deplores her stubbornness, she believes that Felicia had a quality that made up for her being stubborn, that is, adapting to suffering imaginatively. Obviously, this is not what the world thinks. They think she is demented. Herminia justifies her friend's peculiarity as freedom from the maliciousness of ordinary people, that she was more dignified on the edge of sanity.

Also, and most significantly, Felicia was the only one Herminia has ever known who was color-blind. No one, Herminia informs us, admits to racism in Cuba, or talks about such a thing. In this connection, Celia also informs readers in one of her letters to Gustavo of a historical fact in order to prove that racial discrimination does indeed exist in Cuba. To be accepted into membership at the Havana Yacht Club, Batista had to pay a million dollars, because his skin was considered too dark. And in the Little War of 1912, Herminia's relatives had been murdered, as well as thousands of other blacks. "They were hunted . . . like animals, and finally hung by their genitals from the lampposts in Guaimaro" (1992, 185). Still, this war remains a minor footnote in Cuban history.

Herminia, like Celia, claims things are better now under Castro. Women are treated more respectfully. She herself has worked at a battery factory for nearly twenty years and has risen to supervise forty-two other women. She feels that it may not be very prestigious work, but it beats washing floors or working as a nursemaid for strangers. The time is 1980. Yet what Herminia concludes still holds true: that what hasn't changed is that men still control everything.

Felicia had returned to Herminia to confide to her friend that she had murdered her third husband, Otto. Later, the santera's death while in a trance duplicates Otto's, so it is clear that the lwa are taking retribution for this murder. At this point, Celia tries her hardest to convince Felicia to give herself entirely to the Revolution, but Felicia will not be dissuaded from the orishas. Herminia insists that Felicia has a true calling to voodoo and that is why she eventually became initiated as a priestess, a process that Garcia describes in great detail in the text. Nevertheless, the gods have doomed her anyhow, despite all the rituals and necklaces, despite Felicia's fervor.

Celia's response when she sees her daughter near death is to turn against the initiates, destroying all evidence of Felicia's worship. She calls them all murderers and witch doctors and dares to throw Obatala (the chief god) down from his altar. Next, she overturns the tureen with the sacred stones and crushes Felicia's seashells under the heels of her leather pumps. That still not satisfying her, "in a mad flamenco, her arms thrown up in the air" (1992, 190), she throws off her shoes and crushes the shells with her bare feet which begin to bleed. These actions offend Yemaya, goddess of the sea, to whom she had been a devotée. Then she suddenly stops, takes her daughter in her arms, kisses her, and rocks her until she dies. Felicia had requested to be buried as a santera, and by the time she is dressed and all the rituals performed, her facial disfigurements have disappeared. Like Yemaya, the goddess of the sea, her skin is clear and pink as a seashell and her eyes are green again.

Garcia then tells us that a man in rags appears at the cemetery entrance during Felicia's funeral. His face is covered, so that it cannot be seen, and he breathes from the slit near his eyes as though he were "sucking sorrow from the air like venom" (1992, 214). This anonymous and mysterious mourner is Hugo Villaverde, Felicia's first husband and father of her three children. He has outlived Felicia.

Back in New York, Celia's surviving daughter Lourdes mourns her father's death. After his arrival in that city in a fruitless attempt to regain his health, her appetite both for sex with her husband Rufino and for baked goods increased dramatically to the point where she has gained over 100 pounds. As I have previously discussed, Lourdes has been a passionate devotée of her father from infancy. She shares his vision, his dream of life, and how it should be lived. In turn, Jorge adores Lourdes and is inseparable from her. Like Jorge, Lourdes is fanatically conservative, fanatically anti-Castro. Both of them conform entirely to the description of Cuban emigrés, certainly to the one Denis Lynn Daly Heyck gives us:

It is common knowledge that Cubans in the United States, generally speaking, have very strong political views, usually ranging from the merely anti-Castro to the extreme right wing. A case in point is the Cuban American National Foundation, comprised of wealthy exile businessmen such as the well-known Jorge Mas Canosa, the major promoter of Radio Marti, a vehicle for anti-Castro propaganda. The Foundation's political branch, the Coalition for a Free Cuba, supports anti-communist activities, the most notable recent example being the contra war to overturn the Sandinista government in Nicaragua. Cuban Americans tend to vote Republican, and they were strong supporters of Presidents Nixon, Reagan, and Bush. Many Cuban Americans have never forgiven either the Kennedys or the Democrats for the Bay of Pigs fiasco of 1961, in which many Cuban exiles fought and died. (1994, 13)

Lourdes has good reason for her antagonism to the Revolution, as readers later discover. Garcia links Rufino, the scion of landowners who own a farm and extensive holdings, with his father-in-law, Jorge, who, in turn, is linked with Chango. Rufino's attributes are similar to Jorge's–fascination with iron, with material things, with invention, as well as his conservative political values. In turn, Rufino's daughter Pilar, who becomes a feminist artist, is a devotée of Rufino (her father), especially in his creative aspects. Rufino reciprocates his daughter's feelings completely, often interceding with his wife in his diplomatic way on Pilar's behalf.

Garcia describes the mother-daughter relationship between Lourdes and Pilar as a binary: the conservative, gatekeeper mother and second-wave feminist daughter are at loggerheads about everything. The relationship is metaphorical, even allegorical. Eliana Ortega, when she distinguishes between the generations of Cuban women writers in the United States, gives us an understanding of this difference between Lourdes and Pilar:

[M]inority writers in the U.S. usually speak from an experience of marginality and discrimination due to race, class, and/or sex. More to the point, Cuban "writers in exile"–women and men–tend to identify with the establishment and reject the Third World Stance of many native Hispanic writers, and thus do not feel part of an underprivileged ethnic minority. . . . Still, some of the writings done by Cuban women in the United States present a modified vision of cultural reality due to the prevalence of a feminist ideology in their texts, and to the naked, critical portrayal of sociocultural myths, such as the submissive, petit-bourgeois wife and her pathetic Don Juanesque husband.

To put it in general terms, the most distinguishable feature that separates older immigrant generations of Cuban women from their younger compatriots in the U.S., beyond their choice of language, is the problem of their cultural/political identity and affiliations. These vital connections, with their own inner and outer selves, constitute on [sic] artistic mother lode of inquiry, rejection, and affirmation . . . an exciting location at the margins: on the cutting ege of Latina cultural ethnicity and gender awareness. (1989, 127-128)

Pilar accidentally discovers her father having sex with an unknown woman, much as her cousins Pilar, Luz, and Ivanito Villaverde had discovered their father with an unknown woman. In revulsion, she resolves to run away to Cuba, to her grandmother, whom she had been forced to leave when her mother fled to the United States immediately after Castro's accession to power. This is despite Celia's outrage that in so doing, Lourdes was betraying the Revolution. Lourdes, in turn, resents Pilar's feminist political sympathies fully as much as her socialist mother resents Lourdes's conservative politics. The entire family is as torn about as the disparate dreams by which each one lives. Thus is the family a house divided. Jorge, Rufino and Lourdes are anti-Castroites. Celia and Javier are ardent socialists. Pilar, a feminist, is on the same wavelength as her grandmother and uncle, and Felicia becomes a voodoo priestess.

Lourdes' discourse is rabidly anti-Castro, which annoys her American daughter, who feels that she suffers enough as it is from her mother's gatekeeping intrusivenss. As with the other gatekeepers analyzed in this text, Lourdes comports herself as a prying mother, an omnipresent spy for the cultural regime. She reads her daughter's diary without a qualm, declaring that it is her duty as a mother to know her daughter's innermost feelings and thoughts and that Pilar will understand when she had her own children. Similarly, in *How the Garcia Girls Lost Their Accents*, after Dr. Garcia takes it upon himself to read one of his daughter's love letters, a dreadful quarrel and an estrangement ensues between them. Simultaneously they disown each other. He throws her out, while she leaves him.

Lourdes's mode of mothering is like "panopticon" mothering, to apply Foucault's theory of the repressive regime that scrutinizes its prisoner/citizens under its eternal, vigilant gaze. Again, thought-policing righteousness in terms of their children is characteristic of all the gatekeepers discussed in this text. It is characteristic of Cofer's Mama and mother in *Silent Dancing*; of Laura Garcia de la Torre, the mother *in How the Garcia Girls Lost their Accents*; as well as the narrator's grandmother, aunts, and mother in *Happy Days, Uncle Sergio*. They consider this spying element of their conduct toward their daughters as an intrinsic element of the duties and responsibilities of motherhood. Needless to say, their gatekeeping maintains and perpetuates Latino culture, much as gatekeeping in all other cultures globally. Just as Lourdes conducts herself in relationship to Pilar, Dr. Garcia's wife and mother of his five daughters acts toward them like a prison camp guard under the authority of a prison warden, her husband

Symbolically, such mothers conduct themselves as gatekeepers in relation to hegemonic rules and regulations. They impose and enforce them actively. Apparently they do so without any self-reflexivity by stalking their daughters incessantly and keeping tabs on their lives. They maintain that what they are doing–imposing and thereby perpetuating hierarchical restrictions for women into their daughters–is their highest, most sacred duty as mothers. It never seems to occur to any of them, even Celia, a gatekeeper for Cuban State socialism under Castro, that being used and using their daughters, in turn, is a "process." It turns "women qua woman/mother into commodities so as to sustain economic systems and infrastructures that exploit women" (Alarcón citing Irigary, 1988, 158–159). For example, Pilar loves to lie in the tub directly under the shower. However, whenever she is in the bathroom, her mother's reaction to Pilar's activity in the tub is to beat her, pull her hair out, call her a desgraciada and grind her knuckles into Pilar's temples. She then forces Pilar to work in her bakery after school for a pittance, claiming that it would teach her to be responsible and clear her head of "filthy thoughts." Meanwhile, Pilar hears Lourdes pushing herself on Rufino every night.

The direct opposite of her sister Felicia's African-sourced spirituality, intensity, and complete abandon in all matters relating to love, Lourdes has totally internalized the Catholic teaching that unmarried sex and sex with oneself is filthy. Lourdes is a capitalist consumeristic materialist, a successful entrepreneur who loves things, as illustrated in her voracious ingestion of artificial American sweets. Felicia, equally unbalanced on the other end of the scale–indigenism–voraciously consumes coconut ice cream for spiritual reasons.

When her father comes to New York to die, Lourdes gives him Pilar's bed and puts her daughter in a cot next to him. Every day he writes love letters to Celia. Again, note the linking of disparate elements: Jorge, the arch-conservative materialist is a loving and romantic husband. On the other hand, Celia would answer rarely and write only about meetings she was attending. This saddened Jorge. Again, note the clashing linkages, the inconsistency in characters, the endless paradoxes in relationships that Garcia delights in creating. The romantic, idealistic Celia who writes so many unsent letters to a lover who left her is pragmatic, mundane, and factual when it comes to her husband, whom she relegates to that level because his political yearnings are capitalistic and materialistic. Jorge, on the other hand, whose mentality is colonized and who is "Americanized," is romantic with his wife who is a socialist.

He returns to Lourdes, not to Celia, to die and after his death. Commensurate with voodoo belief, he returns to his daughter forty days after burial. He thanks her politely and tells her, laughing, that she had buried him like an Egyptian pharaoh.[2] Her early gratifying, mutually reciprocated love relationship with her father has shaped Lourdes, now a strongly opinionated woman. As already pointed out, when she was a child she used to wait anxiously for him to return from his selling trips. He, in turn, would call her every evening from the road, while over and over again she would plaintively beg him to come home.

She recollects her happiest childhood memories, how Jorge had taken her to baseball games in Cuba, how the sun had darkened her skin, the smell of his cologne, and the warm, acrid smells of the ballpark. Years later in New York, while he is dying, after the Mets won the World Series, Lourdes and her father, both great Mets fans, laughed with joy and embraced each other for a very long time.

Lourdes originally fled from Cuba to Miami, but she left that city precipitously because she couldn't stand her husband Rufino's family, their

eternal complaining about their lost wealth. She made Rufino drive until she felt
it was cold enough to stop. There is harrowing significance in this information
about Lourdes's *driven* search for a cold-enough climate. In Cuba, having
married into a family of wealthy landowners, she moved down to the family villa
on a large ranch. Here she attempted to bring order by removing the corrupt
accountant and doing the books herself, as well as renovating and restoring the
building. When her mother-in-law arrives, however, she undoes every
improvement Lourdes had made: restoring the former furniture and the former
accounting system. The alert gatekeeper vigorously returns everything back to
the patriarchal system of rule, in this case, a farming system. As in every other
system of power relations, the vigilant gatekeeper colludes with the patriarchy,
as usual:

A farming system based on the criterion of who provides the largest labor input serves to
obscure the fact that so-called male agricultural systems still depend on the active
participation of women. . . . [A]dditional criteria in gender classification of farming
systems [warrant] not only labor input but also access to the means of production,
participation in decision making, and control over the outcome of the productive process.
The criteria of access and controls [permits differentiation] between patriarchal and
egalitarian systems–the egalitarian system clearly linked to levels of female access and
control. . . . [F]arming systems [are also linked] to the process of capitalist development
in agriculture and social differentiation of the peasantry. At different stages of capitalist
development in several Third World countries, women were rarely the beneficiaries of
this development process in agriculture. Even during periods of progressive agrarian
reforms, women rarely benefited from these programs. (de la Torre 1993, 169)

    In contrast, after the Revolution, when Felicia and Celia work in the
sugarcane fields in rural areas, they are treated no differently from their male
coworkers. Because Celia also becomes a judge during the Castro regime, El
Lider's ideological commitment to equitable gendered power relations appears
to carry across into professional opportunities. It is observable in vocational
strata, as well, as illustrated in Herminia's improved lot in life. In this way
Garcia tactfully insinuates that women's class rankings have improved under
Castro.
    During Batista's regime, Lourdes's gatekeeper mother-in-law had brutally
erased all of Lourdes's hard work toward the goal of more efficiently and
productively managing the family farm, as well as to improve its living space, a
goal she was about to achieve. This erasure perpetuates the traditional Cuban
culture's "selective amnesia" which in turn fosters the association of masculinity
with power. "When women are erased from the historical record, the public
activism that challenges female confinement to the private sphere becomes
forgotten. . . . By this means the 'norm' comes to be perceived as a monolithic
value–women do seem to be contentedly domestic–instead of as a contested
ideal that is always under construction" (Hassett 1996, 402).
    One day, during her second pregnancy, the horse Lourdes was riding threw
her. After killing a large rodent (portent of things to come) which began to

nibble the toes of her boots, she hobbled nearly an hour until she reached their dairy farm where a worker lent her a horse. Riding at a breakneck pace back to their villa, she found her husband in the custody of two of Castro's soldiers. Lourdes then jumped from her horse and stood like a shield before her husband, shouting to them to leave. The soldiers backed away and left in their Jeep. She then lost her baby "in a pool of dark blood at her feet" (1992, 70).

Her courage is her undoing. For her disrespectful conduct in public toward them as men and as soldiers has humiliated the soldiers in their machismo and triggered their desire for revenge. When Rufino is away on business in Havana, they return. While one of them rapes her, the other holds her down, but only after she has fiercely defended herself with all her strength and will. When he is finished with her, her rapist then carves illegible hieroglyphics on her belly. He then beats her with his rifle before leaving her. For the rest of her life, Lourdes is traumatized by this experience.[3]

In *How the Garcia Girls Lost Their Accents*, we read how Laura Garcia de la Torre handles a similar experience when she also comes face to face with hostile, macho soldiers. Unlike Lourdes's response, however, Laura conducts herself in a servile manner, rather than confronting the soldiers with rage. She understands that, above all, whatever she does and says she must not offend these men's delicate sense of machismo, or the lives of her children and her husband will be weighed and lost in the balance.

Lourdes's direct and bold challenge to this strongest of cultural constructs for men—their machismo—leads to the soldiers' taking direct and awful revenge against her. Laura, in contrast, relies on "the transparency of expressivity" (Desmond 1994, 50). Unlike Lourdes, Laura applies to men of her own culture the belief system about mainstream Americans' assumptions that "Latins are how they dance, and they dance how they are." Laura acts the role expected of her, that "mothers are how they act and they act according to how they are." This is a lack of consciousness or awareness or self-reflexity about an activity or experience representing "a symbolic system" and reality. For example, rape and death are interpretations of given experiences.

Armed with the knowlege of her past trauma, readers can now understand why Lourdes is happy in New York and loves winter with all its layering which she feels protects her physically and psychically. Unlike Rufino, she welcomes English and its possibilities for reinvention. She wants "no part of its wretched carnival floats creaking with lies, no part of Cuba at all" (1992, 73).

Lourdes is still obsessed with the loss of her child and her assault and rape by Castro's soldiers: the kinds of terrorism to which women are continually prey in the patriarchal culture. She has personally experienced the suffering that for too many feminists is the basis for their battle for "abstract equalities." She knows from experience, for example, that "[w]omen have not been able to travel freely," and not only "[b]ecause of racist, misogynist, or homophobic terrorism" or "[b]ecause some 'don't have the fare'" (Gwin 1996, 895), but because they are women caught in a world of endless patriarchal conflict between classes of men, as the Batista and Castro conflicts illustrate.

Lourdes has married into a family of ranching landholders, a class destested by the peasant soldiers of Castro. Thus they consider her open season, vulnerable to the worst treatment imaginable. Ironically, if she had married into the peasant class and Batista soldiers had come for her husband, her treatment also would have been based on her husband's ranking–even lower–because as a woman she is deemed to be the lowest of the low. Women's class, no matter what race, is always based on their men's class ranking. As women, as a gender, they are ranked the lowest of the lowest classes, beneath all men.

Here I disagree with Haunani-Kay Trask, the Hawaiian centric nationalist. Because she shares "many more similarities, both in struggle and in controversy, with our men and with each other as indigenous women than we do with white people" therefore she insists, "culture is a larger reality than women's 'rights'" (1996, 914). In African, Asian, and Indian cultures, "indigenous women" are treated by their men as a different class, a lower class, oppressed sexually, just as in white cultures white women are oppressed. Injustice against women, inequitable gendered power relations crosses cultures and is always a sign of lowering in class ranking, or at best connects women with their men's ranking

Even if Trask succeeded in her "struggle" against "the Gargantua of capitalism and its safeguard, militarism" (1996, 913), she would immediately be beset by the sexism of her own "indigenous" brothers' against her as a woman. She proclaims that "[m]ore than a feminist, I am nationalist, trained by my family and destined by my genealogy to speak and work on my people's behalf, including our women" (1996, 915). In this light, I would ask Trask a question. It can also be directed toward other ethnic and women of color feminists, such as Afracentrics and some Chicana members of La Raza, as well as to all women who advocate their people's nationalist cause as a priority over the cause of women. Why can't they be nationalist and feminist? Are the two causes necessarily irreconcilable binaries? Charlotte Bunch responds tactfully to such thinking as Trask's:

So many women in other countries with whom we work are nervous about the way the difference discourse is going in the United States. They feel it undercuts our ability to talk about the universality of human rights: the notion that all women should have these human rights. . . . My goal has been that people be able to work together better and not be immersed in their difference. During my one year as a separatist, I learned that although separatism is a very good way to learn about your difference and shape your identity, it does not empower you over time. Ultimately, you can become so isolated that you are disempowered. (Bunch in Hartmann et al. 1996, 933, 935)

Lourdes continues to seek to transform herself into an Amazon, a heroic woman warrior, to do feminism in practice rather than theorize. While on duty as an auxiliary policewoman fighting drug dealers, she unsuccessfully attempts to save a boy who has jumped into the East River by jumping in after him. Overtly antifeminist, Lourdes feels that the shoes she wears are purveyors of power for women as specific examples, rather than abstract causes. Lourdes is wearing the shoes as part of a police uniform: "This image embodies middle-class characteristics (a respect for hard work, ambition, and abiding by the law) and persists regardless of former or present class position" (Prieto 1995, 166). On the other hand, again in startling contrast, and again, to expose the paradoxical qualities of Garcia's characters, Celia the socialist habitually wears dressy pumps, thus symbolically catering to male fantasy.

Garcia says of Lourdes that upper-class women believe that work outside the home is beneath them. Not so Lourdes. In this and other ways, her attitude sets the foundation for Pilar's open avowals of feminism without fear of reprisal by her culture. Here again, in the role that Lourdes enacts as gatekeeper, we see Garcia linking similar disparate qualities of character in Lourdes as we have seen in her mother and in some ways the reverse of her mother. Lourdes also suffers from jealousy because Rufino and Pilar are companions, often talking with one another, but neither one talks to her.

Lourdes is conservative politically, yet her actions are feminist, whereas Celia is progressive politically and yet more traditional, especially in her conduct and attitude toward men. Even though Lourdes had married into a class above her own and enjoyed the material pleasures that marriage had brought with it, still she refused to live in Cuba according to the way that class and her husband's family thought were appropriate to a woman. As for her mother-in-law (Pilar's Abuela Zaida), although in Cuba she had controlled eight sons, she now spends afternoons in exile in Miami watching telenovelas on television.

Once back in Cuba, after her honeymoon, Lourdes had realized that she could never be a traditional kind of woman like her mother-in-law. She had gone to work of her own accord on the Puente ranch, reviewing the ledgers, then fired the cheating accountant before taking over the books herself. She also redecorated the whole place. Unfortunately, when a disgruntled servant informed her mother-in-law of what Lourdes was doing in her country house, the matriarch of the family had returned to the ranch in a rage and immediately returned the villa back to where it was before. Lourdes never spoke to her mother-in-law again.

Here again, we see the pattern of female collaborators in the roles of mothers-in-law or aunts generally being deadly enemies to their younger charges. They perpetuate the patriarchal setup, governing all their actions so as to keep the man securely in place at the top of the class system. This is not just a battle between women. It is a battle to keep the status quo, the system, which the male hierarchy runs, as personified in "the cheating accountant." Since Dona Zaida has gained her precedence through unswerving loyalty to the rules of the patriarchal culture and benefited by them, she has a vested interest in the villa being returned to its former condition where once again males will rule. Under these circumstances, women connected to the rulers live peripherally as the dubious beneficiaries of such a system. They live entirely according to the whims of those rulers and their auxiliary gatekeepers.

However, Lourdes is not a rebel against her culture in all ways. There is a crucial part of her being that adores the patriarchy as symbolized by her father and identifies with it. Significantly, she is free to redecorate the ranch so long as her mother-in-law, the gatekeeper, is not informed. But Lourdes identifies, not with her gentle husband, but with her father. Garcia here exposes another major element in her text–father and daughter on the same wavelength, excluding any other member of the family.

The traditional patriarch, Jorge, is proud of his daughter Lourdes, for whatever part of her that replicates him, which emulates his class values. He admires her position on law and order so exactly like his own. He views her training as an auxiliary policewoman as excellent preparation for fighting the communists in the future. Since El Lider's techniques are like those of the fascists who armed the people and kept them in readiness for battle at all times, it would not be possible to fight El Lider unless their side is equally prepared.

Even after his death, Jorge and Lourdes are united in their adoration and pursuit of the American success myth. He wants her to have a sign over her bakery. For her part, Loudes fantasies that her Yankee Doodle bakeries have franchises bearing her name in towns and in malls all across the nation. She is ultraconservative as well, denouncing communists, the media, the Democratic Party, and "those lying, two-timing Kennedys" (because they feel that the Kennedys abandoned their cause at the Bay of Pigs). She and her father would love nothing better than to see Senator McCarthy come back to life to set things right again, because, unlike the Kennedys he would have stood by the Cuban exiles.

Because Lourdes is in such total agreement with her father's politics, it is understandable that she should be incensed when Celia gives Pilar for Christmas a book about Cuba whose front cover contains a photograph of "cheerful, clean-cut children" (1992, 132) posed in front of a portrait of Che Guevara. When she sees that face, Lourdes loses her temper, refusing to read the work on the grounds that all it contains is communist lies. She does not confide in Pilar the awful source of her rage, because she is mortally ashamed of having been raped. She blames herself for being the victim.

Ultimately, Jorge's spectral visits to Lourdes come to an end. And Lourdes grieves again. He leaves her with the profound advice that Dante gives his readers in *The Inferno*, that the dead have no power to see further than the living, preoccupied as they are with hurrying to "their graves" (1992, 194). In her grief, Lourdes melts her weight down and has no sexual relations with her husband after her father dies. She loses the 118 pounds, then immediately eats it back. This problem is due to more than her suppressed grief over the child she has lost and her subsequent rape as a result of the communist takeover.

She also conceives of herself as a failure in her gatekeeping efforts to indoctrinate her daughter into her values, in internalizing the "conservative" tenets of her culture regarding women's expression of sexuality. She worries about her daughter, about her teachers seducing her at the art school she is attending in Rhode Island, about her being murdered by the Son of Sam. She feels very different from Pilar and her mother who break rules, are antireligious, and have no respect for all that she holds meaningful. Neither her mother nor her daughter shows respect for anyone, least of all, for themselves. Her daughter is selfish, "irresponsible," "a bad seed." Because she is conservative and was a virgin when she married, she cannot imagine how she could have borne such a daughter. This is not true, according to what Garcia shows us is the case in each character's meditations or dreams. Going to excess runs in the entire family, not only in Celia and Pilar, but in Felicia and Lourdes as well.

Pilar, like her grandmother and her Aunt Felicia, has strong spiritual powers. Whereas Celia has linked the spiritual with her dream of socialism and her aunt has grounded hers in voodoo, the feminist direction of Pilar's powers are clear, even in childhood. She is strongly class-conscious. Her materialist feminism is congruent with Celia's, as is her political perspective in terms of class. In her attitude toward her art professors, the content of her courses, and in her own work, Pilar is bent on taking "patriarchal myths" and revealing "them for what they are." She would prove to them "how anatomy is never destiny, that gender is constructed within a cultural content, through strategies relying upon the rhetoric of the dream-work that Freud himself was to describe" (Frank 1996, 57–58).

This conclusion is made not without trepidation, except that Bessy Reyna, a Cuban-Panamanian feminist's testimony bolsters me in it. After reading her poems in two languages to "a large bilingual audience" in New York City, she discovered that she got a response from both crowds. "It was one of the most exciting experiences I have had in a long time. I felt the same response from audiences in Boston and Cambridge. This experience taught me that feminist and political issues are the same, regardless of language. Up to that moment, I had always wondered whether my work was culturally limited" (Reyna 1989, 227).

In wanting to return to Cuba, Pilar is seeking to align herself with her grandmother's political position, her identification with the masses versus her mother's elitist, conservative position. True, Lourdes has aligned herself with capitalist materialism, as exemplified in her emigration to the United States and in her career aspirations as an entrepreneur. Despite her choice of vocation as a small-business entrepreneur, a bakery owner who makes very rich cakes which she herself devours, this does not by any means deprive her of equal spiritual powers to those of her mother and sister, according to Garcia. When her nannies had called Lourdes a "brujita, little witch," she caused their hair to fall out so that when they left the family they all had to wear head coverings because they were bald.

As for Pilar, born a rebel with her grandmother's sensibilities, she questions the content of what she learns in school that forwards only the western hegemony. Her father had been the one to tell her what happened to Cuba after Columbus and the Spaniards found it: the deaths from smallpox of more Indians than their guns could kill. Now in a feminist rage she demands why the history books do not include such information She wonders who has the right to decide what issues, what events are significant, and what children should be taught. She concludes that the teachers and the publishers are at fault because all they ever publish is history as battles, one after the other. The majority of what she has learned that has been meaningful and valuable has been on her own or from Celia. She wants the right to decide for herself as to what constitutes history.

Pilar accuses the European patriarchal cultural regime of valorizing as heroic only those humans who fight and make wars, that is, men. She maintains that she would choose other events to historicize if she had the power to do so. She chooses as one example an actual, recorded historical occurrence when Congolese women interpreted a hailstorm as a sign that they should rule instead of men. Here Pilar's choice seems to be an ecofeminist one, essentializing women as linked with natural elements in some intrinsic way. One would think that women in any culture should demand to rule alongside men, because men by themselves have proved themselves so inept. And women should not need hailstorms to justify themselves, because it would be hard to do worse than men have by themselves. Another of Pilar's preferences for recording events and the people involved in them as historic and therefore as meaningful to her would be the life stories of prostitutes in Bombay. Why, however, limit these stories only to Bombay?

By proceeding to dream in Cuban, Pilar has the benefit of learning from her grandmother. As she falls asleep, she can hear Celia's voice telling her about her life and her environment. It seems to Pilar as if Celia knows all about her and that she advises her granddaughter not to pay too much attention to her mother. (Dream on, Pilar!) Through her socialist beliefs and ideals, Celia becomes a rare gatekeeper in a positive sense to Pilar, as she has been to her other granddaughters, encouraging Pilar through these dreams to take an art scholarship. Her father Rufino, in his unobtrusive way, also aids and abets Pilar in a more practical way by persuading his wife to let her attend.

Like Laura Garcia de la Torre in *How the Garcia Girls Lost Their Accents*, Rufino is an inventor of sorts and as much under the spell of capitalistic materialism and late capitalist technology as is Laura. He loves machinery and loves his time period, the age of the machine, the age of technology. As I have already pointed out, this also makes him a devoté of Chango, the god of iron and lightning. Chango is also associated with Pilar's Aunt Felicia, as well as with her father, and Hugo Villaverde. The owner of a Botanica calls Pilar Chango's daughter and gives her rituals to do for free. Fittingly, the last chapter in the text is called "Daughter of Chango." Thus Pilar's title is true literally as well as symbolically, in the sense that an aspect of Chango is forging. Pilar is an art student, and Rufino tinkers with iron elements.

Rufino is also a gentle, tactful man. When infidelity to his wife is combined with the other two jarring characteristics, a triangulation in his character is created. This is a complexity that I have previously noted in other characters created by Garcia. The family does not live in a conventional home, but in a warehouse Rufino bought from the city for one hundred dollars. At the back of this warehouse, he has built a studio for Pilar and a workshop for himself next to hers where he tinkers with his projects. His latest one is a robot voice attached to a typewriter that instructs it how to type and thus does away with human typists. The machine makes females obsolete.

Pilar runs away briefly to Florida, to Coral Gables, where members of her father's family reside. She notes of the shops along the Miracle Mile that they feature mannequins with beehive hairdos. It is her opinion that men "in fashion control centers around the world" (1992, 60) are responsible for thinking up changing fashions. They do this only in order to torture women and to embarrass them in the future. Here Garcia's sarcastic sense of humor should not disguise her crucial insight: that every institution everywhere, including the world of fashion, is part of a vast, linked, and conscious hegemonic male conspiracy against women.

Looking for her cousin Blanquito, Pilar goes to his house and creeps around outside it. By this interesting means, Garcia familiarizes readers on a literal level with other members of the family who have immigrated to America. At a deeper level, she is exposing readers to the diversity of political positions, primarily according to class and gender, which Cuban emigrés have taken in relation to the Castro regime in Cuba.

When she first met Rufino's parents, Celia had felt an immediate dislike to Don Guillermo's appearance and politics. He talked all night about how important it was to maintain a good relationship with the Americans because they hold the keys to the Cuban future. When Celia reminded him of the Platt Amendment that legislated American interference in Cuba, he dismissed her with a wave of his plump hand, covered with rings, and confined his preaching and platitudes to his son. Readers are also asked to believe that this gross and repulsive individual used to fish with Hemingway and that Pilar presumably got her name from the name of Hemingway's fishing boat. But we can more readily believe further information about him: that the Mafia ran Don Guillermo's casinos and that the Cuban dictator Batista had lunched with him at the Havana Yacht Club every Thursday until the Revolution.

Celia had also been horrified to discover that Lourdes's future mother-in-law, Dona Zaida, has a Costa Rican Indian mother who had carried around her children and grandchildren in a sling on her back and still does not wear shoes.[4] For these reasons, Dona Zaida keeps her mother locked up in the attic. Readers are about to meet Dona Zaida again, as well as Don Guillermo, now residents of Coral Gables, Florida. They are Pilar's paternal grandparents.

Crouched outside the window of their home, Pilar overhears a conversation that reveals the same gendered "house slave" perspective that Berta Arango del Pino had taken toward Celia so many years ago. Pilar's paternal Abuela, Dona Zaida, at that moment is in the midst of accusing her daughter-in-law of putting too much salt in the ropa vieja. In this way, the restrictive culture permits those women who collude with it to achieve class status over their juniors in the family. Whenever Abuela Zaida refers to her daughter-in-law, it is never "we," but always "you." Whenever she speaks in the collective "we," she means her husband and her eight sons. She has symbolically risen to equal her husband in terms of class when she bore those sons to Don Guillermo and risen even further to become a powerful matriarch once her sons married and provided her with daughters-in-law. These junior women will all be inferior in rank to her until they repeat the same pattern in their lives–becoming gatekeeping Abuelas, in their turn.

Although Dona Zaida bore all her sons out of wedlock in Costa Rica, she was able somehow to convince her husband to marry her and move to Cuba. She has become the most hypocritical woman in Pilar's acquaintance, now labeling any woman a whore who so much as wears lipstick. Her feminist American(ized) granddaughter views Dona Zaida's conduct from an entirely mainstream American perspective, as that of a hypocrite. She does not seem to know about or understand the common Cuban resolution of marriage to legitimate male children when a mistress produces a precious male heir, let alone eight of them. Using the term "Don" and "Dona" satirically in describing the couple, Garcia tells us that Dona Zaida has successfully aspired to rising in class from Indian peasant stock to the middle class. She has achieved this through motherhood and marriage and is now the perpetuator and upholder of the values and perspectives of that class which are aligned with those of the Catholic Church.

Garcia's critique of this mestizo woman who has internalized the values of Hispanic culture regarding her type and class does not stop with Dona Zaida, however. She also treats her readers to a brief description and analysis of Don Guillermo, the bearer of Spanish culture, which, for my part, could not have been short enough. Originally from Cadiz, he had come to the Caribbean as a stowaway at the age of twelve. Then after the First World War he had become successful in running casinos for the mafia.

Garcia gives readers an equally terrifying example of Don Guillermo's character, as brutal and repulsive as Hugo's. When Pilar was born, her parents were living with Don Guillermo on his ranch. One day she had wandered out onto the road. Cesar, their Doberman Pinscher guard dog who was attached to Pilar, had begun to attempt to drag her back from danger by barking and pulling at her diapers. Believing that the dog was attacking Pilar, her grandfather shot the dog between the eyes and killed him.

Garcia also uses this scene as a foreshadowing of the crucial rape incident that will simultaneously illustrate three levels consistently present in this text. On one level, readers are exposed to the sources for the future bizarre conduct of a major character, Lourdes. On another level, Garcia describes situations in relation to Castro's army, Castro's cause, but not at all as Castro and his supporters would have them described. On a third level, to which we have been introduced through Pilar, Garcia describes situations in relation to Castro's opponents that they too would not want described as Garcia does.

Pilar begins to muse about her mother–after all, she has just run away from her–and about how her Abuela Celia has helped her to be less afraid of Lourdes as a result of her conversations with her in her dreams. Celia explains Lourdes to Pilar so that she can understand her mother: how angry and depressed she is, how frustrated at the current situation in Cuba, how Celia is one of the causes of Lourdes's depression, because Celia plays an active role in that situation and won't change, either. Also as readers will discover, a motivating force to Laura Garcia de la Torre to reinvent herself in *How the Garcia Girls Lost Their Accents* is that in her country of origin she was respected because of her position, but not in the United States. This is literally true, in what readers have discovered in the most ironically powerful way is the source for Lourdes's anguished rejection of her homeland, both political and personal, after the Revolution: lack of respect and acknowledgment.

Garcia uses one character's thoughts about other characters to give us fresh insights. Pilar often talks about her mother in such a way as to give us new information, or information about Lourdes from a different perspective. She sees her mother as becoming a member of the auxiliary out of some misplaced sense of civic duty, rather than out of an intense and complicated response to her prior traumatic experience that she has not confided to Pilar. Her daughter does not know of her mother's brutal rape and mutilation at the hands of one of Castro's soldiers, or the miscarriage of her child.

But Pilar also suffers from the consequences of these events, if only in suffering from loss and the enforced immigration to the United States. Periodically such a strong wave of longing for Cuba comes over her that she has to prevent herself from plotting to "hijack a plane to Havana" (1992, 138). She eloquently expresses her resentment of the politicians and the generals in words similar to those her grandmother had used when she had complained to Gustavo about the Batista regime many years before. Pilar still blames the politicians and the generals (but no longer the priests) who create all the uprooting, force all the migrations. As a result, many Cubans live their lives out in different places and have to change the way they live.

These sad memories are all that the Cuban people in exile will have to look back at in their old age. Her grandmother has already indicted the politicians and the church. Now Pilar adds another significant institution, the military, to the list of offenders against humanity. This is a profound statement on Pilar's part. Many immigrant families have had similar motivations for fleeing their ancestral countries, as well as then experiencing the psychically castrated feeling that ensues, as a result. Each day that Pilar lives in the United States, her memories of Cuba and her memories of her grandmother grow increasingly dimmer until she finds only her "imagination where our history should be" (1992, 138).

When Lourdes commissions Pilar to paint a mural for her second Yankee Doodle Bakery[5] in honor of the Bicentennial, this gives Garcia the opportunity through Pilar's voice to express her insights on gender discrimination in terms of art. She muses bitterly on all the women artists throughout history who managed to paint despite the odds against them. She wonders why there are no "important women painters" and suggests that people should focus on what they did paint and make an attempt

to understand their circumstances. . . . Many people react to good art by a woman as if it were an anomaly, a product of a freak nature or a direct result of her association with a male painter or mentor. . . . Feminism has apparently not reached art school either. The male teachers and students still call the shots and get the serious attention and the fellowships that further their careers. As for the women, we're supposed to make extra money modeling nude. What kind of bullshit revolution is that? (1992, 140)

The situation, alas, is not that much improved today so many years after the bicentennial, although feminist scholars are making strenuous efforts and some inroads into expanding the canon and educational curricula to include women artists. Pilar does see one similarity and only one, between Lourdes and herself, although she is actually similar in many ways to her mother beneath the dissimilarities. Ironically so, for she cannot see this. In having Pilar critique her mother continually, Garcia, is exposing her as doing so about traits in her mother which are most like hers, not only her inability to conceal dislike. She accuses her mother of being arbitrary and inconsistent, as well as always believing that she is right about everything and how irritating she finds that combination of traits. Here Garcia shows subtlety and cleverness and much trust in her readers in this strategy. We could so easily miss this added dimension of pleasure in her representation of an artist daughter with some blinders on and an arch-conservative mother with some sensitivity, both of whom are strong and feminist in their different ways.

Instead of a mural, Pilar does a wonderful painting, a perfect replica of Liberty (as she calls the statue), except for several creative details. Her torch is floating free in front of her while her hand is placed over her heart as if she is singing the National Anthem. Pilar has caught the exact feeling about liberty and equality for women globally.[6] So far it has floated beyond our grasp. Garcia also nicely captures the precise mood and spirit of young intellectuals of the period when Pilar depicts a safety pin piercing the statue's nose, among other punk elements in the painting.

When it is unveiled at the bakery, someone in the crowd yells out in raucous Brooklynese that in his opinion it is a piece of garbage. He attempts to slash at it with a pocketknife. But Lourdes hits him so hard with her handbag that he loses consciousness before he can mutilate it, while she loses her balance and falls. As she does so, she crashes into three bystanders and a table full of her apple tartlets. Pilar's response to this hilarious scene is the first positive statement she has made about her mother, that at that moment she loves her very much. Lourdes's chief quality is great protectiveness when she or her loved ones are threatened. Previously she has shown such foolhardy courage in defense of her husband and then, later, with less success, herself. Now her protectiveness is once again depicted, but this time as slapstick comedy.

Pilar lists to herself the qualities she has inherited from her grandmother. She loves the sea, pearls, music, and talk. She also roots for the underdog, disregards boundaries, and has the self-confidence and the courage to follow her convictions. The last two qualities are like her mother's. Likewise, Lourdes condemns Pilar for qualities like her own. Horrified that her mother could celebrate with cigars and sparkling cider the murder of a journalist in Miami who advocated reestablishing ties with Cuba, Pilar wonders how her mother could be her grandmother's daughter and what she is doing as Lourdes's daughter. She believes that there had to be a scramble somewhere down the line. An ironic thought, because we can see precisely how this could come about. Every character in this text has qualities that are scrambled-up characteristics of another character. Daughter Lourdes is the precise opposite of her mother Celia, as well as her counterpart.

Pilar debates the merits of travel as opposed to staying at home for an artist and concludes that one has to travel widely before talking meaningfully about the world, an ironic statement that applies to Pilar's previous hasty judgments about her mother and grandmother. She has come back to the United States after a semester in an art school in Florence and has changed to majoring in anthropology. She feels as her grandmother had felt as a young woman, as though she is still waiting for her life to begin.

Pilar complains angrily, again from a feminist perspective, about her never making it back to see her Abuela Celia. Again, she uses language similar to her grandmother's, that men who were strangers to her had given her a destiny that did not belong to her, that they had torn her from her dreams when they had separated her from her grandmother. Without knowing it, speaking as a feminist about the patriarchy, about both Castro and President Kennedy, she is yet simultaneously speaking the literal truth. For Castro's soldiers had ruptured Lourdes's dreams when they set into motion her mother's departure from Cuba. Also we see for the first time Pilar's bitterness at the political split dividing her family. Again, it has come about essentially because of "men's power to rupture . . . dreams" (1992, 200).

Pilar and Lourdes do get to return briefly to Cuba, but in tragic circumstances following Felicia's death. They find Celia in a terrible state of grief. As a symbolic gesture of disgust with her mother's politics and the direction Cuba has taken, Lourdes throws her mother's picture of El Lider into the sea. This violent behavior in no way diminishes Celia's desire to have Pilar stay on with her. Pilar does so, spending the time making various paintings of Celia, while the latter talks to her granddaughter. Gatekeeping for her socialism, her convictions, she continues to take advantage of the opportunity of her granddaughter's visit to indoctrinate Pilar according to her perspective, as she previously has done with her other two granddaughters. She informs Pilar that Cuba was a pathetic place, a parody of a country before the Revolution and that she herself was saved because her parents sent her to live with her Great-aunt in Havana who then raised her with progressive ideas. Celia tells her that she believes that freedom lies in having the right to live decently.

Lourdes retaliates, attempting to indoctrinate her daughter into her point of view, her perspective. She reminds her mother about political prisoners, the bad treatment of Catholics, and the loss of property without repayment by the communists. Pilar prefers her grandmother's vision, communism, as opposed to capitalism, her mother's preference. Lourdes is curious about everyone's income and always claims that they can make much more money in Miami, no matter how much they earn. Actually, this is a ploy on Lourdes's part. She will stop at nothing to attract people away from Cuba to the United States, even her nephew Ivanito whom she kidnaps on a visit to Celia, enticing him away with an offer he can't refuse, a trip to Disney World.

In a further reaction against Lourdes, Pilar's dreams now are only in Spanish, the fascination of Havana penetrating her soul: the plant life, the noisiness, the "decay and painted ladyness" of Havana. Here Garcia borders on centricity in maintaining that one's ancestral roots are in the genes, instinctive. However, she does not add, as centrics do, that one would have to be a member of that group to understand and to know its experiences.

Once Pilar and Ivanito leave Cuba, Celia totally loses her incentive to continue living and drowns herself. After the death of Felicia, it is interesting that Celia's first words to Pilar when she and Lourdes find her in Cuba are that she had gone for a swim the night before their arrival and exults that Pilar remembers her, remembers Cuba. The dreaming in Cuban goes on. Celia's granddaughter will remember everything. Furthermore, she will perpetuate what her grandmother represents: a dream of a better future for all, united with compassion for all suffering. Celia walks silent and unseen among sufferers of all kinds all over the world. Ultimately, Garcia's dreaming in Cuban is a dreaming that mourns gender and class and race asymmetry globally and would end it.

NOTES

1. At the end of *War and Peace*, Leo Tolstoy describes his protagonist Levin as experiencing an epiphany from a combination of sweat and idealism while laboring in the fields, much as Celia experiences.

2. This is the way in which Janie buries her beloved husband Teacake in Zora Neale Hurston's *Their Eyes Were Watching God*, like an Egyptian pharaoh with his guitar.

3. In Ralph Ellison's *Invisible Man*, there are both echoes and contrasts to this scene. The anonymous narrator refuses to succumb to the advances of an upper class, white, married society woman filled with delusions of his black animality. He waits until she falls into a drunken stupor. Exulting in simultaneously humiliating her and depriving her of the sexual satisfaction she sought in him as a black man, he writes obscenities on her stomach with her lipstick. Ellison's persona does not physically harm the woman whom he holds in such contempt. Nevertheless, he has the same attitude toward her for the same reasons as the Revolutionary soldier who rapes, then stabs Lourdes in the stomach, and carves his contempt and hatred into her flesh with her own blood. From the narrator's embittered viewpoint in *Invisible Man*, he is enjoying the thought of the white woman's humiliation when she awakens, imagining that he had "gotten over on her," that he has enjoyed her body. In each case, a woman has violated the rules and regulations of gendered power relations. In addition, there are race and class animosities. Both women have acted openly on their conviction of superiority in this regard.

4. "The black (grand)mother who 'stains' supposedly pure Hispanic lineages is a familiar figure in Caribbean literature" (1993, 86), according to Vera M. Kutzinski. Elsewhere she adds the information that this individual, as in Garcia's text, is also kept "hidden or imprisoned in the home, but also her name is concealed "in the registration of newborn children" to avoid "the specter of miscegenation" (1993, 86).

5. Clearly she is becoming economically successful, illustrating the truism that "[t]he predominantly middle-class origin of the Cuban emigrés to the United States has been said to assist the group in becoming economically integrated into U.S. society. Moreover, Cubans' middle-class ideology, in particular their work ethic, is believed to be responsible for the economic success experienced by the group in a relatively short time" (Knouse et al., 1995, 165).

6. Rebolledo and Rivero note that in her manifestation as a failure (for many Chicana writers) the Virgin of Guadalupe "has failed to intercede for her people in the United States. . . . In an interesting juxtaposition, she is often connected with the Statue of Liberty, also a symbol of failure, for this statue promises justice and equality for all, a promise certainly unfulfilled in many writers' opinions" (1993, 191). This list would include Garcia.

Chapter 3

Julia Alvarez, *How The Garcia Girls Lost Their Accents*

Michel Foucault writes that "[f]rom the idea that the self is not given to us, I think that there is only one practical consequence: we have to create ourselves as a work of art" (1982, 777). Applying this idea to women, Luce Irigary would "undo the effects of phallocentric discourse" according to Judith Butler simply by overdoing them, "by miming the mime imposed on woman" (Butler 1990, 140). This is to use "bodies" as so many "'styles' of the flesh,' as an act" (Butler 1990, 39) or, rather, to overact or metaperform (Butler 1990, xii). The goal is to "denaturalize and resignify bodily categories," to shatter the belief that there is a "fixity of gender identity as an interior depth" (Butler 1990, 148) as, for example, Josephine Baker, Mae West, Marlene Dietrich, Cher, and Madonna have done.

If we read Laura Garcia de la Torre's character from this perspective, we can interpret her use of idiomatic expressions and of the stereotypes to which she scrupulously conforms as mother, hostess, and cleaning lady, as acts. They are parodic performances or metaperformances, the conscious performing of gatekeeping in keeping with the "cult of the mother-tenderness, love and the seat of social conservation" (Kristeva 1980, 237). All the while, to paraphrase Madonna, Laura persists in trying to express herself, which should not be mistaken for an attempt to "confess" herself, because. Laura does not seek to be in the public eye in the sense of a famous performer. As bell hooks puts it, "Private life as exhibitionism and performance is not the same thing as a politicized strategic use of private information that seeks to subvert the politics of domination" (1996, 823).

After the family flees the Dominican Republic, Laura works as her husband's cleaning lady in his office and as his interpreter, as well, because he never learns to speak English. Educated at an exclusive all-girls' college in the United States, Laura reads that sign of intellectual élitism, *The New York Times*, for pleasure, while Dr. Garcia confines himself to Spanish papers. Nevertheless, Alvarez depicts Laura as habitually using mixed-up idiomatic expressions.

These scrambled Spanglish malapropisms are corrosively witty combinations, jarring incongruities encoding Laura's experience of discrimination and oppression as political exile in the United States and as gendered exile as woman. In this way, Alvarez is mixing several cultural messages, constructions, and customs by utilizing concepts of hybridity or syncretism through appropriation or borrowing, thereby refashioning (mis)usages of the English language. This is just one of the ways in which Alvarez attempts to capture "the complex interactions among ideology, cultural forms, and power differentials that are manifest in such transfers" (Desmond 1994, 41).

Alvarez describes Laura's English as "a mishmash of mixed-up idioms and sayings" (1992, 135). When her husband orders Laura to speak only in Spanish to their girls so they would not forget their native tongue, she adds that when they are in Rome they should not do as the Romans do, as the readers expect her to say, but to do unto them. This actually makes sense, that is, let's treat the oppressors as they treat us. And when someone was flattering her, she called it spreading gravy on the turkey. One of her wonderfully descriptive statements was that a burro could climb a palm with patience and calm. When ambivalent, she also claimed that it was half of one or two dozen of something else. Indeed, when a group is subordinated, it loses half, at least, of what is lost, whereas its oppressor group gets more than double of what is lost.

When Laura discovers that another inventor had patented the idea for suitcases on wheels, which had been her idea, she exclaims that the other inventor was "no bobo" because he had not been so foolish as to "put all his pokers on a back burner." Again, this is actually a fresh and original variation of the admonition not to "put all your eggs in one basket." Laura states that she continually repeated to her children that she had always felt that some day her ship would pass her by in the night. Again this is a fresh and accurate use of language. To sum up what she perceives as her failed opportunity, her failed life, she then consoles herself with the dramatic and witty truism that there was no use her trying "to drink spilt milk" (1992, 140).

Before she begins to assist her daughter Yolanda in rewriting a speech in celebration of the child's nun-teachers and in emulation of Whitman's *Song of Myself*, she predicts proudly to the child that she would bring their name "to the headlights in this country!" A dreadful quarrel over this speech erupts between the father and daughter, because Dr. Garcia feels it is disrespectful to her teachers. He then buys Yolanda a peace offering, her longed-for typewriter. Laura, who has sided with her daughter all along, consoles her by pointing out that she should pardon her father because he did not mean harm, that it was always better to remember that "bygones be forgotten, no?" (1992, 149). This statement, like the foolishness of trying to drink milk already spilled (although not applicable to felines) also makes perfect sense. After Laura stops inventing, Yoyo thinks of her mother's ghostwriting her speech as her mother's last attempt as an inventor. She imagines her mother as having passed on her pencil and pad to Yoyo, exclaiming that there was "the buck. You give it a shot" (1992, 149). This conveys that they are hunting, tracking down and shooting a male deer, thus productively playing off the statement with the very different meaning of "The buck stops here" or "Passing the buck"

Meticulously carrying out her role of gatekeeper, Laura does not let her girls go to any other school but Catholic school. Other parents who were also Catholic had informed her that only juvenile delinquents attended public schools and their teachers had crazy ideas about human beings evolving from monkeys. Laura is resolved never to permit any offspring of hers to forget their respected birth name and, instead, learn that they were related to monkeys.

Before their sudden, enforced flight from the Dominican Republic,[1] Laura and her husband were involved in an unsuccessful CIA plot to assassinate the dictator Rafael Trujillo, who ruled the country from 1930 to 1961. On one significant occasion, Laura's coolness under pressure saves her husband's life. An undercover CIA agent serves as the consul at the U.S. Embassy. This individual has actually orchestrated the attempted coup. But after stressing the necessity to organize underground and "get that SOB out," he suddenly changed his directives to the rebels to hold off, to rethink it all over again in order to determine precisely what was best under the circumstances. Laura advises her daughter Carla not to tell her friends about what was going on, and when Carla asks why she shouldn't do that, Laura responds that flies do not "fly into a closed mouth" (1992, 209).

Although Alvarez confines pithy and colorful expressions primarily to Laura in her role of gatekeeper, the author provides an exception in Old Chucha, the cook. Back in the Dominican Republic, Chucha had been the family's Haitian cook, saved by the de la Torre family when Trujillo had all the Haitians in that country executed. She served the family with the devotion a nun gives to her calling. Elizabeth Starcevic observes of this situation that it "offers a glimpse into the historical complexity of the relationships of the two countries that share the island of Hispaniola" (1992, 15). Having diapered Laura as a baby, Chucha is privileged to do whatever she wants, once Laura marries. An interesting character, she is grumpy, speaks primarily in idiomatic expressions, wonderfully colorful and descriptive ones, practices voodoo, and always sleeps in a coffin.

Perhaps Chucha has influenced Laura in this regard. Once, when Carla wanders into the servants' quarters, Chucha tells her to leave, but another servant contradicts her, maintaining that Dona Laura would not mind for once, because her husband has just returned home. Chucha responds sarcastically, requesting the young woman to inform her what "hen doesn't peck when the rooster crows" (1992, 259)? Later, when one of the servants dreams of being in New York in thirty-two years, Chucha's opinion is that the girl's head is in the clouds and therefore she should be wary of what is also in the clouds: a thunderbolt.

Alvarez will also expose the nightmarish side of enforced metaperformance in Laura's role of gatekeeper, as well as the humorous side, and rightly so, because as Walters puts it,

Theories of gender as play and performance need to be intimately and systematically connected with the power of gender (really, the power of male power) to constrain, control, violate, and configure. Too often, mere lip service is given to the specific, historical, social, and political configurations that make certain conditions possible and otherwise constrained. . . . Without substantive engagement with complex sociopolitical realities, those performance tropes appear as entertaining but ultimately depoliticized academic exercises. (1996, 855)

Laura reveals such a "substantive engagement" (Behar 1995, 6) in the form of a matter of life and death metaperformance after Dr. Garcia's unsuccessful underground attempt to overthrow Trujillo is discovered by the secret police. It comes to mean life to Laura and her family if she overacts believably, but death, if her mask should crack while she plays her role. When the soldiers come to find Don Carlos and take him away, Laura graciously requests them to enter her home and have a cold drink. Here for very life itself she is consciously exaggerating the gracious hostess of the house act, playing to their belief in this role, this script, for respectable women. She then uses the time-honored Spanish welcome to the men to make themselves at home in her home: " Mi casa es su casa" [My house is your house].

In actuality, Laura is directing rescue operations like a general in the war room of her mind. She is calculating where her husband is hiding; it is only a matter of feet away. She is planning how she can get help; how she can keep the thugs from moving out of her living room to search the house; how she can keep her small children from hysterics and endangering all their lives; how she can most productively play (up) the stereotypical role that conforms to the men's expectations. Acting the hostess, she serves the men food and drinks in the dishes and glasses she reserves for her servants. Because they do not touch anything at first, she remembers the story she had heard about Trujillo. His cooks have to taste his food for him before he dares to eat it. She and Sofia and Yoyo, two of her four daughters, show the soldiers that they are eating the snacks, and then the men take Laura's offerings.

Brilliantly taking advantage of the fact that two of her little girls are clinging to her skirt, Laura simultaneously metaperforms as the doting, distracted mother, while orchestrating the hostess act. For half an hour during their interrogation, she is frightened at every point that she might give the wrong answer. At the same time she is very grateful for the distracting annoyance that Sofia and Yoyo provide by hanging on her and complaining. Their actions give Laura the opportunity to distract the men's attention, to take time out and away from emphasis on her and, instead, to focus on the children by repeatedly inquiring of them what is bothering them. She then has the children give recitations to the visitors and attempts to get frowning Sofia to smile for one of the men who is repulsive and overweight.

By her manipulation of the theory of "femininity as masquerade" (Walters 1996, 858) to exploit the men's unexamined cultural expectations about women as hostesses and mothers, Laura succeeds in distracting them, in delaying the search for her husband, and therefore of evading his capture. When the U.S.

Consul finally arrives, Alvarez lets out all the stops in order to expose Laura's great courage, all the while suffering through a triple range of conscious, enforced metaperformances:

[1. Society lady, gracious hostess act]: She calls out to the consul to come in before informing the soldiers that the new arrival is none other than Victor Hubbard, the American consul at the American Embassy. She does this as if not to humiliate the soldiers, should they happen not to be fully aware of his identity, his importance.

[2. Her real self]: She then moves out to the patio, gives the consul a quick kiss on his cheek, and informs him that she has told the soldiers that her husband was playing tennis with Hubbard.

[3. The devoted mother act]: She greets Carla and Sandi (her two other daughters who came in with Hubbard) very enthusiastically and affectionately, calling them by pet names as though she were thrilled to see them, inquiring solicitously as to whether they have eaten. (As if she gives a damn.)

[2. Again, back to her real self]: The children silently indicate that they have done so, while staring at her. Laura understands with a deep sense of pain caused by the intensity of their gaze that they already know they are living in a police state. They already know how one must speak and gesture, be careful what to say, and be sure where one is going.

Here Laura is taking advantage of what Kristeva calls "language-symbolism-paternity," the unholy trinity of patriarchal culture in relation to motherhood. As long as "the controlling eye of surveillance establishes and maintains power relations" (Boer 1996, 53), "there will never be any other way to represent, to objectify, to explain this unsettling of the symbolic stratum, this nature culture threshold, this instilling the subjectless biological program into the very body of a symbolizing subject, this event called motherhood" (Kristeva 1980, 242).

After fleeing to the United States with her husband and children, Laura tries to invent items that can be used every day by women, which they would really appreciate. Because she no longer receives the respect and notice that she assumed was always going to be accorded to her due to being a member of the de la Torre family. She resolves to show the Americans what a woman of intelligence can do. Profoundly alienated from the world run by men, Laura dismisses male constructions such as the Statue of Liberty, the Brooklyn Bridge, or Rockefeller Center, with contempt. In my opinion, her examples are ill chosen, because they are some of the best results of male-only building efforts. In addition, due to the disability, illness, and eventual death of Washington Roebling, with great efficiency and aplomb, his wife headed the operations as his representative until the completion of the Brooklyn Bridge.

Still, at this point in Laura's life, this separatism is her attempt to resolve her feeling of "powerlessness in a dehumanizing and technological consumer society" (Ortega 1989, 130–131). Through inventing, she is trying hard to resist her feeling in the most productive way she can that "individual agency," at least for women who have no "control over social practices and discursive conventions . . . is but a delusion" (Kutzinski 1993, 111).

Like Benjamin Franklin, the American prototypical model of capitalistic invention and entrepreneurship, Laura is also obsessed with the problem of time saving in her own life as well as in her inventions. She sketches her domestic inventions in bed, only after everyone else is asleep, after she has satisfied all her family's needs as efficiently and rapidly as she can in order to get on with her own work. In the scene where she outsmarts the secret police, we have seen Laura performing motherhood publicly according to the accepted cultural script. In reality, Laura's drive for self-expression as an inventor, traditionally conceptualized as a male activity, clashes violently with her mothering role. For example, had their father, Dr. Garcia, presented himself to them as an inventor, the girls would not have dismissed his inventions as rough sketches, as they do their mother's. Realistically, the patriarchy cannot be subverted or even destabilized by such private means and measures as Laura attempts. As Lisa Disch and Mary Jo Kane remind us:

The patriarchal reversal does not take place whenever a woman challenges the typical gender hierarchy by taking a position in a traditionally male profession; rather, it occurs only when such a challenge to traditional gender roles also destabilizes the certainties on which the conception of gender as a social construction based on a natural binary depends. (1996, 293)

Laura's daughters are products of what Mary G. Dietz calls "a patriarchal discourse of maternity," which they have internalized without question. Laura's style as a mother does not fit this discourse. Therefore, as one of my female students angrily proclaimed about her: "She's a bad mother!" She confuses their names, their varying birthdates and professions, husbands and boyfriends, dresses them all alike, and calls every one of them by the generic pet name, Cuquita. All these faux pas give her daughters the impression that she is too organized and rigid–an assembly-line mothering.

Most damaging of all to her image as a good mother, Mami Laura has the nerve to wave her children out of her room dismissively when they come to her with their problems. Their attempt to get her attention away from her inventions is part of becoming Americanized. Laura's outraged and indignant Americanized daughters believe that they and their problems should come first, last, and in between in the family hierarchy. As a matter of course in American culture, children are the focus of attention at all times, with grown-ups, especially mothers, remaining in the background. Alvarez reveals here that the grown-up daughters, like most American children, have remained infantile in their expectations and conceptualizations of motherhood. "For the infant, the mother is not someone with her own life, wants, needs, history and social relationships, work. She is known only in her capacity as mother" (Chodorow and Contratto 1982, 65). A Latina woman, as well as any woman in most cultures, who becomes a mother, is denied "a subject position" (Fregoso 1993, 143).

To Laura's daughters, now becoming Americanized, only topics of significance to them, such as their efforts to assimilate, should be sufficient for Laura's interests. She should concern herself only with helping them while they are trying to find their identities, or trying to figure out why their Irish schoolmates–who were called "micks"–do not try to understand, and instead call the Garcia girls "spics." They want her to explain to them why it had been necessary for them to immigrate to the United States. These were the significant issues in their lives, and at a time when she should be helping them solve them, their mother refused to do so; instead, she spent her free time "inventing gadgets to make life easier for the American Moms" (1992, 138). What is heresy to her Americanized daughters actually represents Latina tradition where children are doted on, but considered of less consequence than adults and therefore expected to remain silent and unobtrusive when an adult is working or with other adults.

Even more silent and of even less consequence than women and children are members of the lower classes, especially peasant workers. When Yolanda visits the Dominican Republic, her sympathy and compassion for and identification with this group lead her to detest her wealthy relatives based on their use of their class and gendered relations of power over workers and women. Alvarez describes this position powerfully in her poem "Homecoming." In this poem about a visit to relatives in the Dominican Republic, she characterizes her uncle as a dirty old man, as well as a callous exploiter of the workers on his large estates. He pats her shoulders lecherously when he dances with her and otherwise admires her looks and her brains. Boasting that it was all hers as he pressed himself into her dress, he urges her to return to the country.

Alvarez claims that it is her education, the courses she took, that gave her a different slant on class issues than that of her relatives. This was the case because attending "schools paid for by sugar from the fields around us," it had taken her years to understand "how one does not see the maids when they pass by" (1984, 14). But she does see them, finally, as well as the contrast between the genders and classes, the paradox of their lives. She prophesies revolution. At a family wedding that she attends, she imagines that the fields around them are on fire. While the bride and groom cut the wedding cake and all the wealthy, upper class guests are filled with food and drink, Julia notices the maids and the male workers seated on stoops behind the sugarhouse. They are eating also, but with their fingers, although the wealth to construct all the family's fine buildings and furnish everything in the building–the windows, shutters, walls, pillars–came from the cane that their workers had cut in the fields.

The daily witnessing of the exploitation and the general and specific injustice to the peasants by her own family causes Yolanda to flee from the Dominican Republic again and return to the United States, to her mother, also trapped in her prison of domesticity. At first, Laura's inventions provide her with her only respite. As is the case with her Spanglish malapropisms, they combine the jarringly incongruous with the unexpected. When the tap is turned in a certain direction, soap is emitted from the showerhead. Instant coffee already contains creamer. Previously timed water capsules release themselves. A timer in a keychain emits an alarm when the parking meter runs out of time (lost keys can also easily be located because of the ticking). A car bumper also somehow becomes a can opener. And, finally, the invention that ultimately came to fruition was Laura's idea of a suitcase on wheels.

When Yolanda angrily wants to know what the point is to these inventions, Laura retaliates by asking of her daughter why everything has to have a point and why she writes poems. Alvarez, however, gives Yolanda the writer the last word over Laura the inventor. Although she has to admit to herself that her mother has a valid point, still, she feels that given the grand scheme of things, somehow poetry seemed more significant than "a potty that played music when a toilet-training toddler went in its bowl" (1992, 138). If Yolanda had been a toddler's parent, however, she might well have come to a different conclusion.

Eventually, furious because her idea for a suitcase on wheels has been stolen, the disheartened Laura gives up inventing and apparently seems to resign herself to being her husband's drudge for the rest of her life. Late at night she does the bookeeping, duly noting down the income her husband has taken in that day. She tells herself that she did not have the time any more to invent "silly things" (1992, 141). As another de la Torre puts it:

Perceptions of women's roles affect women's economic contribution and influence the division of labor within the home. Both in less developed and more developed nations, capitalist economic growth has not diminished the traditional gender-specific division of labor in the home. Indeed, the euphemism of the "double day" is readily accepted in most advanced capitalist nations, even though the term is used to obscure the loss of control women experience in the sphere of production and in the home. (1993, 176)

However, Laura's metaperformance as her husband's cleaning lady is designed to conceal the fact that she is still tunneling her way through to self-expression and self-fulfillment. The novel ends without answering the question as to whether Laura ever did get to express herself. Was she forced to live out her life as just a Foucauldian postmodern subject, doomed forever to be a female push-me pull-you at the mercy of the external global police forces of male authority?

In her earlier work, as in the poetry collection, *Homecoming*, Alvarez is not sanguine about the possibility of Laura eventually being able to subvert the rut of her life. In fact, she sees her mother as entirely a gatekeeper, a conservator of her culture's model of housewife-woman, "as the perfect housewife and wonderful cook, as befits women who value their place in the system: the Betty Crockers, the Julia Childs. With their technique and assimilation to the established order, they destoy the identity of 'unrefined' humanity, of those who would be different and thus be who they truly are" (Horno-Delgado 1989b, 139).

To illustrate my point, in "Dusting" Alvarez describes her mother as a gatekeeper extraordinaire, as suppressing her daughter's individuality. The perspective is youthful. In rebellion against this threat to her selfhood, the young Alvarez imposes her identity on all things around her. She writes her name on all the dusty furniture in the dining room, practicing her signature "like scales" while her mother follows her, conscientiously polishing everything in sight, erasing the poet's "fingerprints" wherever she has put them. Eventually her mother removes all of them with the towel "with which she jeweled the table tops." Nevertheless, the poet ends on a note of triumph, with the declaration that she kept putting her fingerprints on the furniture because "every mark" she made signified her "refusal" to become "anonymous" (1984, 19) like her mother.

By the time Alvarez wrote *How the Garcia Girls Lost Their Accents*, the author is able to perceive far more nuances to her mother's constricted lifestyle than serving loyally as her daughter's jailer gatekeeper. For at the end of the demeaning list of Laura's activities as a cleaning lady, we discover an interesting item. Mami, we are informed, just might have "her own little revolution brewing." She "had begun spreading her wings." She had enrolled in "adult courses in real estate and international economics and business management." Secretly Laura is now "dreaming of a bigger-than-family-size life for herself." (1992, 116). In the world as it is constructed, however, Laura gets to act in public only according to the script, according to how she is expected to act, and only in private in the darkest reaches of the night can she finally do what she wants to do. Like Alvarez's vision of the contemporary, archetypal woman, Laura is still a rough draft in progress. Alvarez encourages other women who feel confused, lost, oppressed, who yearn for freedom to understand that it is a continual process, that the poet herself at one time had gone through "as many drafts as" other women, but to put it "briefly, essentially, here I am" (1984, 93), a woman.

Cher and Madonna publicly strut, exaggerate, and posture, continually stretching the bounds of the culture's parameters, the patriarchal rules, the masculine signifiers for women, the "gendered discourse that generates female sexuality as a discursive effect" (Kutzinski 1993, 117). In Laura's case, that of a wife and mother who continually attempts to become an individual in her own right and fulfill her own needs, she turns, at the end of this text, to education. Privately, Laura is attempting to subvert her culture's maternal "ideology" through what Alvarez terms "lip service." But as Wendy Luttrell points out, Laura's "reasons for attending adult basic education programs" were like those that many "women gave for returning to school" in a survey she conducted. She perceives that these reasons only "illuminate the hidden structure of schools that are organized around women's work as mothers and the ideology of maternal omnipotence" (1993, 509).

Laura Garcia de la Torre steals the show from her daughters, as well as stealing readers' hearts. She also ends by running away with the book, becoming one of those marvelously unforgettable, quirky, loveable characters who live on in our memories. For me, her attraction is that she is not drawn with consistency as a character, as are all the others in the text. I would not advise Julia Alvarez to make up her mind, or to do a better job of bridging between all the short stories that she published separately before stringing them into this novel. I maintain that in Laura's inconsistency resides her charm and credibility as a character, her great claim to three-dimensionality, to life-likeness. Starcevic concurs:

Although Carlos García is drawn as the patriarch and all the girls seek his approval, it is Laura de la Torre who plays the significant role as a mediator between two cultures. Educated in the United States, she merges the self-confidence of her wealthy background with a receptivity toward the new challenges. Energetic and intelligent, she is always thinking of new inventions. Her creativity is stymied, yet she finds other outlets in the activities of her children and her husband. She is a vivid, alive character whose contributions to the necessary adjustments of her new life are both critiqued and appreciated by her daughters. (1992, 15)

At times she is depicted as a silent, passive, insignificant onlooker at the action, at other times, as the center of the stage, or as rather dim and slow. Sometimes she is witty and sharp and ironic, sometimes conventional and limited, a hawk-eyed-and-souled gatekeeper. Sometimes she is heroic and courageous, at other times a Franklinesque genius inventor, whose ambitions as an inventor are minimized by her daughters. In an instant Laura can turn to helping them with a speech, with the most sensitive display of feelings imaginable, or turn into a scientifically practical and abstract mother who color coordinates her daughters' belongings and accessories with hers.

Overtly an extremely traditional Latin wife and mother in deferring to her husband, she is simultaneously as powerful as he is, if not more so. She changes consistently, conforming to Judith Butler's suggested means of out-maneuvering static, rigidly set categories of woman, wife, and mother through metaperforming them. But if Laura Garcia de la Torre is consistent about one thing, it is her attitude toward that white western, late-twentieth-century patriarchal attempt to apply abstract and objective science to the human mind–to psychoanalyze it. Laura's playful contempt for psychology–most probably is that of her creator's.[2]

It takes thirty-one pages before Laura Garcia de la Torre is actually mentioned, and then only in passing, seemingly only to be included in the fact that her youngest daughter Sofia (Fifi) sends both her mother and father posctcards while she is on her honeymoon. Sofia and her father, Dr. Carlos Garcia, had become estranged because she walked out while he was ordering her to leave, furious about having found intimate love letters in her dresser. The letters reveal that she has had sex with her German boyfriend. The proud and obstinate father and equally proud and obstinate daughter then begin a feud that ends for the father only after the birth of the young couple's second child, a boy. Because the baby is the first male in Dr. Garcia's line of succession and is very Germanic looking, the hidebound old man relents because he not only has a male descendant, but icing on the cake for him, a descendant with "fair Nordic looks." Now he feels that there is "good blood in the family" just in case one of his daughters marries darker in the future, that is, makes "a bad choice" (1992, 26–27).

The previous birth of a baby girl to the young couple had not changed Dr. Garcia's adamant disowning of his daughter. But at that point, and it is only then that she begins to figure in the text, Laura had vowed that he could continue to disown Sofia until he dies. However, she felt differently and was going to visit the young family and see the new baby. The result is that Dr. Garcia does accompany his wife to his daughter's home, but he remains unbending. Little noticed by the reader early in the text is the subtle power of his wife. Even in the midst of his feud with his daughter, obstinate in his fixed position, in which for him all his values and teaching are at stake, Dr. Garcia nevertheless trails after his wife.

On the old man's next birthday, Sofia appears at her parents' apartment with her little girl, where, under Laura's watchful eye, the grandfather gets to hold the baby. Laura is still a seemingly minor character in the background at this point. It is her husband's relationship to his daughters that is detailed: a relationship fully revealing his macho personality and patriarchal character. Dr. Garcia predictably spoils and dotes on his four daughters within those parameters. In questions of morals differing from Catholic heirarchical decrees for women, he is hidebound, opinionated, and fixed in his belief in what Haleh Afshar terms "social architecture" (1995, 206).

His wife is shown in scene after scene as in total agreement with him–as holding the same views. She acts as her husband's and the culture's subaltern by ruthlessly and rigidly policing the girls to grow up according to traditionally valorized dictates. For instance, she is depicted as patting his arm in silent sympathy whenever tactless people comment on the disappointing fact that her husband has sired no sons. She then agrees with him in an apologetic manner.

At Dr. Garcia's seventieth birthday party, his wife is mentioned in passing as having given him a gold watch among the many other gifts bestowed on him by his daughters and sons-in-law. When his drunken daughters play a game where their blindfolded father has to guess which one is kissing him, he guesses his wife on the first go-round. Exhausted, Laura has fallen onto a couch and requests not to be included in the game. The point to this chapter seems to be that Sofia wins out over her father by humiliating him sexually (as he has her in the past). Underneath all his moralistic blustering and posing, he is like most other human beings, both men and women, sexual by nature. When Sofia gives him an innapropriate kiss, running her tongue in his ear and nibbling at its tip, he tears off his blindfold, enraged that he should be aroused in public by one of his daughters. But which one? Then he notices on Sofia's face the same expression she had had when she had torn her love letters away from him. Clearly, Sofia has inherited her father's intransigency, his unforgiving and proud nature.

In the chapter called "the four girls," Laura in her role of mother is described as the one who still calls them that, even though they are all grown. She colorcoded their clothing in different sizes from hers, but in the same styles, so that the husband sometimes jokingly called them all "the five girls" (1992, 40). This provokes the question of whether Laura as gatekeeper considers her daughters younger versions or extensions of her female self. They all have the same things, only color coded, ranging from fancy dresses, school clothes, and underclothing to toothbrushes, cups, towels, brushes, and combs.

In a devastating and sardonic critique of psychology, Alvarez has Carla, a psychologist, write a paper about herself in which she complains that her mother's color coding of her daughters had weakened the four girls' identity differentiation abilities and made them forever unclear about personality boundaries. She also hinted that this habit signified that her mother might be mildly retentive. Actually, Laura imposed mathematical precision into chores that wasted precious time. For example, there is the disorder of buying individually, caring for different items, and having to satisfy the varying tastes of four different children. This actually reveals a quality of character that foreshadows the ending of the text when Laura enrolls in night school. As an individual and as a mother, she displays a certain kind of practical, efficient, and yet inventive mind-set. This creativity, this inventiveness toward everyday living is not applied to exotica, but to that which is at the end of her nose.

Instead of appreciating this quality, her daughters, all growing up in America, dismiss these talents in their mother. Laura does realize that her daughters criticize her, even though she claims not to comprehend their use of psychological terms. Since she has graduated from an American college, such ignorance is impossible to believe. The next time they all get together, Laura retaliates by laying on the guilt trip. She cries, claiming that she had always done her best as a mother, whereupon her husband responds that "[g]ood cows breed cows," his oft-repeated expression of sympathy for Laura for never having succeeded in bearing him a boy.

Laura has a favorite story she tells about each child. In doing so, she again shows this odd streak of inventive, yet efficient practicality about what should be highly individualized. At Dr. Garcia's seventieth birthday party, Laura, somewhat drunk, took advantage of the band going on break to take the mike and tell her special story about Carla. As psychologists, both Carla and her husband had already thoroughly analyzed the story in order to determine whether Carla still retained any "unresolved childhood issues." Because it was her story, however, Carla still took pleasure in hearing it, no matter how often repeated. Besides, whenever Laura told it, this was a sign to Carla that for the moment she was the favored of all her siblings.

Alvarez continues her sarcastic treatment of psychology and psychologists in a witty duel between two jealous siblings–Carla, the psychologist, and another sister. But Laura wins the verbal duel over both of them. The other sister complained about hearing the mother tell the story about Carla again, and Carla had angrily appealed to everyone present to notice the negativity of her sister's attitude. In response, her sister mocked her back, appealing to everyone present to notice Carla's use of psychological jargon. Laura interjects at this moment, thereby ending the sibling rivalry, by bringing the attention back to her. She demands that everyone listen to *her* story.

Yet once again, in the middle of her story, the mother is interrupted by some sparring between her daughters to which she again puts an end. When Laura happens to roll her eyes in the same way that her second daughter had rolled her eyes at her older sister, Carla expresses mock disbelief because her younger sister had rolled her eyes in the same way. Annoyed, the younger sister retorts that she can indeed believe it. Carla strikes back, requesting the group to notice her sister's hostility. Her husband then adds his weight to the quarrel by siding with Carla, whispering something about her sister in his wife's ear that makes them both laugh. Again, nipping the ugly sibling rivalry in the bud, Laura interjects with the request that they let her finish *her* story. And once again at the end of her story, she tops her daughter when the second daughter in her exasperation groans out a loud appeal to Jesus to which her mother adds that he always provides. More of Laura's character begins to emerge after this point, even though the novel is ostensibly not about her, but about the Garcia girls, primarily the third of her daughters, Yolanda. Nevertheless, the book really focuses on Laura.

In relation to the special stories she tells about each of her daughters, she had always intended to tell one in which she prophesied Yolanda's eventual fame. Now she is disappointed. She could not tell that story because Yolanda has indeed become a famous poet. This does not stop Laura from attending her daughter's public poetry readings with great pride.

Here Alvarez's conception of the character of Laura begins to take on a derisive tone at Laura's expense, transforming her into a slapstick buffoon. Alvarez now writes about her as if she were some kind of a one-dimensional stock character, a guileless fool. This lovable airhead quality doesn't jibe with what readers learn about her before or afterward–her upper class background, her education, and intelligence, her wit and grace under fire, her inventive abilities. Such a gross discrepancy in characterization between the beginning of the text and the end could only be accounted for by the fact that Alvarez originally published the book in separate parts as individual short stories standing on their own merits.

Be this as it may, Laura is depicted as acting silly and obtuse during Yolanda's reading. She always sits in front row center from where she applauds each poem and gives her daughter standing ovations to Yolanda's intense embarrassment. For this reason, Yolanda attempts to keep her readings secret, but her mother somehow always discovered them. Naturally, when Yolanda reads intimate poems to lovers whose settings are bedrooms, Yolanda is embarrassed by her mother's presence. However, Laura never seemed to notice the subject matter of her daughter's poems, perhaps because she thought all of it was creative license, the product of Yolanda's wonderful imagination.

During Yolanda's readings, Laura boasts about her daughter and tells intimate and embarrassing anecdotes about her to whomever happens to be sitting in a neighboring seat, even though sometimes it turns out to be one of Yolanda's current lovers. This is the case in the hilarious scene depicted by Alvarez when Yolanda, in excruciating embarrassment, watches from the platform where she is performing her poetry an intense dialogue taking place between Laura and Clive, her current lover. Laura is expatiating at great length about Yolanda as a baby at the time when she lost all her hair and was taken to a specialist. On the way home, the parents exit the bus, somehow without Yolanda. They have to run after it to catch it. When they do, they find Yolanda surrounded by a crowd of people. She is reciting a poem about a blackbird.

Here Laura breaks down, unable to remember the author. Her neighbor, in addition to being Yolanda's lover, is also the department chair at the university where Yolanda works. He first erroneously guesses (Wallace) Stevens. Then he finally comes up with the name of Poe. In her excitement that he has guessed correctly, Laura begins to recite "Annabel Lee" very loudly. Suddenly she looks around her and realizes that the entire audience is staring at her in silence. She blushes with embarrassment, and the poet's lover, amused, squeezes her arm to make her feel better. Meanwhile, back at the podium, the poet who has already been introduced, is waiting "for the white-haired woman in the first row to finish talking" (1992, 50). She reads her poem, a hot one, called "Bedroom Sestina" and dedicated to Clive who smiles with embarrassment at her mother who is busy smiling with pride at Yolanda. Clearly at this point Laura is no more than an exasperating but lovable figure of fun, an impercipient, naive, one-dimensional gatekeeper mother figure.

Combining her contempt for stupid psychologists in confrontation with this naïve Laura, Alvarez informs readers that her mother no longer tells a story unique to her second daughter, Sandra, because the story was not celebratory but an explanation of her daughter's mental illness. Laura and her husband have committed their daughter to a private mental hospital. The dense Dr. Tandlemann is the senior staff psychiatrist at Mount Hope who uses psychobabble language. When he makes the mistake of telling Laura that Sandra is not "clinically crazy," she frowns and invalidates him, demanding what that phrase means, adding once again that she does not understand his talk. Again, a lack of understanding of psychology and its terms is not in keeping with Alvarez's depiction of Laura as a well-educated woman who reads *The New York Times*.

Alvarez then starts up a hilarious duel between Dr. Tandlemann and Laura, with the mother always in all seemingly simple earthy innocence revising the slow, bemused doctor's terminology and topping him, of course. When she claims that she and her husand have had their share of problems from all of their daughters, the doctor jumps to a logical, but erroneous conclusion that other daughters had had nervous breakdowns. The mother frowns at him and announces that what her daughters have had are "[b]ad men."

Then she puns on the doctor's use of the word "breakdown": that it does make some kind of sense, because the word "heartbreak" (which is causing Sandra's problem) is related to the word "breakdown." The doctor, allergic to layman's terminology, tries to protest, but Laura ignores him. Once again, when Laura informs him that Sandi, who had inherited her Swedish light skin from a great-great-grandmother, nevertheless longed to be dark complected like her sisters, the doctor again falls into her trap when he states that he can understand Sandi's feelings. But Laura shouts angrily that this is what is crazy about Sandi.

When the doctor asks about whether Sandi got along with her other sisters, Laura blinks disapprovingly because he is asking too many questions. He makes the mistake of attempting to explain to her what he means by using the term "siblings." Laura loudly objects to the word, expressing her antagonism to the use of psychological terms by explaining that her children are sisters, not siblings. Again, according to Alvarez's earlier descriptions of Laura's education, she would have understood the word "siblings," unless, of course, she is pulling the psychiatrist's leg from start to finish, expressing her antagonism to his use of specialized jargon in relation to human beings.

When her granddaughter is born, Laura is again depicted as a buffoon figure of fun in the scene before the baby-viewing window. In carrying on a conversation with a doting father next to her, she quickly reveals some of her inner values to the stranger. As a Catholic she doesn't believe in polytheism, she confides to him. She herself takes on the guilt and shame of having borne only four girls to her husband, but in reality she doesn't feel it is all her doing. She also confides to the stranger that she doesn't believe in a girl's traveling without a chaperone, or she and her husband would never have let her go. She justifies her position on the grounds that she and Don Carlos do not approve of such freedom for females.

In another scene, although Laura does not appear, the mother still ends up present in terms of her gatekeeping influence, again, as Alvarez's vehicle for deflating psychology:

When one of the sisters calls Clive a "turd" for leaving "Yo," Carla informs her that Yolanda wishes to be called Yolanda, not "Yo." Yolanda then protests that her name is indeed Yolanda, and that her wish to be called by her own name is nothing new. Carla, assuming her professional calm, asks her why she is so angry, whereupon Yolanda rolls her eyes and tells her to stop doling out cheap therapy. Carla then goes on to favor her sister with compliments. She tells Yolanda that she is really a good poet and that she has saved all her poems, that she should think more of her talents and not belittle herself. Every time she reads another poet she thinks to herelf how much better "Yo" is. How manipulative Carla is to force the nickname on her sister against her wishes! Yolanda remains silent, busy thinking about Carla's tendency to mix her compliments with calls to self-improvement, as she has just done. This reminds her of her mother's style and technique, mingling compliments with "constructive criticism" (1992, 61).

The chapter closes with the prophetic words: "Everyone listens to the mother" (1992, 67). Mami Laura is becoming an important character.

When second–wave feminism spreads, Yolanda brings home *Our Bodies, Our Selves*, which provides readers with an opportunity to observe Laura in her role as a gatekeeping mother. She claims that Laura could not put her finger on the source of her objections to the book. Here Alvarez is punning on the conviction of the authors of this classic feminist text that women should pride themselves on their private parts and explore them with a speculum. Perhaps the book bothered Laura because it did not contain pictures of men, only women and their bodies. At any rate, Laura knew it wasn't a sex book as she had been trained to understand what sex books were like. Still, a book about women examining their own bodies, which included a chapter about lesbians, caused Laura to decide that it must be a disgraceful book, especially after she saw the illustrations. Here Laura reveals herself in still another, less admirable, and lovable manifestation: as the punitive watchdog mother of conventional cultural values, the gatekeeper role that the author defines even more clearly in the following incident.

One summer, the four girls are allowed to visit relatives in the Dominican Republic. Just before their departure, Sofia tossed a plastic bag of marijuana behind a bookcase when the girls hear their mother coming toward their room. Mami flies out from New York to confront them after a maid finds it. At first, the two women think that the substance in the bag is oregano, but after sniffing and tasting it, they realize it is marijuana. From the moment they had attained puberty, Laura had focused all her concern, all her attention on the girls' maintaining their virginity "in this land of wild and loose Americans." Still, "vice had entered through an unguarded orifice at the other end" (1992, 114), Yolanda quips.

Seeking aid and assistance from other cultural standard bearers, Laura goes to a psychiatrist who is an uncle by affection. Of course no reader is surprised by now at Alvarez's stabs at psychology and psychologists. Again, a source of confusion arises as to why Laura, so inimical to psychologists/psychiatrists, should go to one to help her to cope with her children. Yolanda justifies her doing so by claiming that Laura wanted to uncover the truth and to shield Papi from suffering a heart attack, which she was certain would kill him if he learns about the marijuana. The psychiatrist gets Mami to free associate about other things that the girls might be doing to upset her. By the time he is finished with her, Laura is convinced that the girls were drug addicts, prostitutes, and pregnant from married lovers.

The girls attempt their best to discredit their Uncle Pedro by informing Mami that he is a lecher, habitually ending their sessions with overlong hugs and by patting their behinds, but Mami does not bite. Carla then inquires caustically what Saint Peter could possibly know about grass, to which Mami, frowning, responds that it was marijuana. Carla is finally silenced. Laura then launches into an inquisition of her children. Sofia pleads guilty, begging her mother to be the only one punished. Mami agrees, adding a request to the girls that they had better not tell their father about the situation unless they all wanted "wholesale Island confinement " (1992, 116).

As usual, Carla pontificates afterward to her siblings in psychological terms about the situation. She tells Sofia that because she is in the midst of adolescence she is supposed to be miserable and disturbed. On the other hand, her decision to stay in the Dominican Republic under her aunt's strict chaperonage, instead of returning home with her other sisters, is just going to make her condition worse. When Sofia is reported, instead, as having become well adjusted to island life, Carla hilariously defines Sofia's behavior as "a borderline schizoid response to traumatic cultural displacement" (1992, 117).

Alvarez then informs readers of Laura's motive for concealment, for not rocking the boat with her husband. It is not due to maternal motives, or her role of gatekeeper, but to attain the fulfillment of her own needs and desires. Although she has stopped inventing and donned a cleaning lady's uniform, she still has hopes of following her own path to full and free self-expression. This is why she does not wish to "blow the whistle on her girls and thus call attention on herself" (1992, 116) in relation to her discovery of their use of marijuana.

It is not until the chapter "Daughter of Invention" that Mami finally becomes an individual character called by her full name, Laura Garcia de la Torre. Sadly her inventions leave her daughters unimpressed. They are also unsupportive because they are jealous of her attention. In the much closer quarters they all now share, as was characteristic of American nuclear families, but not of upper-class families in the Dominican Republic, Laura's great energy drained their burgeoning independence whenever she focused her attention too closely on them for their comfort. This is in great contrast to when they were younger, when they gave her very little privacy to invent. In their arrogance they resolve to allow her to have her harmless little distractions. This is not support.

Discouraged for a while, Laura turns to more practical, down-to-earth employment. She takes to driving with her husband to his office in the Bronx. Garbed in a nurse's uniform and a name tag and armed with cleansers for his office, she brings order to the car's glove compartment. Once in the office, Laura also makes certain to prudently remove all stickers from the magazines in the waiting room because she fears that patients who are drug addicts may otherwise discover their address and rob their home.

Meanwhile, she makes sure never to express disagreement with her husband's plans for her, although secretly she plots a "revolution" of her own. This revolution consists of Laura's ultimate decision to go to school. It also indicates that Laura is getting used to the life here in the United States. She does not want to return to the Dominican Republic where "de la Torre or not, she was only a wife and a mother (and a failed one at that, since she had never provided the required son). Better an independent nobody than a high-class houseslave" (1992, 143–144).

Of what, exactly, does this "revolution" consist? Laura has "begun spreading her wings" by registering for "adult courses in real estate and international economics and business management." She is secretly "dreaming of a bigger-than-family-size life for herself," although "she still did lip service to the old ways, while herself nibbling away at forbidden fruit" (1992, 116). In contrast to Mama of *Silent Dancing*, who subverted the system only when it was a matter of life and death, Laura consciously does so to fulfill her own needs and desires, while playing her role of gatekeeper to the hilt.

NOTES

1. The author's family fled the Dominican Republic in 1960.

2. This critique is common to Latina writers. For example, the most trenchant one is that of the Puertorriqueña Nicholasa Mohr in "I Never Even Seen My Father," *In Nueva York*. She compares and contrasts ethnocentric Freudian psychology with Santería, exposing the fact that both are equally based on the patient's will to believe in myths which she also exposes as equally irrational and ridiculous.

Chapter 4

Rosario Ferré, *The Youngest Doll* and Other Stories

Rosario Ferré's position is that women do not have any real class assignments. They are actually outside of the class system which is for men only, whether a woman is a gatekeeper, a prostitute, or a high born lady. In her essay "How I Wrote 'When Women Love Men'" in *The Youngest Doll*, she blames gatekeeper nuns as "allies" of the "patriarchal system." The nuns of her town did everything in their power "to assure male liberties as to sexual and economic activities, while it tyrannized the wife as well as the prostitute." To this end, they taught their female charges that "erotic sensations" were "sinful," so that when they grew up they would become Isabel Luberzas" (1991b, 150–152). Isabel Luberza is the lady wife of her story "When Women Love Men."

In "When Women Love Men," Ferré shows two women actually merging into one another—a whore into a lady wife and a lady wife into a whore. Her purpose in doing this is to forward her belief that it makes no difference in a culture run by men to what class women are assigned and situated. This is the case, even though one, a brunette, goes shoeless and ragged, whereas the other, a blonde, wears elegant clothes. The future prostitute first sees the lady beside the man they both love, their lord and master, the "tall handsome man dressed in white linen and Panama hat, who stood leaning out on the balcony" (1991b, 139). Both become equally enslaved to this patriarch, who, at the end of the story—which is where the story actually begins—has just died. Without his patronage both women are now equally devoid of any meaningful identity. "Now we know that what you really wanted was to meld us, to make us fade into each other" (1991b, 134), they declare angrily to his spirit by the end of the story.

By twinning these women, although outwardly from very different classes, Ferré contends that the solution to the problems of enforced sexual repression and "social exploitation" like prostitution "is prostitution itself" (1991b, 151). In this author's view, as well as in that of all the other authors explored in this text, all women are basically prostituted, enslaved under male hegemony, in one way or another.

In Ferré's feminist horror fairy tale "Milk and Rice," a "blond and fair-skinned young man named Rice" is the "richest young planter in the whole province." He decides to choose a bride whom he would also make "sole heir to his sugarcane plantation" on the basis of whether she could answer his questions over a period of three days as to how a wave can be sawed and a mirror sheared "without scissors." He also stipulates that his bride should "knit," "purl," and "gather, stitch and interlace" at an excellent "pace," and then know how to put her "needles" into the "perfect place" (1993, 133).

One day he passed by a house on his horse and he saw there a beautiful visitor named Milk. Their courtship begins, based on each one challenging the other with riddles. He invites her to dinner and tells her to request any delicacy she wishes. If it isn't served immediately, then he promises to marry her and give her the keys to his house. Milk grows sad because she wants his love, not his money. She proceeds to request "a slice of baked ice." When this proves impossible, Rice announces that Milk had won and that he will make her his bride.

As in Mama's tale and in "The Youngest Doll," another tale by Ferré, both heroines are aware that their husbands intend to kill them and both avoid this fate by outsmarting them. Milk locks herself up in the bridal suite after the wedding, sews up all the openings of her wedding gown, fills it with honey, and lays it out with great care on the bed. Then she cuts off some strands of hair from her head, places them above the dress, and hides herself. Just as in Mama's tale of Maria Sabida, but with a different twist at the end, when the husband enters, he repeatedly stabs what he believes to be his new bride's body. When the honey spills out all over the bed and the floor, some drops fall on his lips. Then Rice wails and cries that if he had realized how "sweet" (1993, 135–136), she was, he would never have murdered her. The next day, Rice's friends found him lying on the bed with a long knitting needle buried on the left side of his chest. When Milk, now dressed in widow's weeds, went back home to her family, the people of the town sang as she rode by that Rice had "at last" found himself a bride who was able to do everything with her needles he had demanded. This included putting them in the "perfect place" (1993, 136).

Through Mama's and her tales of Maria Sabida, Cofer deplores both the class system and woman's place in that system. Ferré also uses the myths of "Rice and Milk" and "The Youngest Doll" for the same ends. In "Rice and Milk," however, Ferré goes further to expose patriarchal oppression than Mama in her myths, or even Cofer in her feminist "fairy tale," "Maria Sabida." Cofer describes Maria Sabida's husband as a reformed character once his bride has outsmarted him, but the savvy woman never trusts her husband again for the rest of her life. Ferré's bride kills her husband in retaliation for his attempting to kill her. Like Cofer, Ferré questions "the feminine stereotypes common in" Puerto Rican culture, but more pointedly questions "the feasibility of the female existence" as a subaltern in "a capitalist society based on gender inequality" (Bilbija 1994, 887).

In "Out of the Frying Pan," Ferré tells readers that her motives for writing were also political, because external forces in some large measure created her interior reality. It is noteworthy that like Santiago and Ramis she resents the United States. As a writer, she chose to depict the destruction of the plantation class, to which she herself belonged, by nouveau riche, a "metamorphosis" of one set of values based on familism with another based on individualism and the profit motive. She attributes the transformation in her culture to a new "value system implanted among us by strangers from the United States" (1991a, 475).

This does not mean that Ferré is nostalgic about her country's value system prior to North American incursions. Ferré refuses to repeat her aunt's paeans of praise for the glories of past times when peasant laborers in the fields of the cane plantation suffered and died from malnutrition while the plantation owners gave their daughters dolls filled with honey.

In fact, Ferré's feminist perspective involves a difficult personal and political repudiation of the elite plantation class into which she was born, a choice that has led to the power of her allegories, especially in her finest work, *The Youngest Doll*, a collection of short stories. She also tells us in "Out of the Frying Pan" that she created characters based on her own experience of divorce. Because of her love for her husband she had renounced her "own intellectual and spiritual space for the sake of the relationship with the one I loved." Her basic motive in doing so was not so much love as her enculturation into inequitable gendered power relations, which caused her to determine to be "a perfect wife." After her divorce, she began to understand her mistakes, her lack of strength, her "failings," why and how she had been the way she was. While grieving over "her passivity, her acceptance, her terrifying resignation" during her failed marriage, she nevertheless was empowered by her illumination to create heroines in her future works, such as *The Youngest Doll*, who were "braver, freer, more energetic and positive" (1991a, 476–477).

Ferré's perspective, as well as those of the heroines she delineates, is recognizable as similar to the other authors analyzed in this text. All these writers are inimical to their cultures' system of inequitable gendered power relations. At some previous point in time, the authors have rebelled and distanced themselves from such relations in order to critique them through their writing. Like Ferré and Cofer they write from a knowing perspective in the present, whereas their heroines do not necessarily reflect their own current situation, but may be re-creations from their past states of constraint, feelings of impotency, and rage.

Sometimes they are triumphant composites, as in the case of "Rice and Milk" and "The Youngest Doll," where the woman's frustrated rage at the patriarchal system, festering inside for too long, turns suddenly outward, always in tragic ways. In "Rice and Milk," it is the knitting needle to which women are relegated, which is turned into an instrument of death for the heartless sugar plantation owner. Symbolically, Milk, as "Everywoman," kills the force that she loves and hates because it would destroy women if they are so foolish as to yield to their feelings for their oppressors. In "The Youngest Doll," claws embedded and festering in the aunt's leg have kept her from moving around, that is, the claws of the system which confines, stifles, and shackles women. Ultimately the heroine uses the claws as deadly weapons against the embodiment of the system, her status-seeking, social-climbing husband.

There are other authors, such as Alvarez, for example, who apply patriarchal cultural role models for men to their female characters for the purpose of provoking laughter–at the patriarchy. However, in Cofer's and Ferré's work the results are always tragic. Regardless of whether they choose tragedy or comedy, the gaping chasm thus exposed by contemporary Latina writers between one set of infallible prescriptions for one gender and another set for another gender never fails to reveal a crucial indicator for defining inequitable gendered power relations between men and women.

In "The Youngest Doll," perhaps the finest feminist horror story written since Charlotte E. Perkins Gilman's "The Yellow Wallpaper," both the heroine and her aunt are unnamed, as are all her elder sisters. After each child's birth, their aunt, seated on the porch of her brother-in-law's plantation house facing the canefields, sews magnificent dolls for them. When she was younger she had been bitten while bathing by "an angry river prawn." It remains to form an ulcer on her leg, "slimy" and hard as a stone. The maiden aunt has internalized her rebellion against the patriarchal culture that has constrained her movement. Her doctor claims that he cannot remove the ulcer because if he does so, it will then endanger her entire leg. The malevolent patriarchy has hobbled the aunt's free self-expression. The aunt's consciousness now harbors an internal, hostile, festering element which voids the beguiling, but destructive "perfumed" myths that take women in, that women internalize.

The house she lives in is decaying, as are all plantation houses depicted by Ferré, for they symbolize the condition of its owners. Ruination is where the excesses, greed, oppression, and exploitation of this class have led them, according to Ferré, who critiques this class, her own class, her family's corrupt inheritance through such imagery every chance she gets.

The aunt's dollmaking, her gift of dolls to each of her nieces, is the external expression of the prawn of outrage living within her. The dolls become ever more extravagant, the objects of ritual celebrations. They begin to represent each girl in height and measurements–one doll for each of the nine girls, so that by the time the eldest turned eighteen, there were 126 dolls.

The only item that the aunt did not use for the making of the dolls was the glass eyes. However, she considered them useless unless she had "submerged" them in the stream for several days. Then the brides would be able to interpret the slightest moves of the prawn's "antennae" (1991b, 5). This represents the necessity on the part of the brides, who will have to deal with their treacherous menfolk daily after marriage, to be ever conscious and alert to their perilous endangered situation. They must use their "antennae" at all times, or suffer the consequences, a moral reminiscent of the moral of Mama's "Maria Sabida" cuento. Women, according to both Mama and Ferré, must know and understand that their husbands are the representatives of the patriarchal system and as such are their enemy. Their husbands embody that system in all its ways and institutions and act on it every day in every way. Women must remain alert, even at night, all night and every day.

The married life of each bride demands that she turn into a perfect decorative object like the kind of doll that used to be placed on piano tops (1991b, 4). Significantly, the aunt fills the wedding doll with honey, rather than with the cotton ordinarily used for stuffing. At this point, readers realize that "The Youngest Doll" is going to play a variation on the grisly fairy tales of Mama's "Maria Sabida" and Ferré's "Rice and Milk": about love, betrayal, conflict, and death involving a man and his wife.

The maiden aunt is her nieces' subversive ally: a guerrilla, a saboteur of the hegemony, the direct opposite of the gatekeeper role she plays on the surface. This is illustrated when she reassures the grooms, one and all, as each girl marries, that the wedding doll she is giving her niece is "merely a sentimental ornament." It represents the good, old-fashioned, submissive, obedient wife, the housebound kind–on the surface. The bride, like the doll, must be a covert saboteur of the regime.

Eventually the last suitor arrives for her last niece. He is the son of the maiden aunt's attending doctor. Upon examination of the maiden aunt, the young man realizes that his father could have cured her ulcer from the very beginning. Her disability–being hobbled, held down and out (that is, the cultural constraints against her) had unnecessarily prevented her from leading a meaningful life of her own. Instead, the suitor's father, the aunt's doctor, has brutally used his services to treat the ulcerated prawn to pay for his son's education. Without remorse, instead of objecting and correcting the problem, the last suitor colludes with his father, thus callously permitting the maiden aunt's unnecessarily crippled condition to continue.

Like his father, this suitor is totally given over to capitalistic materialism and is a social climber, a member of the nouveau riche, as evidenced by his "ostentatious tiepin of extravagant poor taste" (1991b, 5). The last niece nevertheless decides to marry him out of curiosity. This continues the association of the internalized prawn preyed upon by powerful sea creatures.

On the girl's wedding day, the maiden aunt embeds her own diamond earrings into the pupils of the wedding doll. Her aim in doing this is to assure the return of the girl's clarity of vision and as a symbol of her own continuing concern and watchfulness.

All too soon the bride discovers that her husband is entirely given over to materialism, that his "silhouette" and "soul" were "made of paper." He makes his first decisive constraining move against his wife when he forces her to seat herself in the hot sun on the balcony so that anyone who passes by could see with their own eyes that his wife is a woman from the upper classes. Next he pries the diamonds from the eyes of his wife's wedding doll "with the tip of his scalpel" (1991b, 5) and pawns the diamonds in exchange for a gold pocket watch and chain for himself. Throughout his increasing depredations, his wife's wedding doll remains on the piano lid, but after the man's heartless excision of her aunt's diamond earrings from the wedding doll, the doll's attitude changes. She begins to sit with her eyes lowered "modestly," a position identical to that which the wife assumes in her enforced balcony appearances.

Aware of her danger in the face of her husband's intention to break up the doll's body parts even further–that is, to deprive her altogether of her freedom–the wife continues her aunt's legacy of covert deceit. When the doll suddenly disappears, she gives her husband the excuse that ants had sensed that the doll contained honey, had marched up the piano and consumed the doll in the night (1991b, 6). Her husband frantically digs up the ground all night without finding any trace of the doll. Gulled by her appparent obedience to the culture's appropriate submissive model for wifehood, the doctor totally believes in his wife's veracity.

Years pass, and the doctor, still unaware of his wife's enmity, becomes very wealthy by charging enormous fees to the townspeople, like a barker at a circus, for them to come to his home in order to view "a genuine member of the extinct sugarcane aristocracy up close" (1991b, 6). Ferré then satirizes the crude and ignorant nouveau riche "draped in necklaces and feathers and carrying elaborate handbags and canes . . . coughing or sneezing, or shaking their doleful rolls of flesh with a jingling of coins" (1991b, 6) who come to stare at his wife. Meanwhile, his wife sits forever "motionless in her muslin and lace, and always with lowered eyelids" (1991b, 6), exactly like the doll that used to sit on the piano.

When they come to sit near her, these vulgar, insensitive women, however, are disconcerted by her strange odor which creates "an uncontrollable urge" in these women "to rub their hands together as if they were paws" (1991b, 6). The wife's mood is contagious, although her visitors pretend to ignore it in her and in themselves. Ferré is here revealing that the wife has internalized the animosity of the prawns toward the rapacity of her husband and his nouveau riche friends. At the same time as the nouveau riche women are the parasites and tools of their menfolk, they are also their victims, preying on their sisters and themselves by colluding with the men who own them. They could, however, at any time, turn against their men, because they do, after all, suffer from the same conditions as women of the upper classes suffer.

While the doctor ages inexorably, somehow his wife's skin remains like porcelain (1991b, 6), exactly as it had appeared when he had courted her. Clearly the youngest doll represents the youngest sister, his wife. The wedding doll has become his wife. They are one and the same: forces of repressed fury and vengeance. One night, fired by his curiosity as to the secret of her eternal youth, he intrudes into her bedroom while she sleeps. There "[h]e noticed that her chest wasn't moving. He gently placed his stethoscope over her heart and heard a distant swish of water. Then the doll [no longer his wife] lifted up her eyelids, and out of the empty sockets of her eyes [that he himself had pried out] came the frenzied antennae of all those prawns" (1991b, 6). Notice that the single prawn embedded in the aunt has now become a multitude inhabiting the niece. The forces of hierarchy and materialism have harbored the monsters of vengeance which have multiplied with each wrong and which now turn on him and tear him to pieces. His own greed and cruelty have brought about his destruction.

Like Celia of *Dreaming in Cuban*, the youngest doll's aunt is a gatekeeper in reverse, sewing/internalizing into her charges the courage to sabotage, subvert, and, if necessary confront and destroy the capitalistic materialistic patriarchy.

Chapter 5

Magali García Ramis, *Happy Days, Uncle Sergio*

In *Happy Days, Uncle Sergio,* Magali García Ramis is concerned about the constraints of gatekeepers on the younger generations, as well as about political issues from a historical perspective. The book takes place during the presidency of Luis Muñoz Marín who devised Operation Bootstrap after World War II. This period has been described as "a terrible time . . . in a period of official optimism" (Ruta 1995, 11). Marín sought to modernize Puerto Rico by attracting U.S. industry to exploit indigenous workers. The United States got wealthier, many poor Puerto Ricans were out of work than before, and Puerto Rico became even more dependent on the United States. Dams and electric power stations are built according to the advice of the Americans. Significantly, it became a routine part of Lidia's Uncle Roberto's job as a representative of the government development corporation, Fomento, to pick the Americans up when they land in Puerto Rico at the new futuristic international airport. Ramis also writes sarcastically of this period by juxtaposing ugly, man-made modern improvements, identified with Americans, with natural imagery. Mountains are destroyed by laying asphalt roads on them and constructing suburban developments. Cement and hotels blossom instead of flowers.

As I have shown in a previous chapter on Judith Ortiz Cofer, both Cofer's parents are profoundly conservative, whether separatist or assimilationist. They sought to indoctrinate Judith and her brother into the same class and race values into which Lidia and her brother are indoctrinated by their family who are all female gatekeepers. According to Nicholasa Mohr, who makes Ramis her exception among only a few others, most Puerto Rican writers lack "the universality that bonds the common human family, regardless of language, class, or geography." Ramis however, exposes "her privileged middle-class background" in a way "that reveals much of the sickness that is prevalent in that class system. It is a system that continues to stifle attempts to eliminate the

Spanish/European-style legacy of race and class that was deposited on that island centuries ago" (1989, 115). Lidia's voice from *Happy Days* illustrate Mohr's analysis when she informs readers in a lengthy list about her family's preferences for the Catholic Church, the Pope, anything American, European, Spanish, German, Swiss, and all whites. The family detested the nazis, African countries, nonbelievers like communists, Puerto Rican proindependents and nationalists, mambo, and the dictators Trujuillo and Batista.

The Cubana Coco Fusco omits class as an element, let alone a major one in terms of shaping the identity of women. Given Lidia's struggle with her identity, Fusco's point about social construction of identity is valid in political terms: "There will not be a really open dialogue until it is understood that those debates on sexuality, ethnicity, and cultural politics are crucial to defining 'identity,' American or otherwise, and that they are just as important as the well-worn discourse against cultural imperialism" (1995, 164–165). American ethnocentric policy is objected to universally by all the Puerto Rican writers studied in this text, as well as by other writers from other Caribbean countries. The title of Julia Alvarez's text, *How the Garcia Girls Lost Their Accents*, and the work itself deals with the Americanization process, although the author focuses primarily on gender issues, rather than on educational demands by the school system to assimilate and integrate. Similarly Ramis's young narrator, Lidia, writes to her Uncle Sergio about the glories and pitfalls of her education by the nuns, an education that was enlightening in many ways, except for its valorization of English, American, and Spanish cultures. She was taught primarily American literature, because the nuns were American. For example, the children read *Uncle Tom's Cabin* and learned about slavery and the Civil War; Henry James's *Portrait of a Lady* was followed by a lecture on the feminist movement. The nuns also liked Peter, Paul, and Mary. Meanwhile, Puerto Rican culture was obliterated. Everything had to be thought and said in English so that the children "learned to think and feel in English, and to distance ourselves more and more, some forever, from Spanish."

Once the nuns required the children to write a comprehensive twelve-page essay on Longfellow's "Evangeline" during the Christmas break when Lidia's family traveled to El Yunque tropical forest. She recited the poem over and over again while in the rain forest, in the vain hope that she would be inspired to write a wonderful essay in a wooded environment. But as she intoned, "This is the forest primeval, the murmuring pine and the hemlock" (the opening line of Longfellow's "Evangeline,") she was perspiring heavily in the tropical forest, with its prehistoric palm trees and enormous ferns. Such a forest was completely alien to the poem she had been assigned to study and to what she wanted to become. Nevertheless it was her forest, far more real for her than the forest she had been assigned to learn about. What bothered her most of all was that she could not translate the word "primeval" into Spanish because she felt that the Spanish word "primigenio" was not poetic enough.

The same experience is true for Puerto Ricans in the United States, as Roberto Santiago's parallel indictment reveals. Like Ramis in Puerto Rico, he learned about U.S. history from the Anglo perspective only. They had kindly asked the indigenous people they found here to have Thanksgiving dinner with them. They had founded a country here where all men were created equal. They were taught to valorize July 4, Independence Day from the English colonizers. They were taught Christianity–that Christians "treat one another with love and respect." They were taught how vital a clean environment was, the air and the water. But they were never taught who the Puerto Ricans were and their history, and they never even realized this. Only the Puerto Ricans had no idea who they were, whereas all the other minority groups in the city, such as the Jews and blacks, did have a sense of their own identity. One of Santiago's teachers, a nun, assured him, as Ramis's family had assured her, "that Puerto Ricans had no culture" and made him feel that he was somehow "stupid" to have wondered about this.

A priest defined the term "oppressed" as characteristic of those who were shiftless and were only interested in blaming others for the problems they experienced as a result. Like Ramis, Santiago concluded that Puerto Ricans were "worthless people" because they had "no identity" as a group, "no culture" and "no history." Although he saw many Puerto Ricans in New York, everywhere he went, asserting that they were "proud" of it, none of them could justify such a claim. Nevertheless he did realize that Puerto Ricans were strongly linked in a unified goal, "to claim our identity," no matter how difficult it might be to achieve.

Priests lectured to him about being patriotic, being a good Christian with good Christian values. Showing him the American flag, they told him that he was "an American," that it was his duty to love the United States and to die for his country, if necessary. They showed him a crucifix and told him to turn his other cheek in the face of injustice and oppression. Finally they told him that he was a member of his school. But meanwhile, Santiago was called "nigger" and "spic" by his white schoolmates, and the Jesuit priests ignored them. His classmates told him where they thought he belonged, back in Puerto Rico, and they told him that his people "were all lazy welfare and food stamp cheats," too ignorant to be able to speak English.

Continually inscribed on all sides of him was the belief system, the "conviction" that to be white was to be "superior" to people of color. It took Santiago many years to understand that some of his schoolmates had absolutely nothing else "going for them" other than their white skin color. He concludes that racism "either makes you withdraw from yourself, hate yourself, or discover yourself" (1995, xiii–xvi).

Lidia is taken on a trip to Spain because her relatives claimed that their roots were there. Somehow she is intelligent and perceptive enough to notice that her gatekeepers–her grandmother, aunts, and mother–are denying that there are other unacknowledged roots, that is, Taino Indian and African roots. Some of her Spanish cousins are very dark, and when she returns home, her brother Andrés corroborates her suspicions when he reminds her that the Moors were in Spain for 800 years. He also tells her not to bring her convictions to the family's attention, and she does not do so. Clearly Lidia is confused at this point and has not yet sorted out her identity as a Puerto Rican from the elitist class identity that her gatekeepers would impose on her. After she attends college she finally does so, also discovering paradoxically that her close-minded, antinationalist family were actually "less assimilated, more naively Puerto Rican, than she is" (Ruta 1995, 11).

Ana Lydia Vega, another Puerto Rican writer, like Ramis, writes in Spanish; she has openly stated that her work is fuelled by a natural, spontaneous feminism. This is the case because the experience she has had since infancy "with repression, this constant negotiation with a male-dominated world, leaves an imprint on one's self." Vega claims that it is not necessary to read feminist theories to know them, "to be a feminist in practice, to arrive at some positions that frame what one chooses to write about." Although she did study feminist theory while attending university, feminism for her is "more a response to decisions I have made in my life . . . grew out of decisions and positions that are ˙lived experiences" ("Interview," Hernández and López Springfield 1994, 816-817). This is clearly the case with Ramis who shows her heroine Lidia in *Happy Days, Uncle Sergio* growing up in search of her Puerto Rican identity and coming to her feminism as the product of lived experiences within a world of female gatekeepers ruled by her grandmother.

Compared with the other young narrators discussed in this text, Lidia attempts, even as a child, to battle against her gatekeepers. Wild and courageous, she is always getting into trouble because of her independent spirit, quick temper, and sassiness, which her family interprets as bad manners. These qualities, perhaps those of the author herself, are temporarily suppressed in her childhood and adolescence. But they will reemerge one day and enable her to break through her cocoon of indoctrination. Once she does so, she powerfully critiques her culture's inequitable gendered power relations through the mediation of her gatekeepers. Had Lidia not possessed a rebellious spirit from the beginning, she might never have undertaken her painstaking, epic quest to eventually grow past her training and find her own Puerto Rican identity. She might have remained forever brainwashed. Lidia has more gatekeepers hovering over her than any other character in any other text I have discussed so far.

Happy Days, Uncle Sergio contains very few male characters, and they play minimal roles, except for Sergio. Lidia has lived with women all her life, and the women in her family ran everything in the home. In its exposure of a woman's world composed entirely of gatekeepers, this text, therefore, should theoretically provide the clearest proof of my thesis: gatekeepers' willing collaboration with the patriarchy and the ways in which they do so. It should also provide evidence of covert subversion or deviance, as, for example, we have seen with Judith's Mama. Not surprisingly, then, readers discover that even when they are physically absent for the most part, it is clear that the patriarchy rules the world of *Happy Days, Uncle Sergio*; its women are all obedient to their training without one iota of self-reflexivity. Her family, Lidia's personal group of gatekeepers, act in strict obedience to men's rulings, even after their death. The Catholic Church and its teachers reinforce this acculturation.

Lidia lives with her widowed grandmother, the matriarch of the family, her daughters, and widowed daughter-in-law, Lidia's mother. Aunt Ele, a doctor, like her deceased father, was the oldest daughter and therefore had the right of decision making for the family. But Lidia's mother, María Angélica, called Marí A, made all the decisions in relation to her children. Also in the household were Sara Fernanda, another aunt, a secretary and movie buff; and a cousin, Nati, brought up as one of their own. They are all uniformly loyal to their male god in heaven and their deceased husband and father whose pontifications are quoted by his widow and daughters as though they were sacred commandments. Mamá Sara rules, as the substitute for and in deference to the absent patriarch, husband, or any other male. She sits in a high-backed chair at one end of the table, like a queen, and places a chair opposite her for any man to sit in who would visit. Otherwise it is kept empty. The Man, even in absentia, is the King, the ruler, the authority over the female authority.

Sara has three other married daughters–María, Meri, and Clara, and one son, the Sergio named in the title. A revolutionary nationalist, Sergio lives in New York where, together with his radical Independista group, he plots the overthrow of the government–of American rule over Puerto Rico–through violent means. For a brief period, he goes into exile at his mother's home until he can return again to his underground activities in New York. Unable to work as a professional, a teacher, or government worker, which he is trained to do, he remains virtually housebound, because the government will not allow him access to any meaningful employment. During this period of Sergio's inactivity, while he waits for permission to return to the mainland, the children of the family– Lidia, her brother Andrés, and her cousin Quique–are of necessity exposed to him, his habits, his moods, and his philosophy, as he is to them.

Sergio's influence on Lidia, how he conducts himself in various situations, what he says and does, form a major element in the text because they form a major element in her thinking, which eventually reinforces her own tendency to disagree with her gatekeepers on politics, religion, and gender issues. He is wonderful with the children, never talks down to them, joins them in their activities, teaches them about art and, inadvertently, about Puerto Rican politics and history, in the few moments when he lapses from being on guard. The children follow him everywhere and hang on him as much as they can, especially Lidia, who falls deeply in love with him.

Whatever Sergio and his group plotted or did is not disclosed to the reader until the end of the book, but he evidently became a *persona non grata* to the American government. This is why his group hurriedly bundles him back to Puerto Rico, to lie low for a while until it is safe for him to return to New York. Apparently he has left his male lover there, as well, so sexual frustration adds to his personal loneliness and isolation, his intense unhappiness during this period. Once he even appeared in the morning with eyes red from crying after having read a letter from New York. To Lidia, this is unheard of in a grown man. At one point Sergio attempts to have sexual relations with a sympathetic maid, but he is unable to perform. To his niece, who has observed this scene by accident, his impotence is a symptom of a crucial loss of will. She believes that this attempt is a defeat for him, for his attempt at heterosexuality. She believes that he has been defeated in the past and would be again in his political project because he has hardly any faith left in himself or his cause.

A dutiful son and brother, Sergio obeys his mother's and sisters' provisos that he not expose his niece and nephews to his perspective about the politics and history of Puerto Rico and only does so rarely, for example, when Andrés puts down the Russians and communism. He cautions the children not to be naïve, not to believe everything that is published. He then immediately stops giving his opinions to the children because he realizes he has inadvertently broken his promise to his mother and sisters not to talk politics or pass on his version of Puerto Rican history to the children.

Another time during a walk, they pass a school named Segundo Ruiz Belvis. When Andrés asks for an explanation of the name, his aunt speaks dismissively and disrespectfully of Belvis as one "of those shitheads" (1995, 71) as a political figure, something of a hero to the nation. Too offended to remain silent, Sergio contradicts his sister, telling the children that Belvis was a significant force in Puerto Rican history: he believed in abolition. He then stops talking, and the children sense that something unpleasant was happening among the grown-ups. Many years later, Lidia and her brother question their family about this. They deny ever having ordered Sergio not to talk to the children from his perspective about Puerto Rican history. The children believe that their family lied because he never tried again, and they never again asked him to do so.

Even as a child, Lidia is remarkable for her irrepressible spirit, the courage to always question and openly rebel at situations that do not make sense to her. Ever curious and possessed of an abundance of wit, Lidia copes at every point with her gatekeepers' omissions and lies, as well as their constraints on her. She responds with mockery, sarcasm, and irony to explanations that are irrational. She is, of course, reined in at every turn by her chief gatekeeper, her mother, and eventually, tragically, does become the unwilling, acutely uncomfortable product of her training. She is continually pressured to keep her temper under control. It is acceptable for a man to have a temper, but a woman who shows such a thing is considered vulgar and arrogant. Another reason for avoiding anger, according to Lidia's mother, is adrenaline, a substance causing someone who is angry to get angrier. Instead, Lidia should pray to be granted humility, a quality that will enable her to control her anger and insolence.

Ramis writes from a present feminist and politically aware sensibility, different from that which she held as a child after being indoctrinated by her gatekeepers. The process of the originally independent child's indoctrination and then painful and painstakingly arduous efforts to emerge from her benighted state to one of full knowledge is just as difficult for Lidia as for all the other narrators in all the other texts I have discussed in this work. What her translator,

Carmen Esteves, writes about Ramis's current perspective in her Afterword to the novel could be said of the other authors, as well:

Despite the apparent identity between the narrator and the protagonist there are temporal, spatial, intellectual and life experience differences that distinguish the narrative "I" from the "I" in the story. The narrative "I" is generally a reflexive being who relates a story in which she appears as a younger and more innocent person seen through the filter of an older and wiser "I." Experience and knowledge mediate between the two "I's." The retrospective nature of this type of narrative suggests the existing temporal disparity between the time of the story and the time the story is enunciated. (1995, 172)

Furthermore, like the other Latina authors, Ramis writes from a current feminist perspective, as well as a current knowledge of and pride in her Puerto Rican identity, past and present. She has achieved this only after tremendously hard-fought battles, not the least of them within herself. Like the other authors, as well, Ramis has only come to this current moment in time after much difficulty and reflection about how and what she was taught. *Happy Days, Uncle Sergio* is also about her Uncle Sergio's role, however inadvert, in assisting Lidia to eventually come to see her acculturation for what it was.

The book is also about her love for him, written to tell the world about it. She spent her time planning how she would write to him some day and tell him about her love for him. But then she would question why she should bother to do so; he might not welcome her admission of her love for him, he would think it was disgusting, a sin, depraved. What point would there be in confiding her feelings if he did not reciprocate, especially because in her view he had abandoned her when he returned to New York? "It would be pathetic, wrong, in bad taste. But I wanted to embroider you in a cloth, to draw you in a book, to paint you with words, to possess you, to duplicate you, and then to let the whole world know you" (1995, 155).

At the same time, this book is Ramis's feminist dissection of her "indoctrination," an indictment of all that she was taught. She was taught to valorize the European and to despise whatever was Puerto Rican as either nonexistent, or so crude as not to be considered worthy of consideration. Her gatekeepers loved the English and adored the French. Americans were not refined like the French, but were good, as well as being technological geniuses. Lidia's mother also blesses the unknown American inventor of the washing machine, and with good reason, for previously she had had to wash by hand. When Columbus Day would come to an end, Lidia was taught to give thanks to God for permitting Columbus to discover Puerto Rico and to bring the island the Catholic religion and Spanish. Anything Spanish was wonderful. The family even owned a Majorcan sheep dog, so intense was their drive to be connected with that culture. As Lidia quips sarcastically, the children in the family did not learn about the atrocities of Franco's Moorish Guard during the Spanish Civil War until they were grown.

But Latin America is not included in the countries to admire. Her Aunt Ele, an intrepid traveler, cautioned Lidia never to roam freely around there as can be done in European cities. The region was very depressing because it is only populated by poverty stricken, starving, filthy Indians. Ele does make an exception of Argentina as worthy of visiting because the population there resembles Europeans.

The family also doesn't like Cubans and is opposed to homosexuality as well as ignorant about it. They believe that a man is necessary as a role model for boys; otherwise, if they live only with women, they become "faggots." It is never clear whether they are aware that Sergio, their son and brother, is a homosexual, or whether they are surrounding him with a conspiracy of silence, or whether they are willing to acknowledge it to to him or themselves.

The family is also racist, an attitude that Lidia protests, even as a child. They remark of an apparently white Cuban that they would have to see her relatives in Cuba in order to see whether she is indeed white. Andrés, who is studying genetics in school, points out that even if the Cuban woman does have black relatives her children will not necessarily turn out black. Lidia inquires sarcastically whether if someone were only a little black, would it therefore not matter? She and her brother are then told that the children of black and white parents are never happy because whites will not accept them because they are not white, and blacks won't accept them because mulattos are superior to them. They are also told not to stroke a black child's head because their hands would then get tangled in the hair. In addition, blacks aren't as healthy as whites because of their different blood. Even if a blood transfusion was given and even if the blood type was identical, it would still be preferable if the transfusion would come from someone of the same race because the blood is more homogenous. This is the training to which whole generations of her family had been subjected for centuries, rationalizing their racism. Whenever Andrés and Quique (Lidia's cousin) wished to get a rise out of the family, they would announce that they intended to marry black women when they came of age.

Closely aligned to their racism is the family's class snobbery. To a large extent, their elitism is connected with the cultures they admire or detest, according to what their culture has decreed is the high or low level of the civilization in question. The children are not permitted to play with their neighbors, and Uncle Sergio is criticized for neglecting himself, for walking around the house unshaven, sloppily dressed in only a T-shirt, the way the market vendors dress. Such criticism provokes a response from Lidia's Uncle Germánico, who idolized the English and always took every opportunity he could to compare their superior practices with any inferior ones such as Sergio's. The English, even when they were prisoners of war never failed to shave and dressed themselves carefully every day because it was the only way they could maintain their pride in themselves.

It takes her years, until she goes to the university, before Lidia learns anything to counteract her training, to refute her gatekeepers. In *Happy Days*, Ramis focuses her rage primarily against her training by her gatekeepers in relation to gender and to the nonexistence of Puerto Rican history, culture, and art. Lidia's hopeless and passionate love for her uncle is interwoven with her hopeless and passionate commitment to correcting the wrong done to her country by brutally suppressing its history, culture, and art, as Sergio's homosexuality and nationalism has been suppressed.

She remains in love with him all her life, even though he never reciprocates, not even to the letter she sends him when she is in college in which she eloquently expresses her passionate feelings for him. She likens him to a spider and herself as a victim caught in a spiderweb. He is her "temple," her "sacred cow," her "everything," her "relative . . . son . . . brother . . . uncle." There were other men who aroused deep feelings in her, and she went to bed with some of them, allowing them to lie on top of her. But could she have had her way, she would "only be under" him, "always with" him, only have him inside her, only his "smell" and his "truth" (157).

Although he could not and did not fulfill the role of lover or husband that Lidia would have wanted for him, Uncle Sergio did give her what he believed to be the truth compared with the lies fed her by the rest of their family, the church, and her teachers. His perspective became a gift to Lidia so that the chasm between what he taught Lidia and what the others taught her became one of the major motives for writing this book. For example, Lidia had been taught that there were no Puerto Rican artists. When her brother Andrés spouts the belief that both of them had internalized, that no famous artists are Puerto Rican artists because of the lack of culture and the insignificant size of the island, Uncle Sergio provides the antidote to their training by setting them straight immediately. Art is not a by-product of the size, wealth, or power of any given culture, but a global phenomenon that all cultures possess in different ways and forms.

For a long time Lidia did believe her family about the inferiority of all things Puerto Rican. In her unanswered lengthy letter to her adored Uncle Sergio, much as Celia's Querida Gustavo does not answer her letters (in the latter case because she never sends them), Ramis details three stages to the long, epic internal journey Uncle Sergio had first set Lidia in order to arrive at her current perspective. First, before her Uncle Sergio's arrival in her life, she loved English and believed it to be the best language. As a young student she was exposed to an enlightened, liberal, but Eurocentric education that gave her a colonized mentality. She became pious and devout as well, in her desire to be a good girl, according to the notions of those who were molding her. At the age of fourteen, one of the nuns put her in charge of censoring the *Paris Match* magazine. Her job was to cut out any illustrations containing any indication of breasts, women's undergarments, or bathing suits for fear that the boys would be tempted to commit sin. Gradually she internalized her oppressor's influence, as she had her own family's, to the point where she buried her Puerto Rican identity, wishing to escape from being Puerto Rican and whatever she felt as such. This lasts until she gets to the university level.

Interestingly in her letter to her Uncle Sergio, Lidia blames him for her having grown up in a state of uncertainty and doubt, with the incapacity to make decisions for herself and where to direct her ideals. She blames him for having deserted her, Andrés, and Quique. He had left them suddenly without providing any guidelines for them as to how to think independently, how to question as they struggled to achieve their identity, although he had started them off in the right direction.

Second, the lengthy process of losing her Puerto Rican identity was reinforced in Lidia's adolescence when her teachers taught her about traditional Greek and Roman myths and traditional epic heroes, including El Cid and King Arthur. Her adoration for Arthur paradoxically ignited her into self-reflexivity for the first time. The questions she then asked herself at that point eventually gave her illuminations, but at that time they only reinforced her conviction that she was different in a negative sense, that she was inferior. She demanded of herself why she was not like what she was supposed to be; why she does not like what she is supposed to like; why she does not want to learn about what she is supposed to learn; why she does not know how to adapt herself to all the things she does not like, as others apparently do. She did not like opera, although paradoxically she did want to learn Italian. She liked mambo and merengue. She did not like French, nor memorizing Greek gods. She wanted to know about the Aztec and Inca gods.

One day while shopping with her mother in Old San Juan, Lidia looks around. Everything bothers her about the place: the dirty and peeling Town Hall, the appearance of abandonment, the two dry fountains, the decaying statues, the drunks hanging about. The heat bothered her, the dirty town, the dirty island, the stunted trees, and the same feeling as a human being, of being stunted, deprived. Nothing was like Paris, or the way Switzerland looked.

She then enters another stage, seemingly descending to the lowest point in her lack of personal self-esteem as a Puerto Rican. She begins another litany with a series of rhetorical questions to her uncle as to why Puerto Rico has nothing valuable: not one world famous artist, poet, painter, or saint. The Puerto Rican flag is never placed on a dictionary flap because the country does not count as a country, or even a colony or a commonwealth. Puerto Rico is worthless because it does not exist. She concludes that she does not want to be part of this country because Puerto Ricans and Puerto Rico "are shit" (153).[1]

Before Lidia can move up to the third level where she can begin the process of political self-identification independent of her gatekeepers, she enters yet another phase in her ongoing efforts to resolve her misery. She begins to consciously attempt to think like her gatekeepers. She tries to become like their definition of what it means to be a civilized person: to accept the situation as it is, as her family does, by Europeanizing herself, by traveling through Europe, fantasizing herself assimilated. Lidia describes this stage as her way of escaping her insecure feelings and colonized mentality as a Puerto Rican. In doing so, Ramis exposes to readers the chasm between the author's current perspective and her previous travail. This is reflected in her terminology about what the immature author had undergone, defining herself as having been psychically "colonized." By using the conditional, even though at that time she did not understand why she was insecure and how she was colonized, nor even the meanings of those terms, Ramis thereby reveals her full awareness and understanding of these feelings and terms at the time of writing.

When she allows herself to have lovers, to be loved by others, Lidia's shell breaks open and she enters into a final stage, self-awareness, which enables her to start to learn about herself and her country. First she determines to learn all the songs Sergio had liked, the ones he had listened to on WKVM, which her aunt used to define with contempt as the station to which only maids listened. These were Puerto Rican songs, for the most part. Lidia then began to learn the boleros, the traditional music and Christmas songs, *plenas* and *danzas*. These are all examples of Puerto Rican music that her family disdained in their elitism, confining themselves only to Spanish *pasos dobles* and songs from American movies.

At some point she and Quique suddenly realized that they had truly become Puerto Ricans. Armed with this revelation, Quique and Lidia went to a craft fair at a festival on the beach run by the proindependence group. There they proudly buy a Puerto Rican flag pin that Quique attaches to his shirt and a leather bracelet for Lidia with the flag used at Lares in the revolt against Spain. Their family reacts predictably, maintaining that the communists have brainwashed them. They also expose a hilarious sense of humor that enables us to see for the first time where Lidia got hers. They mock the young people for talking so much about the Puerto Rican flag and the Puerto Rican motherland, while not being able to tell one Puerto Rican root vegetable from another, one town from another, or the identity of the first Puerto Rican governor. Lidia mistakenly tries Munoz Marín's name, but they triumphantly inform her that Piñeiro had been the first governor, that Lidia and Quique are not really knowledgeable about Puerto Rican history, although they think they are superior to the rest of the family.

Lidia admits ruefully to the reader that the reason why she did not know anything about her country was because not one of her gatekeepers taught her about it. The problem arose because her family believed and taught her that whatever was worthwhile from that past was from Europe and whatever was going to be worthwhile in the future was going to be from the United States. Interestingly, she distinguishes between herself and her family in that as Eurocentric as they are, they still knew who they were. They were more Puerto Rican than she was herself. True, they each had an American passport. Nevertheless their lives contained a certain sense of what was enduring. The only changes they experienced were the changing seasons and holy days, tropical storms, and war.

Passionately loyal to the United States, continually avowing this loyalty, the family was somehow still less colonized and insecure than she and Quique. They did not have to continually struggle with their identities, as was the case for Lidia and her cousin because of the continual changes going on around them. Even though they could not answer the questions their relatives taunted them with, they attended study groups, read Puerto Rican poetry, and researched Puerto Rican history. They fantasied coming upon remains of Taino culture, distributed fliers about proindependence marches, and never stopped trying to find their Puerto Rican identity.

Once Lidia discovers her identity as a Puerto Rican, she feels she has at last achieved cohesiveness within herself. She can finally put all that she was beginning to learn into a context that gave her a meaningful identity in the present as well as the past, linked to her personal experiences. For the first time in her life she feels connected to people beyond members of her family. Knowing who she is, and the same is true for Quique, makes them both feel related to and part of a larger extended family.

Ramis's condemnation of Lidia's gatekeepers for their failure to provide her with a secure identity as a Puerto Rican is not all that *Happy Days, Uncle Sergio* is about. Her condemnation of her gatekeepers extends into every area of Puerto Rican culture because the gatekeepers mediate inequitable gendered power relations through the various institutions dedicated by the culture for that purpose. The intense indoctrination to which her gatekeepers submitted Lidia illustrates the gender specifics of her training. From her family she got the impression that sex was a mental state or a form of activity linked to the concepts of original sin, women's evil-doing, and men's disgustingly dirty bodies. Anything related to men was considered dirty by virtue of their being men, because men were dirty by nature, by definition. Men lacked the capacity to keep themselves clean and moral. They were weak and helpless without women to watch over them.

Ramis ascribes the source of sex stereotyping as the Catholic Church. To inform her son about what a man was and to inform her daughter about menstruation and becoming a woman, their mother buys two books for them, which have the church's stamp of approval. This guaranteed the officially sanctioned Catholic perspective and also the perpetuation of human experience from the Catholic perspective. The books teach Lidia and her brother that sex is the cause of filth and evil. Sex was caused by Eve who tempted Adam. Somehow there had to have been a Hebrew scribe (male, of course) present to observe all this so that the decree could be made with certainty. One imagines that the Hebrew scribe saw for himself that it was Eve who talked Adam into doing the dirty deed. He had to have seen that it was a terrible thing that she did, or he did, or they both did. This Hebrew scribe had to have heard God rage and immediately expel them from the Garden of Eden for having sex and then punish them for all eternity for it: men to have to toil and women to suffer in bearing children for the sin of tempting Adam. One has to imagine all this happening and being observed, then to believe that it is true, and not a myth made up by some misogynist Hebrew scribe to explain human origin and the cause for human suffering and death as due to women.

At any rate, to continue with what poor Lidia had to learn, according to the Catholic Church, God then assigned to women alone the complete "responsibility" for "holy matrimony," which the book described as a present from God, a "divine grace." In actuality, throughout history and in all known cultures, men created marriage as a control and constraint on women in order to assure that posterity were really theirs so that they could leave what they had amassed in their lifetimes to their own sons. How was Lidia to know this until she went to university and could study evolution and Engels and Veblen et al.?

Women were also somehow responsible for the sacred and honorable priesthood that was superior to marriage. Women were also responsible for raising the children Catholic because only women were generically and naturally good to their children. Men were responsible for respecting pure women and only having sex with them after a Catholic priest had joined them in holy matrimony. Apparently they could have sex with "impure" women also, but as Lidia complains, nowhere was she informed how to make love.

When her brother watches a nursing woman with lust and fantasies unimaginable to her, Lidia rages against her brother's mingling the sexual with the maternal. She rages also at the culture, at its God, at Catholicism, at the Catholic Church, and her own family. Instead of productively assisting her in finding out and experimenting freely, she was taught about a concept called love, entirely without sex, except in the dark when a married couple wished for a baby.

She rages most at the double standard. Her brother confesses that he purchased books about sex for the purpose of masturbation, yet the priest forgives him for it without a problem. For Lidia, on the other hand, there is an excruciatingly difficult and different standard to which she is bullied into conformity on all sides. As a woman she is not supposed to do anything sexual or even think such thoughts until she finds a boyfriend who will marry her. But she will never have a boyfriend or be able to marry if she is not pure. Further, and most important to her brother, the priest would disapprove if he discovered that Lidia knew anything about sex. He might then "tell on Lidia" (1995, 101) to their mother. Lidia, traumatized, because she knows that she is no longer pure by these standards, at least in her thoughts, believes that what her brother told her was true. Men have a wolf inside of them and therefore when they sin they cannot avoid it. Unlike men, women do not have the demands of the wolf on them, and women can only be evil and impure because they chose to. Through God's grace women had been given the strength to resist sexual temptation which men with their wolves howling in them could not.

By depicting Lidia's great suffering at having to lie at confession because of her curiosity about sex and about men, Ramis eloquently, powerfully vents her continuing sense of outrage against the church's successful indoctrination of a binary system for men and women. Lidia, the child on the verge of adolescence, concludes that she was vicious, lost, evil, and a liar, that she would be liable to excommunication, that she had forfeited the grace of God forever. She would be ostracized out of the kingdom of all those who were just, pure, Catholic, and the grown-up members of her family. She was now one of the culture's outcasts and weirdos, a "pariah" like her Uncle Sergio.

She calls her uncle a "pariah" here and once again, at the very end of the work, after his death, when she has put the missing pieces of his life together, when the family finally learns that Uncle Sergio was not a political fugitive so much as an outcast. He was hounded by the FBI because he belonged to a Trotskyite literary circle, had attempted to organize unions in factories and warehouses where he worked, and had collected money for the Algerian revolution against France. It got to the point where he had to use false identities in order to secure employment because he had served a six-month sentence for joining a protest demonstration. Gradually the family learned that he had been "a pariah, a rebel, and probably a homosexual" (1995, 164–165).

Lidia's chief gatekeeper is her mother, although María Angelica does differ from the rest of her family in several respects. She has compassion for pariahs, even though she feels it right that they are ostracized, as when she gives baby clothes to her neighbor who has borne an illegitimate son (as it turns out, thanks to her own brother-in-law). She is not racist, and trains her daughter to respect people from other races. She is respectful and generous to the poor and the downtrodden. She is very much a product of her training about gender.

At one point, Lidia dares to question her mother as to why women are the cause for men's sinning; why they are depicted in *Exemplary Lives* as the devil's emissaries to saints to tempt them sexually, and whether men were then devil's emissaries to tempt female saints. Her mother answers that this is symbolic, an allegory. When the paintings depict women, they are really depicting sexual temptation. Clearly Lidia's mother is unreflexive, unquestioning, uncritical of the Catholic Church's teachings, like the rest of her family. Her daughter is not, however. Lidia goes right to the heart of the feminist critique in relation to the Catholic Church's view of women. She demands to know why women were singled out to signify temptation and why Saint Contardo Ferrini was considered so wonderful for never noticing any women, no matter how beautiful. Ramis/Lidia then distances herself from herself and makes a statement about herself as she was. From her current feminist perspective, she indicts the Catholic Church:

All the saints had given up women, even those who were in love like Saint Augustine. The married ones abandoned them to become priests, or they waited until their wives died to reach true peace as monks. In our religion complete happiness was never reached with a woman. And I, almost a woman, and in love as I was with the idea of love, didn't understand why. I asked them again . . . why were women bad, why did Eve tempt Adam, why did God punish us by making childbirth painful, why wasn't it as dignified to be a woman as it was to be a man? Why couldn't we touch the Holy Sacrament? (1995, 115)

Her mother's response was to mumble cliches about grace and human beings in relationships before telling her daughter that she would go for clarification to the American priest because Americans could give better explanations for such things than the Spanish could.

Through Lidia's voice, Ramis openly informs us that she not only wrote this book to expose the difficulties of being Puerto Rican, but to expose the precise nature of her gatekeepers' training and her epic struggles to free herself from their "indoctrination" as a Puerto Rican woman. They do this through the perpetuation of inequitable gendered power relations. The method used to train her was with "speeches, containing a mixture of Catholicism and (pseudo)science . . . the true and false, the liberal and conservative, products of their fears and prejudices, their wisdom and beliefs–information which took us a lifetime to reorganize and debunk" (1995, 40–41).

Sadly, Magali García Ramis still lives in a world where she writes in order to question her gatekeepers. Sadly, she still retains her sense of outrage as a woman at the irrational "indoctrination" of females (and males) generation after generation into cultural conformity. This appalling (mis)information takes only .the strongest and most courageous of women (and men) a lifetime to reorganize and debunk in their lives and their work: writers such as Cofer, Garcia, Ferré, Alvarez, and Ramis herself, not the least of them all. Sadly, most generations of women and men, as well, remain obedient and good citizens of their culture; they are loyal to their training without the painful eternal questioning of information that feminists continually force themselves to engage in at a great price, most of the time for an entire lifetime.

Hopefully, this generation will be succeeded by a postfeminist generation in a sense much like that of a postethnic generation coming into being. Hopefully this generation will live on into a future time, "post" or after, influenced by the feminist movement and by the work of writers such as Cofer, Garcia, Alvarez, Ferré, and Ramis. Hopefully this generation will live past a seemingly endless time when critics such as myself have to defend the validity of an ethnicity different from that of the canonical Anglo-American ethnicity, as well as fight for equality of men and women. Hopefully, future generations will live in a time after these issues needed to be resolved.

NOTE

1. I myself as a professor have noticed over the years how violently students would react after the possibility of a different way of being and knowledge dawns in them. Prior to a complete shift in their perspective on some issue from what they had had been taught previously by their family, teachers, and members of the clergy and had unquestioningly internalized, a passionate venting, like Lidia's, almost like a verbal regurgitation, would take place in the classroom.

Afterword

As Kutzinski describes an Afrocentric perspective, specifically an Afro-Cuban one, it views whites as only capable of identifying or empathizing "with blacks only in a quasi-mythic space untroubled by history and social realities" (1993, 157). On the one hand there is African "lyric intuition," and on the other hand, there is western "burdensome historicism and sociology." As she puts the truth of the matter when speaking of "a white man and an admirable black poet," Luis Palés Matos, "The quid is not in genealogy but in genius" (1993, 162). The claim for ability (as well as interest), regardless of whether one belongs to a given group, seems far more rational than the claim for ability as necessitating the belonging to whatever one studies and writes about by bloodlines, by "genealogy."

Mirtha Quintanales, a Cubana who has emigrated to the United States, expresses how I feel when my work in other ethnic areas is dismissed on the grounds that my voice is therefore not authentic, unless I confine myself to my own ethnicity. I am a first-generation American Jew whose European relatives all perished in the Holocaust. Far from feeling resentment, I am delighted to have found someone who has put into words exactly what my experience has been, when she complains about African-American women or others equating her with white mainstream women because of her light skin. What is being denied in that questionable affirmation is her "history . . . culture . . . identity . . . [her] "very being," her "pain" and . . . struggle" (1981, 153). It is racist to claim that the light skin such as some lesbians and certain minorities and ethnicities might have privileges them more than African-American women. To achieve such privileges means for most of us, and not least of all, for Jewish women, to deny our Jewish selves, to assimilate, to integrate into a mainstream American society, to undergo "ethnic death." How can it possibly be considered a privilege to achieve acceptance only if we are willing to become "invisible, ghost-like, identity-less, community-less, totally alienated"? (1981, 153–154).

These words resonate for me individually–the price an ethnic white-skinned woman must pay to become mainstream–is the denial of her ethnic identity (and in my case, religious identity, as well, which has been the cause of universal persecution of my people historically and in the present). Women of color feminists should not jump to the conclusion that on the surface of the whiteness of ethnic skin lies willingness to sell out our ethnic identities. Would we pretend to be/or merge with our oppressors because we more or less evolved over centuries of rape and intermarriage to look like them? Some women of color feminists concentrate too much on how easy superficial skin color apparently makes assimilation and integration into the mainstream in order to evade discrimination. They are unaware of or discount our different history and differently internalized cultural training. These experiences of eternal oppression are so strongly inscribed into us that even if we do have skin color similar to whites, still we cannot and do not "pass" into Euro-American white Christian mainstream culture or do we even wish to.

This refusal to pass as mainstream on the part of many Jews is not just a refusal from recent times, but goes back over aeons. However we have appeared externally, the retention and claiming of the religion is what has demarcated our group as separate. This is an internal, psychic, voluntary separatism. Some women of color critics claim that because there is the opportunity "to pass" given to certain ethnics, such as Chicanas and Latinas, white ethnics would want to be "with our own kind." The only similarity we have with Anglo-Americans is skin color. Ironically, in the history of oppression and the experience of genocide, most first-and second-generation Jews initially experience far more identification with African-American and women of color feminists than they do with white mainstream English and western European-American women. That is, until and whenever they are lumped in with the latter by women of color critics.

Nevertheless I am disappointed with Quintanales's solution, although I respect it. She has decided "to turn away from my American sisters" to become "separatist," to work only with her "Latina sisters." On what basis? Ultimately, she maintains, we are all "culture bound." A "cultural mold" is set in each of us, and we are never quite "able to break away from it. At least not completely." The impact of our differences, at least "in the most private activities of our lives– how we express and share feeling in the context of our intimate inter-personal relationships" (1981, 149) apparently provides too much of a challenge for her.

Rosario Morales, however (perhaps because of her experience of marrying a Jew, as well as being a Puertorriqueña) is willing to cross the boundaries.[1] Beginning by deploring inequitable gender power relations, in *Getting Home Alive* (co-authored with her daughter Aurora Levins Morales) she states that she is strongly opposed to each group claiming that they are oppressed more than any other group, that is, that there is a hierarchy of oppression. (1986, 157). Lourdes Rojas details Morales's solution as:

[A] pluralistic women's allegiance based precisely on their diversity and held together by their awareness of shared condition of marginality as daughters and granddaughters of immigrants in American soil. . . . Instead of "scissors" to separate and accentuate the different colors, and forms of oppression, Morales offers a unifying "thread" for women's solidarity that will bring together an awareness of each and all the different textures of the fabric of women immigrants. (1989, 169)

Unfortunately this solution does not include Native American and African American women, as well as other women of color whose ancestors were here before most of us. However, both Rosario Morales and her daughter Aurora Levins Morales, explicitly include all women in their vision of "[a] multilingual, multireligious, many-colored and -peopled land where the orange tree blooms for all" (1986, 208), in what Rafael Peréz-Torres sees as then necessitating "an endless engagement with contradictory positions" (1994, 185). Nevertheless Rosario Morales sums up my position when she affirms that "[c]olor and class don't define people or politics" (1981, 91). Would that this were so.

Still, how might we achieve such a solution? Judit Moschkovich also disagrees with Quintanales' separatism when she calls for all women to move past their need to have to continually "explain and defend our different cultures" to others. In order to learn about other cultures, she believes that we must share our experiences with one another. Acceptance can only be achieved through caring and respect for one another. I believe that class and race elitism, a product of the global patriarchy, prevents us from achieving acceptance of one another because after having internalized their cultures' class-and race-based values, women in all cultures discriminate against each other on the basis of class and race.

Elsewhere, Moschkovich complains about white mainstream feminists who imagine that they are creating and building a "new feminist or women's culture" (1981, 83) when, as products of their culture, they replicate their culture's inequitable gendered power relations with perspectives that emanate from well within their oppressive culture's paradigms. Thus the new-world order they envision "would still be just as racist and ethnocentric as patriarchal American culture" (1981, 83). But so would hers be, and so would an Asian or African woman's "new culture" include the influence of their cultural paradigms, because they are also the products of their cultures. How would they be any less influenced by their respective cultures than Anglo-American women? Than Latinas?

The only solution, then, according to Rosario Morales, is to stop defining people by their race, class, sex, and so on, and define them, instead, by the fact that they are struggling against those injustices (1981, 92–93). In spite of many artificial barriers created between women and women (and men and women) by social constructs, we can nevertheless each strive to become, as Maria Lugones suggests, an individual who possesses

[t]he desire and ability to explore reality from the perspective of "wearing the other's shoes." This means recognizing wherever one goes, that the other's perspective is fully realized, not a bit of exotic "difference" to be incorporated within one's own world. . . .

The world-traveling thinker will always be ready to abandon familiar territory when human understanding and communication seem to require it" (1996, 286–287).

Not only Cofer's "essentially Puerto Rican work" but other Latina and ethnic works, in general, have "great resonance for Americans generally." This is the case because "[t]he pursuit of cultural identity is an often unquestioned part of our intellectual baggage. . . . [T]hat pursuit is at best a partial solution, an attempt to replace what [is] irretrievably lost" (Ruta 1995, 11). Kutzinski also believes that "[t]he outmoded paradigm of an abstract citizen of one given nation or state, of one religion, one given color" (or gender perspective) will not make it. Likewise the advocates and followers of traditional canonical cultural mainstreams will fall and perish by the wayside like so many dinosaurs. For at the very least, they dismiss ethnic feminist literature as "political," without redeeming aesthetic value. These traditional critics are ironically unconscious to the fact that they themselves "disguise political choices as purely aesthetic ones" (1993, 179). They dismiss this literature on supposedly aesthetic grounds, thereby justifying and rationalizing their continuing to remain comfortably ignorant and thereby unconscious of all its richness and complexity. This is the case because essentially they do not care about its significance and how rewarding it is to study. Still this literature provides models of complex global problems and issues, especially in relation to the major topic of this text, to the characters and roles of gatekeepers in mediating to their young charges inequitable gendered power relations characteristic of patriarchy in Latino and other cultures globally.

Finally this body of work by contemporary Latina authors provides models of complex global problems and issues. It also provides suggestions and solutions for the future–especially in relation to the major topic of this text, to the Procrustean bed of culturally constructed inequitable gendered power relations as mediated by the culture's gatekeepers. For these Latina authors maintain that without the ongoing tragedy of such women's active assistance, the patriarchal system of gendered inequitable power relations might not prevail and endure. Contemporary Latina writers believe that patriarchal cultures, both Latino and American mainstream, create overwhelming obstacles to women's advancement into equitable treatment in the twenty-first century and future centuries to come. They bring to their readers' attention that female gatekeepers impose these obstacles upon succeeding generations through brainwashing and intimidation. Children naturally trust, respect, and internalize the cultural messages that perpetuate patriarchal hegemony's inequitable and irrational constraints upon female lives.

Latina authors believe that it is vital for future generations of young females to question and reject these female collaborationists with love and compassion. They offer their work as witness to the unjust and irrational havoc that patriarchy wreaks upon the lives of untold generations of women, the role of the cultural gatekeepers in perpetuating the suffering of their own kind, and the effects upon their charges. But they offer no solutions to their readers, except attempts at private, individual solutions. On some rare occasions, they are content to offer stories about women who have somehow survived and flourished like these authors themselves. But they do not show readers how this is possible.

Far more frequently, as my work has revealed, they offer testimony to women who have not succeeded. In great detail, out of rage and frustration, they depict how and why succeeding generations of women fail. In doing so, they indict gatekeepers as well as the patriarchy. Tragically women have always been "saddled" by inimical patriarchal systems as pushy "la gringas." But instead of assisting their young charges to freely pursue whatever goals each child desired, gatekeepers have aided and abetted the patriarchy in its aim of perpetuating inequitable gendered power relations locally and globally. Gatekeepers, instead, should teach younger generations about diverse ancestral and contemporary cultures of humanity, not just their own group's culture. The greater the knowledge and understanding of other cultures, the greater the reach, the more global the perspective. Such human beings will traverse the pitfalls of the twenty-first century and future centuries to come.

NOTE

1. In an earlier piece, "I Am What I Am," Morales identifies herself as a "U.S. American" which she proudly and defiantly lists as including "Puerto Rican . . . Boricua" with "an English accent," and "yiddish . . . "I am what I am and I'm naturalized Jewish-American wasp is foreign and new but Jewish-American is old show familiar schmata [rag] familiar and its me dears its me bagels blintzes and all I am what I am Take it or leave me alone" (1981, 14–15).

Bibliography

Afshar, Haleh. 1995. "Book Review." *Signs: Journal of Women in Culture and Society* 21(1): 205–208.

Alarcón, Norma. 1995. "Cognitive Desires: An Allegory of/for Chicana Critics." In *Chicana (W)rites on Word and Film*. Series in Chicana/Latina Studies, ed. María Herrera Sobek and Helena María Viramontes, 185–200. Berkeley: Third Woman Press.

———. 1989. "The Sardonic Powers of the Erotic in the Work of Ana Castillo." In *Breaking Boundaries: Latina Writing and Critical Readings*, ed. Asunción Horno-Delgado, Eliana Ortega, Nina M. Scott, and Nancy Saporta Sternbach, 94–110. Amherst: University of Massachusetts Press.

———. 1988. "Making *Familia* from Scratch: Split Subjectivities in the Work of Helena María Viramontes and Cherríe Moraga." In *Chicana Creativity and Criticism: Charting New Frontiers in American Literature*, ed. María Hererra-Sobek and Helena María Viramontes, 147–159. Houston: Arte Publico Press.

Allen, Paula Gunn. 1989. *Spider Woman's Granddaughters: Traditional Tales and Contemporary Writing by Native American Women*, ed. and intro. Paula Gunn Allen. Boston: Beacon.

Alvarez, Julia. 1996. "Gorilla in the Midst: A Conversation with Jennifer Russell." *Women's Review of Books* 13(5): 31–32.

———. 1992. *How the Garcia Girls Lost Their Accents*. New York: Penguin Plume.

———. 1984. *Homecoming: Poems by Julia Alvarez*. Grove Press Poetry Series, ed. Robert Pack. New York: Grove Press.

Bakhtin, Mikhail. 1988. "Dialogism in the Novel." In *The Dialogic Imagination: Four Essays*, ed. Michael Holquist, trans. Caryl Emerson and Michael Holquist. Austin: University of Texas Press.

Behar, Ruth. 1995. "Revolutions of the Heart: Review of *In the Time of the Butterflies* by Julia Alvarez." *Women's Review of Books* 12(8): 6–7.

Beltrán, Carmen Celia. 1993. In *Infinite Divisions: An Anthology of Chicana Literature*, ed. Tey Diana Rebolledo and Eliana S. Rivero, 65–66. Tucson: University of Arizona Press.

Bhabha, Homi K. 1984. "Of Mimicry and Man: The Ambivalence of Colonial Discourse." *Cultural Critique* 28: 125–33.

Bilbija, Kisenija. 1994. "Rosario Ferré's 'The Youngest Doll': On Women, Dolls, Golems and Cyborgs." *Callaloo* 17.3: 878–888.

Blea, Irene J. 1991. *La Chicana and the Intersection of Race, Class, and Gender.* Westport, CT: Praeger Publishers.

Boer, Inge E. 1996. "Despotism from Under the Veil: Masculine and Feminine Readings of the Despot and the Harem." *Cultural Critique* 32: 43–73.

Boesing, Martha. 1996. "Rushing Headlong into the Fire at the Foot of the Mountain." *Signs: Journal of Women in Culture and Society. Special Issue Edition: Feminist Theory and Practice* 21(4): 1011–1023.

Brady-Clarke, Cherry. 1997. "A Controversial Revisiting of the Right to Consortium" in *Gender: A Caribbean Multi-Disciplinary Perspective*, ed. Elsa Leo-Rhynie, Barbara Bailey, Christine Barrow, 106–117. Kingston, Jamaica: Centre for Gender and Development Studies, University of the West Indies.

Brown, Barkley, Elsa. "African-American Quilting: A Framework for Conceptualizing and Teaching African-American Women's History." *Signs: Journal of Women in Culture and Society. Special Issue Edition: Feminist Theory and Practice* 14(4): 925-929.

Bruce-Novoa, Juan. 1989. "Deconstructing the Dominant Patriarchal Text: Cecile Pineda's Narratives." In *Breaking Boundaries: Latina Writing and Critical Readings*, ed. Asunción Horno-Delgado, Eliana Ortega, Nina M. Scott, and Nancy Saporta Sternbach, 72–81. Amherst: University of Massachusetts Press.

Brush, Lisa D. 1996. "Love, Toil, and Trouble: Motherhood and Feminist Politics." *Signs: Journal of Women in Culture and Society* 21(2): 429–54.

Butler, Judith. 1991. "Imitation and Gender Insubordination." In *Inside/Out: Lesbian Theories, Gay Theories*, ed. Diana Fuss, 13–31. New York: Routledge.

————. 1990. *Gender Trouble: Feminism as the Subversion of Identity.* New York: Routledge.

Castañeda, Antonia I. 1993. "Sexual Violence in the Politics of Conquest: Amerindian Women and the Spanish Conquest of Alta California." In *Building with Our Hands: New Directions in Chicana Studies*, ed. Adela de la Torre and Beatríz M. Pesquera, 15–33. Berkeley: University of California Press.

Castillo, Ana. 1995. *Massacre of the Dreamers: Essays on Xicanisma.* New York: Penguin Plume.

Chodorow, Nancy, and Susan Contratto. 1982. "The Fantasy of the Perfect Mother." In *Rethinking the Family: Some Feminist Questions*, ed. Barrie Thorne and Marilyn Yalom. New York: Longman.

Cixous, Hélène. 1983. "The Laugh of the Medusa." In *The Signs Reader: Women, Gender and Scholarship*, ed. Elizabeth Abel and Emily K. Abel, trans. Keith Cohen and Paul Cohen. Chicago: University of Chicago Press.

Cliff, Michelle. 1984. *Abeng.* Trumansburg, NY: Crossing Press.

Cofer, Judith Ortiz. 1995. "The Story of My Body." In *Boricuas: Influential Puerto Rican Writings–An Anthology*, ed. Roberto Santiago. New York: One World Ballantine Books.

————. 1990. *Silent Dancing: A Partial Remembrance of a Puerto Rican Childhood.* Houston: Arte Publico Press.

————. 1987. *Terms of Survival.* Houston: Arte Public Press.

de la Torre, Adela. 1993. "Hard Choices and Changing Roles among Mexican Migrant Campesinas. In *Building with Our Hands: New Directions in Chicana Studies*, ed. Adela de la Torre and Beatríz M. Pesquera, 168–180. Berkeley: University of California Press.

de la Torre, Adela, and Beatriz M. Pesquera, ed. 1993. *Building With Our Hands: New Directions in Chicana Studies*. Berkeley: University of California Press.

Dernersesian, Angie Chabran. 1993. "And, Yes . . . The Earth Did Part: On the Splitting of Chicana/o Subjectivity." In *Building with Our Hands: New Directions in Chicana Studies*, ed. Adela de la Torre and Beatríz M. Pesquera, 34–71. Berkeley: University of California Press.

Desmond, Jane C. 1994. "Embodying Difference: Issues in Dance and Cultural Studies." *Cultural Critique* 26: 33–63.

Dewey, Janice. 1989. "Doña Josefa: Bloodpulse of Transition and Change." In *Breaking Boundaries: Latina Writing and Critical Readings*, ed. Asunción Horno-Delgado, Eliana Ortega, Nina M. Scott, and Nancy Saporta Sternbach, 39–47. Amherst: University of Massachusetts Press.

Dietz, Mary G. 1992. "Introduction: Debating Simone de Beauvoir." *Signs: Journal of Women in Culture and Society* 18(1): 74–88.

Disch, Lisa, and Mary Jo Kane. 1996. "When a Looker Is Really a Bitch: Lisa Olson, Sport, and the Heterosexual Matrix." *Signs: Journal of Women in Culture and Society* 21(2): 278–308.

Domino, George. 1995. "Acculturation of Hispanics." In *Hispanics in the Workplace*, ed. Stephen B. Knouse, Paul Rosenfeld, and Amy L. Culbertson, 56–74. Newbury Park, CA: Sage Publications.

Ebert, Teresa L. 1991. "The 'Difference' of Postmodern Feminism." *College English* 53(8): 886–904.

Ferdman, Bernardo M., and Angelica C. Cortes. 1995. "Culture and Identity among Hispanic Managers in an Anglo Business." In *Hispanics in the Workplace*, ed. Stephen B. Knouse, Paul Rosenfeld, and Amy L. Culbertson, 246–277. Newbury Park, CA: Sage Publications.

Ferré, Rosario. 1996. *Sweet Diamond Dust*. New York: Ballantine.

———. 1994. "The Bitches' Colloquy." *Callaloo* 17(3): 889–899.

———. 1993. "Rice and Milk." In *Pleasure in the Word: Erotic Writings by Latin Americn Women*, éd. Margarita Fernández Olmos and Lizbeth Paravisini-Gebert, 133–136. Fredonia, New York: White Pine Press.

———. 1991a. "Out of the Frying Pan." In *Ourselves among Others: Cross-Cultural Readings for Writers*, ed. Carol J. Verburg, 471–477. New York: Bedford Books of St. Martin's Press.

———. 1991b. *The Youngest Doll*, foreword by Jean Franco. Lincoln: University of Nebraska Press.

Foucault, Michel. 1990. *The History of Sexuality, Volume I: An Introduction*, trans. Robert Hurley. New York: Vintage.

———. 1982. "The Subject and Power." *Critical Inquiry* 8(4): 777.

Frank, Lawrence. 1996. "Dreaming the Medusa: Imperialism, Primitivism, and Sexuality in Arthur Conan Doyle's *The Sign of Four*." *Signs: Journal of Women in Culture and Society* 22(1): 52–85.

Fregoso, Rose Linda. 1993. "The Mother Motif in La Bamba and Boulevard Nights." In *Building with Our Hands: New Directions in Chicana Studies*, ed. Adela de la Torre and Beatríz M. Pesquera, 130–145. Berkeley: University of California Press.

Frye, Marilyn. 1996. "The Necessity of Differences: Constructing a Positive Category of Women." *Signs: Journal of Women in Culture and Society* (21)4: 991–1010.

Fusco, Coco. 1995. *English is Broken Here: Notes on Cultural Fusion in the Americas*. New York: New Press.

Garcia, Cristina. 1992. *Dreaming in Cuban*. New York: Knopf.

Gómez, Alma, Cherríe Moraga, and Mariana Romo-Carmona, eds. 1983. *Cuentos: Stories by Latinas.* New York: Kitchen Table Women of Color Press.

Gwin, Minrose. 1996. "Space Travel: The Connective Politics of Feminist Reading." *Signs: Journal of Women in Culture and Society* 21(4): 870–905.

Haaken, Janice. 1996. "The Recovery of Memory, Fantasy, and Desire: Feminist Approaches to Sexual Abuse and Psychic Drama." *Signs: Journal of Women in Culture and Society* 21(4): 1069–1091.

Hall, Stuart, and Donald James, ed. 1985. *Politics and Ideology: A Reader.* Philadelphia: Open University Press.

Harding, James M. 1995. "Adorno, Ellison, and the Critique of Jazz." *Cultural Critique* 31: 129–158.

Hartmann, Heidi, Ellen Bravo, et al. 1996. "Bringing Together Feminist Theory and Practice: A Collective Interview." *Signs: Journal of Women in Culture and Society* 21(4): 917–951.

Hassett, Contance W. 1996. "Siblings and Antislavery: The Literary and Political Relations of Harriet Martineau, James Martineau, and Maria Weston Chapman." *Signs: Journal of Women in Culture and Society* 21(2): 374–409.

Hernández, Elizabeth, and Consuelo López Springfield. 1994. "Women and Writing in Puerto Rico: An Interview with Ana Lydia Vega." *Callaloo* 17(3): 816–825.

Heyck, Denis Lynn Daly. 1994. *Barrios and Borderlands: Cultures of Latinos and Latinas in the United States.* New York: Routledge,

Hodge, Merle. 1970. *Crick Crack Monkey.* Oxford: Heinemann

hooks, bell with Tanya McKinnon. 1996. "Sisterhood: Beyond Public and Private." In "Feminist Theory and Practice," ed. Barbara Christian, et al. Special issue of *Signs: Journal of Women in Culture and Society* 21(4): 814–829.

Horno-Delgado, Asunción, Eliana Ortega, Nina M. Scott, and Nancy Saporta Sternbach, eds. 1989a. *Breaking Boundaries: Latina Writing and Critical Readings.* Amherst: University of Massachusetts Press.

Horno-Delgado, Asunción. 1989b. "'Señores, don't leibol me, please!!: ya soy Luz Maria Umpierre." *Breaking Boundaries: Latina Writing and Critical Readings,* ed. Asunción Horno-Delgado, Eliana Ortega, Nina M. Scott, and Nancy Saporta Sternbach, trans. Janet N. Gold, 136–145. Amherst: University of Massachusetts Press.

———. 1983. *Cuentos: Stories by Latinas,* ed. Alma Gómez, Cherríe Moraga, and Mariana Romo-Carmona, 7–15. New York: Kitchen Table Women of Color Press.

Hurston, Zora Neale. 1978. *Their Eyes Were Watching God.* Urbana: University of Illinois Press.

Irigary, Luce. 1985a. *Speculum of the Other Woman,* trans. Gillian G. Gill. Ithaca: Cornell University Press.

———. 1985b. *This Sex Which Is Not One,* trans. Catherine Porter. Ithaca: Cornell University Press.

———. 1981. "And the One Doesn't Stir Without the Other," trans. Helene Vivienne Wenzel. *Signs: Journal of Women in Culture and Society* 7(1): 64–65.

Jameson, Frederic. 1986. "Third World Literature in the Era of Multinational Capitalism." *Social Text* 15: 65–88.

Kafka, Phillipa. 2000. *(Out)Classed Women: Contemporary Chicana Writers on Inequitable Gendered Power Relations.* Westport, CT: Greenwood Press.

———. 1997. *(Un)Doing the Missionary Position: Gender Asymmetry in Contemporary Asian American Women's Writings.* Westport, CT: Greenwood Press.

King, Lourdes Miranda. 1995. "Puertorriqueñas in the United States: The Impact of Double Discrimination." In *Latinos in the United States: History, Law and*

Perspective. Volume 2, *Latina Issues: Fragments of Historia (Ella) (Herstory,* ed. Antoinette Sedillo López, 102–109. New York: Garland Press. (Orig. ptd in *Civil Rights Digest* 6 [1974]: 20–27.)

Knouse, Stephen B., Paul Rosenfeld, Amy L. Culbertson, eds. 1995. *Hispanics in the Workplace.* Newbury Park, CA: Sage Publications.

Kosta, Barbara, and Richard W. McCormick. 1996. "Interview with Jutta Brückner." *Signs: Journal of Women in Culture and Society* 21(2): 343–374.

Kranz, Rachel. 1995. "Culture Crosser." Review of *English is Broken Here: Notes on Cultural Fusion in the Americas,* by Coco Fusco. *Women's Review of Books* 12 (12): 11.

Kristeva, Julia. 1982. *The Power and the Horror.* New York. Columbia University Press.

———.1980. *Desire and Language: A Semiotic Approach to Literature and Art,* trans. Thomas Gora, Alice Jardine, and Leon Roudiez. New York: Columbia University Press.

Kutzinski, Vera M. 1993. *Sugar's Secrets: Race and the Erotics of Cuban Nationalism.* Charlottesville: University Press of Virginia.

Leps, Marie-Christine. 1995. "Empowerment through Information: A Discursive Critique." *Cultural Critique* 31: 179–196.

Leví, Lillián. 1993. "La Mano Vuelta [a hand extended]: A Letter From Lillián Leví." *Women's Review of Books* 10(10–11): 15.

Levinson, Marjorie. 1995. "Postmodernism and Post-Dialectical Materialisms: Modeling Praxis without Subjects and Objects." *Cultural Critique* 31: 111–127.

López, Antoinette Sedillo, ed. 1995. *Latinos in the United States: History, Law and Perspective.* Volume 2, *Latina Issues: Fragments of Historia (Ella) (Herstory).* New York: Garland Press.

López Springfield, Consuelo. 1994. "'I am the Life, the Strength, the Woman': Feminism in Julia de Burgos' Autobiographical Poetry." *Callaloo* 17(3): 701–714.

Lugones, María. 1996. "Playfulness, 'World'-Traveling, and Loving Perception." In *The Woman That I Am: The Literature and Culture of Women of Color,* ed. D. Soyini Madison, 626–638. New York: St. Martin's Press.

Luttrell, Wendy. 1993. "'The Teachers All Had Their Pets': Concepts of Gender, Knowledge, and Power." S*igns: Journal of Women in Culture and Society* 18(3): 505–546.

Majid, Anouar. 1996. "Can the Postcolonial Critic Speak? Orientalism and the Rushdie Affair." *Cultural Critique* 32: 5–42.

McCormick, Richard W. 1993. "From Caligari to Dietrich: Sexual, Social, and Cinematic Discourses in Weimar Film." *Signs: Journal of Women in Culture and Society* 18 (3): 640–668.

Michie, Helena. 1987. *The Flesh Made Word: Female Figures and Women's Bodies.* New York: Oxford University Press.

Mintz, Sidney W. 1974. *Caribbean Transformations.* Baltimore: Johns Hopkins University Press.

Mohr, Nicholasa. 1989. "Puerto Rican Writers in the U.S., Puerto Rican Writers in Puerto Rico: A Separation beyond Language (Testimonio)." In *Breaking Boundaries: Latina Writing and Critical Readings,* ed. Asunción Horno-Delgado, Eliana Ortega, Nina M. Scott, and Nancy Saporta Sternbach, 111–116. Amherst, MA: University of Massachusetts Press.

———. 1977. *In Nueva York.* New York: Dial Press.

———. 1975. *El Bronx Remembered.* New York: Harper & Row.

Moore, Henrietta L.1986. *Space, Text, and Gender: An Anthropological Study of the Marakwet of Kenya*. Cambridge: Cambridge University Press.

Moraga, Cherríe, and Gloria Anzaldúa, ed. 1981. *This Bridge Called My Back: Writings by Radical Women of Color*. Foreword by Toni Cade Bambara. New York: Kitchen Table Press.

Morales, Aurora Levins. 1995. "Child of the Americas" from *Getting Home Alive* by Aurora Levins Morales and Rosario Morales. In *Boriquas: Influential Puerto Rican Writings–An Anthology*, ed. Robert Santiago, 79. New York: One World Ballantine Books.

Morales, Aurora Levins, and Rosario Morales. 1986. *Getting Home Alive*. Ithaca: Firebrand Books.

Morales, Martita. 1995. "The Sounds of Sixth Street." In *Boriquas: Influential Puerto Rican Writings–An Anthology*, ed. Roberto Santiago, 8–11. New York: One World Ballantine Books.

Morales, Rosario. 1981. "I Am What I Am," 14–15; "And Even Fidel Can't Change That," 53-56; "We're All in the Same Boat," 91–93; "I Never Told My Children Stories," 120–123. In *This Bridge Called My Back*, ed. Cherríe Moraga and Gloria Anzaldúa. New York: Kitchen Table Press.

Moschkovich, Judit. 1981. "But I Know You, American Woman." In *This Bridge Called My Back*, ed. Cherríe Moraga and Gloria Anzaldúa, 79–84. New York: Kitchen Table Press.

Naiman, Eric. 1996. "When a Communist Writes Gothic: Aleksandra Kollontai and the Politics of Disgust." *Signs: Journal of Women in Culture and Society* 22 (1): 1–29.

Nin, Anais. (1966–1980). *The Diary of Anais Nin*, ed. Gunther Stuhlmann. 7 vols. New York: Harcourt, 2:233.

Ocasio, Rafael. 1992. "Puerto Rican Literature in Georgia? Interview with Judith Ortiz Cofer." *Kenyon Review* 14(4): 43–50.

Olmos, Margarita Fernández, and Lizbeth Paravisini-Gebert, eds. 1993. *Pleasure in the Word: Erotic Writings by Latin American Women*. Fredonia, New York: White Pine Press.

Ortega, Eliana. 1989. "Poetic Discourse of the Puerto Rican Woman in the U.S.: New Voices of Anacoanian Liberation." In *Breaking Boundaries: Latina Writing and Critical Readings*, ed. Asunción Horno-Delgado, Eliana Ortega, Nina M. Scott, and Nancy Saporta Sternbach, 122–135. Amherst: University of Massachusetts Press.

Pérez, Emma. 1993. "Speaking from the Margin: Uninvited Discourse on Sexuality and Power." In *Building with Our Hands: New Directions in Chicana Studies*, ed. Adela de la Torre and Beatríz M. Pesquera, 57–71. Berkeley: University of California Press.

Pérez-Torres, Rafael. 1994. "Nomads and Migrants: Negotiating a Multicultural Postmodernism." *Cultural Critique* 26: 161–189.

Piper, Karen. 1995. "The Signifying Corpse: Re-Reading Kristeva on Marguerite Duras." In *Cultural Critique* 31: 159–177.

Prida, Delores. 1991. *Beautiful Señoritas and Other Plays*, ed. Judith Weiss. Houston: Arte Publico Press.

———. 1989. "The Show Does Go On (Testimonio)." In *Breaking Boundaries: Latina Writing and Critical Readings*, ed. Asunción Horno-Delgado, Eliana Ortega, Nina M. Scott, and Nancy Saporta Sternbach, 181–188. Amherst: University of Massachusetts Press.

Prieto, Yolanda. 1995. "Cuban Women in the U.S. Labor Force: Perspectives on the Nature of Change." In *Latinos in the United States: History, Law and Perspective*.

Volume 2, *Latina Issues: Fragments of Historia (Ella) (Herstory)*. ed. Antoinette Sedillo López, 163-181. New York: Garland Press. (Orig. ptd. in *Cuban Studies* 17 [1987]: 73–91. University of Pittsburgh.)

Quintanales, Mirtha. 1981. "I Come with No Illusions," 148–149; "I Paid Very Hard for My Immigrant Ignorance," 150–156. In *This Bridge Called My Back*, ed. Cherríe Moraga and Gloria Anzaldúa. New York: Kitchen Table Press.

Ramis, Magali García. 1995. [1986]. *Happy Days, Uncle Sergio*, trans. Carmen C. Esteves. Fredonia, New York: White Pine Press.

Rao, Aruna. 1996. "Engendering Institutional Change." *Signs: Journal of Women in Culture and Society* 22(1): 218–221.

Rebolledo, Tey Diana, and Eliana S. Rivero, eds. 1993. *Infinite Divisions: An Anthology of Chicana Literature*. Tucson: The University of Arizona Press.

Resnik, Judith. 1996. "Asking about Gender in Courts." *Signs: Journal of Women in Culture and Society* 21(4): 952–990.

Reyna, Bessy. 1989. "A Cuban-Panamanian-American-Lawyer-Writer Now in Connecticut (Testimonio)." In *Breaking Boundaries: Latina Writing and Critical Readings*, ed. Asunción Horno-Delgado, Eliana Ortega, Nina M. Scott, and Nancy Saporta Sternbach, 223–228. Amherst: University of Massachusetts Press.

Rhadakrishnan, R. 1993. "Postcoloniality and the Boundaries of Identity." *Callaloo* 16(4): 750–771.

Rivera-Ramos, Alba N. 1995. "The Psychological Experience of Puerto Rican Women at Work." In *Hispanics in the Workplace*, ed. Stephen B. Knouse, Paul Rosenfeld, and Amy L. Culbertson, 194–207. Newbury Park, CA and London: Sage Publications.

Rodriguez, Clara E. 1995. "Puerto Ricans: Between Black and White." In *Boricuas: Influential Puerto Rican Writings–An Anthology*, ed. Roberto Santiago, 86. New York: One World Ballantine Books.

Rojas, Lourdes. 1989. "Latinas at the Crossroads: An Affirmation of Life in Rosario Morales and Aurora Levins Morales' *Getting Home Alive*." In *Breaking Boundaries: Latina Writing and Critical Readings*, ed. Asunción Horno-Delgado, Eliana Ortega, Nina M. Scott, and Nancy Saporta Sternbach, 166–180. Amherst: University of Massachusetts Press.

Romany, Celina. 1995. "Ain't I a Feminist?" In *Latinos in the United States: History, Law and Perspective*. Volume 2, *Latina Issues: Fragments of Historia (Ella) (Herstor)*. ed. Antoinette Sedillo López, 389–399. New York and London: Garland Press. (Orig. ptd. in *Yale Journal of Law and Feminism*.)

Rosenfeld, Paul, and Amy L. Culbertson. 1995. "Hispanics in the Military." In *Hispanics in the Workplace*, ed. Stephen B. Knouse, Paul Rosenfeld, and Amy L. Culbertson, 211–230. Newbury Park, CA: Sage Publications.

Ruíz, Vicki L. 1993. "'Star Struck': Acculturation, Adolescence, and the Mexican American Woman, 1920–1950." In *Building With Our Hands: New Directions in Chicana Studies*, ed. Adela de la Torre and Beatriz M. Pesquera, 109-129. Berkeley: University of California Press.

Ruta, Suzanne. 1995. "Struggling for Independence." *Women's Review of Books* 13(2): 10–11.

Sandoval, Alberto. 1989. "Dolores Prida's *Coser y cantar*: Mapping the Dialectics of Ethnic Identity and Assimilation." In *Breaking Boundaries: Latina Writing and Critical Readings*, ed. Asunción Horno-Delgado, Eliana Ortega, Nina M. Scott, and Nancy Saporta Sternbach, 201–222. Amherst: University of Massachusetts Press.

Santiago, Esmeralda. 1995. "Island of Lost Causes." In *Boricuas: Influential Puerto Rican Writings–An Anthology*. New York: One World Ballantine Books, 22–24.

Santiago, Roberto, ed. 1995. *Boricuas: Influential Puerto Rican Writings–An Anthology*. New York: One World Ballantine Books.

Sasaki, R[uth] A. 1991. *The Loom and Other Stories*. St. Paul, MN: Graywolf Press.

Scorczewski, Dawn. 1996. "What Prison Is This? Literary Critics Cover Incest in Anne Sexton's 'Briar Rose.' " *Signs: Journal of Women in Culture and Society* 21(2): 309–342.

Scott, Nina. ed. 1989. *Breaking Boundaries: Latina Writing and Critical Readings*, ed. Asunción Horno-Delgado, Eliana Ortega, Nina M. Scott, and Nancy Saporta Sternbach, 243, 244. Amherst: University of Massachusetts Press.

Segura, Denise. 1993. "Slipping through the Cracks: Dilemmas in Chicana Education." In *Building with Our Hands: New Directions in Chicana Studies*, ed. Adela de la Torre and Beatríz M. Pesquera, 199–216. Berkeley: University of California Press.

Soland, Birgitte. 1996. "Book Review." *Signs: Journal of Women in Culture and Society* 21(2): 502–506.

Stacey, Judith. 1996. "La Mano." *Woman's Review of Books* 13(5): 15.

Sternbach, Nancy Saporta. 1989. In *Breaking Boundaries: Latina Writing and Critical Readings*, ed. Asunción Horno-Delgado, Eliana Ortega, Nina M. Scott, and Nancy Saporta Sternbach, 48–61. Amherst: University of Massachusetts Press.

Tan, Amy. 1991. *The Kitchen God's Wife*. New York: Putnam.

Tolstoy, Leo. 1991. *War and Peace*, ed. Henry Gifford, trans. Louise and Aylmer Maude. Oxford: Oxford University Press.

Trask, Haunani-Kay. 1996. "Feminism and Indigenous Hawaiian Nationalism." *Signs: Journal of Women in Culture and Society* 21(4): 906–916.

Turner, Faythe, ed. 1991. *Puerto Rican Writers at Home in the USA*. Seattle, WA: Open Hand Publishing

Vargas, Yamila Azize. 1989. "A Commentary on the Works of Three Puerto Rican Women Poets in New York," trans. Sonia Crespo Vega. In *Breaking Boundaries: Latina Writing and Critical Readings*, ed. Asunción Horno-Delgado, Eliana Ortega, Nina M. Scott, and Nancy Saporta Sternbach, 146–165. Amherst: University of Massachusetts Press.

Vega, Ana Lydia. 1994. "Miss Florence's Trunk." *True and False Romances: Stories and a Novella*, trans. Andrew Hurley. New York and London: Serpent's Tail.

Vélez, Diana L. 1988. *Reclaiming Medusa: Short Stories by Contemporary Puerto Rican Women* Writers. San Francisco: Spinsters/Aunt Lute.

Walters, Suzanna Danuta. 1996. "From Here to Queer: Radical Feminism, Postmodernism, and the Lesbian Menace (Or, Why Can't a Woman Be More Like a Fag?)." In *Feminist Theory and Practice*, ed. Barbara Christian, et al., special issue of *Signs: Journal of Women in Culture and Society* 21(4): 830–869.

———. 1995. *Material Girls: Making Sense of Feminist Cultural Theory*. Berkeley: University of California Press.

Wegner, Phillip E. 1993–1994. "'Life as He Would Have It.' The Invention of India in Kipling's *Kim*." *Cultural Critique* 26: 129–160.

Zamora, Margarita. 1991. "Abreast of Columbus: Gender and Discovery." *Cultural Critique* 17: 127–50.

Index

About the Author

PHILLIPA KAFKA is Professor Emerita of English and former Director of Women's Studies, Kean University. Her previous books include *(Un)Doing the Missionary Position: Gender Asymmetry in Contemporary Asian American Women's Writing* (Greenwood, 1997), and *The Great White Way: African American Women Writers and American Success Mythology* (1993).